VISUAL DICTIONARY
UPDATED EDITION

Written by Simon Beecroft, Elizabeth Dowsett, Jason Fry, and Simon Hugo

Contents

CHAPTER 3:
The Rise of the First Order

CHAPTER 4:
Specialist Sets

CHAPTER 5:
Beyond the Brick

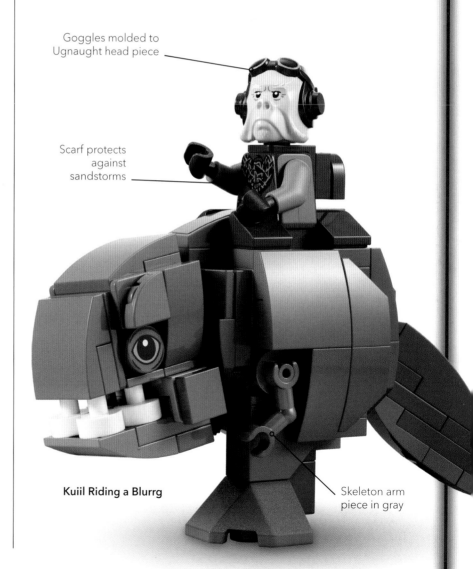

Goggles molded to Ugnaught head piece

Scarf protects against sandstorms

Kuiil Riding a Blurrg

Skeleton arm piece in gray

Introduction

For 25 years, the LEGO Group has been building the *Star Wars*™ galaxy in LEGO® bricks, to the delight of adults and children alike.

Back in 1999, along with launch of the Prequel Trilogy, the LEGO Group and Lucasfilm came together in a partnership that was the first—but not the last—of its kind. The appeal of LEGO *Star Wars* carries across generations and brings families together, with action-packed sets for imaginative play as well as highly detailed models for display.

For two and a half decades, LEGO designers have been innovating for the *Star Wars* theme by creating brand-new elements and reinventing existing ones. *Star Wars* minifigures, for example, were the first to get short minifigure legs and sculpted heads. Meanwhile, familiar elements, including the LEGO skate and castle spire pieces, have been put to exciting new use as part of various LEGO *Star Wars* vehicles.

Originally published in 2009, LEGO® *Star Wars*™: *The Visual Dictionary* has been updated and expanded over the years. This fourth edition celebrates the theme's landmark 25th anniversary.

Since the last edition of this book, the *Star Wars* galaxy has grown, with new heroes and villains; new movies, live-action series, and animation; and even themed lands. This richness has been translated into LEGO sets, minifigures, and inventive new lines, such as the Helmet and Mech series, which are detailed in these updated pages.

It's time to hop aboard and travel far, far away into a minifigure-size galaxy of imagination and an ever-expanding roster of LEGO sets, models, and minifigures.

Data Boxes

Throughout the book, LEGO *Star Wars* sets are identified with a data box, which lists the official name of the set, its LEGO identification number, how many LEGO pieces or elements are in the set, the year it was first released, and the *Star Wars* source that inspired the model.

Set name Rey's Speeder	
Number 75099	Pieces 193
Year 2015	Source VII

Source abbreviations:

AH	*Star Wars: Ahsoka*	**L**	*Star Wars* Legends (non-canon stories)
AN	*Star Wars: Andor*		
BB	*Star Wars: The Bad Batch*	**M**	*Star Wars: The Mandalorian*
BBF	*Star Wars: The Book of Boba Fett*		
		O	*Star Wars: Obi-Wan Kenobi*
CW	*Star Wars: The Clone Wars*		
		REB	*Star Wars: Rebels*
I	*The Phantom Menace*	**RES**	*Star Wars: Resistance*
II	*Attack of the Clones*	**R1**	*Rogue One: A Star Wars Story*
III	*Revenge of the Sith*		
IV	*A New Hope*	**S**	*Solo: A Star Wars Story*
V	*The Empire Strikes Back*	**TFA**	*LEGO Star Wars: The Freemaker Adventures*
VI	*Return of the Jedi*		
VII	*The Force Awakens*	**TYC**	*LEGO Star Wars: The Yoda Chronicles*
VIII	*The Last Jedi*		
IX	*The Rise of Skywalker*	**YJA**	*Star Wars: Young Jedi Adventures*
JFO	*Jedi: Fallen Order*		

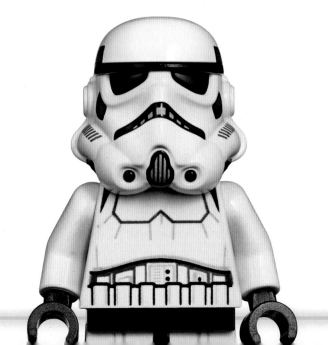

25 Years of LEGO® *Star Wars*™

From the first simple playsets a long time ago, to far, far, and away the largest, most complex builds any LEGO® theme has ever seen—the LEGO® *Star Wars*™ galaxy has it all!

Mini
AT-AT

The first LEGO *Star Wars* sets go on sale. They showcase scenes and characters from the newly released *Star Wars: The Phantom Menace*.

The first LEGO model of the *Millennium Falcon* (set 7190) is released.

A unique, 1,868-piece bust of Darth Maul (set 10018) is released as part of the Ultimate Collector Series.

The first sets based on the new movie, *Star Wars: Attack of the Clones*, include the Republic Gunship (set 7163).

A new range of Mini Building Sets includes pocket-size AT-ATs, X-wings, and more.

1999   **2000**   **2001**   **2002**   **2003**

TIE Interceptor

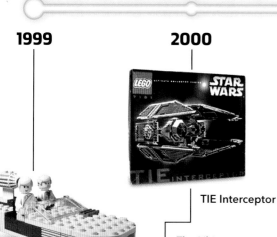

The first LEGO Jabba the Hutt features in Jabba's Palace (set 4480).

Yoda, two Ewoks, and Young Boba Fett are the first minifigures to have short legs.

The first Imperial Shuttle (set 7166) features red Royal Guard minifigures.

The UCS Imperial Star Destroyer (set 10030) is the first LEGO set to top 3,000 pieces.

The Ultimate Collector Series (UCS) launches with the 703-piece TIE Interceptor (set 7181, above) and the 1,300-piece X-Wing Fighter (set 7191, below).

C-3PO gets the LEGO® Technic treatment (set 8007).

Builds based on the Original Trilogy (1977–1983) are also introduced.

Cloud City (set 10123) includes Lando Calrissian, who is the first LEGO *Star Wars* human character to have a non-yellow head.

X-Wing
Fighter

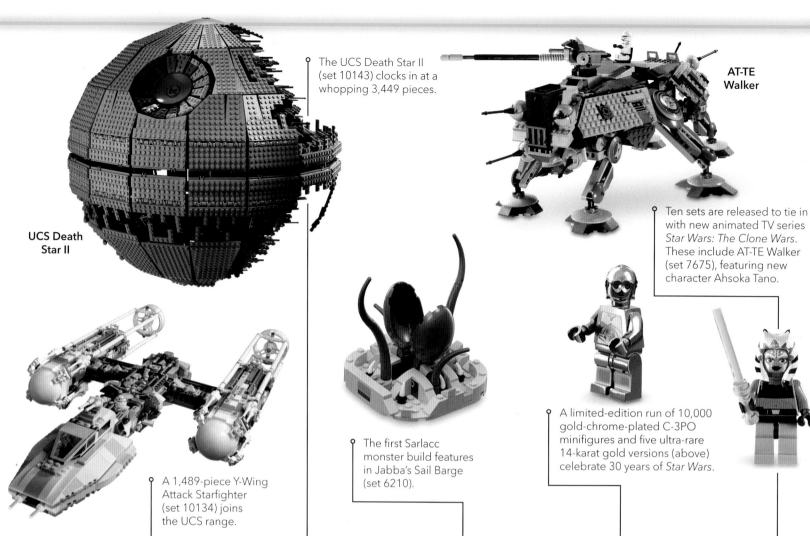

The UCS Death Star II (set 10143) clocks in at a whopping 3,449 pieces.

UCS Death Star II

AT-TE Walker

Ten sets are released to tie in with new animated TV series *Star Wars: The Clone Wars.* These include AT-TE Walker (set 7675), featuring new character Ahsoka Tano.

A 1,489-piece Y-Wing Attack Starfighter (set 10134) joins the UCS range.

The first Sarlacc monster build features in Jabba's Sail Barge (set 6210).

A limited-edition run of 10,000 gold-chrome-plated C-3PO minifigures and five ultra-rare 14-karat gold versions (above) celebrate 30 years of *Star Wars.*

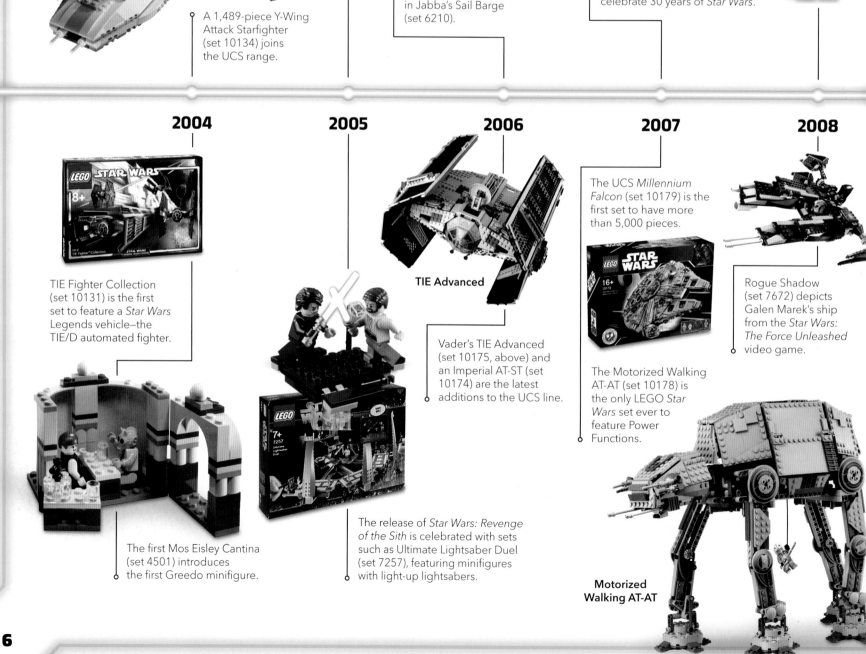

2004

TIE Fighter Collection (set 10131) is the first set to feature a *Star Wars* Legends vehicle—the TIE/D automated fighter.

The first Mos Eisley Cantina (set 4501) introduces the first Greedo minifigure.

2005

The release of *Star Wars: Revenge of the Sith* is celebrated with sets such as Ultimate Lightsaber Duel (set 7257), featuring minifigures with light-up lightsabers.

2006

TIE Advanced

Vader's TIE Advanced (set 10175, above) and an Imperial AT-ST (set 10174) are the latest additions to the UCS line.

2007

The UCS *Millennium Falcon* (set 10179) is the first set to have more than 5,000 pieces.

The Motorized Walking AT-AT (set 10178) is the only LEGO *Star Wars* set ever to feature Power Functions.

2008

Rogue Shadow (set 7672) depicts Galen Marek's ship from the *Star Wars: The Force Unleashed* video game.

Motorized Walking AT-AT

To mark the 10th anniversary of LEGO *Star Wars*, 10,000 chrome-effect Darth Vader minifigures are randomly inserted into sets.

UCS Imperial Shuttle

The first LEGO *Star Wars* Advent Calendar (set 7958) includes a Santa Yoda minifigure.

Jek-14's Stealth Starfighter (set 75018) is released. It's based on the first original LEGO *Star Wars* character, Jek-14.

The UCS Imperial Shuttle (set 10212) is released. It is made from 2,503 pieces, most of which are white.

Anakin Skywalker's and Sebulba's podracers get their first update since 1999 (set 7962).

A UCS R2-D2 (set 10225) measures more than 31 cm (12 in) tall.

The *Clone Wars* version of Darth Maul (with mechanical legs) makes his debut in Mandalorian Speeder (set 75022).

New sets for *Star Wars: The Clone Wars* include Count Dooku's Solar Sailer (set 7752).

2009

The 1,758-piece Republic Dropship with AT-OT Walker (set 10195) is the largest LEGO *Star Wars* set outside of the UCS range.

2010

A new wampa figure features in Hoth Wampa Cave (set 8089).

2011

At close to 124 cm (50 in) long, UCS Super Star Destroyer (set 10221) becomes the longest ever LEGO set.

2012

Two sets are released to tie in with the *Star Wars: The Old Republic* video game, including the Sith *Fury*-class Interceptor (set 9500).

2013

New UCS sets include the elaborate Ewok Village (set 10236).

UCS Super Star Destroyer

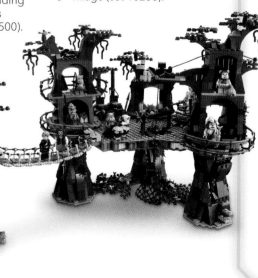

**UCS
Sandcrawler**

Animated TV series LEGO *Star Wars: The Freemaker Adventures* launches, along with tie-in sets *Eclipse Fighter* (set 75145) and *StarScavenger* (set 75147, below).

StarScavenger

As *Star Wars: The Last Jedi* soars into cinemas, LEGO *Star Wars* releases new sets including the First Order Heavy Assault Walker (set 75189).

The Kessel Run *Millennium Falcon* (set 75212) is one of eight sets marking the theatrical release of *Solo: A Star Wars Story*.

The UCS Sandcrawler (set 75059) has 3,296 pieces.

The Microfighters range launches with six sets, including the TIE Interceptor (set 75031).

The theatrical release of *Star Wars: The Force Awakens* heralds a new wave of LEGO *Star Wars* heroes in sets such as Poe's X-Wing Fighter (set 75102).

2014   **2015**   **2016**   **2017**   **2018**

The *Ghost*

The UCS Death Star (set 75159) is updated, and includes more than 4,000 pieces.

Animated TV series *Star Wars: Rebels* blasts onto screens and into LEGO sets, starting with the *Ghost* (set 75053, above) and the *Phantom* (set 75048).

New buildable figures such as General Grievous (set 75112) allow for character battles on a whole new scale.

Fifteen years after it was first made into a LEGO set, Cloud City gets the Master Builder Set treatment (set 75222).

A new UCS *Millennium Falcon* (set 75192) is the first LEGO set to have more than 7,000 pieces.

Meanwhile, an aged Luke Skywalker makes his LEGO debut in Ahch-To Island Training (set 75200).

**Buildable
General Grievous**

An adorable Yoda-style tiny figure appears in two sets that tie in with the new live-action series *Star Wars: The Mandalorian*. In 2021, this character's name is revealed as Grogu.

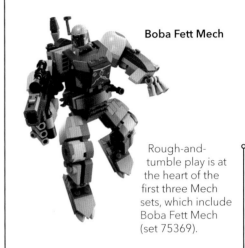

In a new range, explicitly for adult fans, the first three Helmets designed for display are produced, including TIE Fighter Pilot Helmet (set 75274).

Continuing the innovation of 18+ sets, the first three Diorama sets hit the shelves. Now fans can display iconic movie moments like Dagobah Jedi Training Diorama (set 75330).

To celebrate 20 years of LEGO *Star Wars*, a range of anniversary sets is released. Updates of classic sets, they have commemorative plaques and the packaging carries the anniversary logo.

The Bad Batch are on the loose in The Bad Batch Attack Shuttle (set 75314), which accompanies their new animated series *Star Wars: The Bad Batch*.

Boba Fett Mech

Rough-and-tumble play is at the heart of the first three Mech sets, which include Boba Fett Mech (set 75369).

2019 **2020** **2021** **2022** **2023**

To mark the final movie installment of the Sequel Trilogy, Kylo Ren's Shuttle (set 75256) is one of five sets to accompany the release of *Star Wars: The Rise of Skywalker*.

Following Season 2 of *Star Wars: The Mandalorian* a fleet of five new sets are released, which include Din Djarin and Grogu on a speeder bike in Trouble on Tatooine (set 75299).

Wrapped against the desert sand, Obi-Wan's minifigure is in one of two sets about the new live-action series *Star Wars: Obi-Wan Kenobi*.

A youthful Yoda appears in Tenoo Jedi Temple (set 75358). The Junior build is packed with play features and is the first set based on the animated series *Star Wars: Young Jedi Adventures*.

Resistance I-TS Transport (set 75293) is the first *Star Wars* set based on a themed land following the 2019 opening of *Star Wars: Galaxy's Edge* at Disneyland and at Walt Disney World Resort.

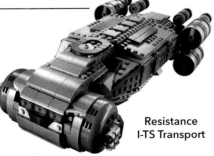

Resistance I-TS Transport

Boba Fett gets a live-action series of his own with *Star Wars: The Book of Boba Fett* and a new minifigure with freshly painted armor in Boba Fett's Throne Room (set 75326).

Along with the live-action *Ahsoka* series, a range of new sets is released, including Ahsoka Tano's T-6 Jedi Shuttle (set 75362)—a remake of the *Rebels*-era craft.

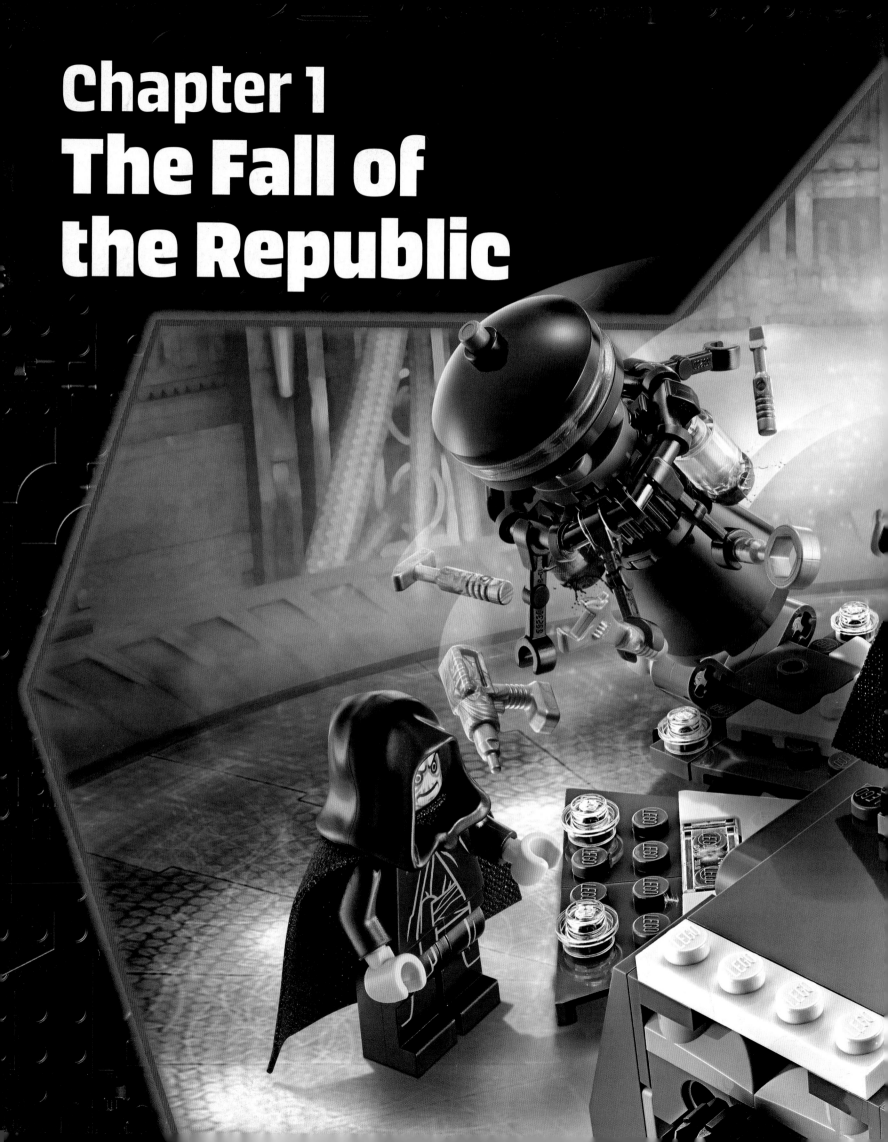

Chapter 1
The Fall of the Republic

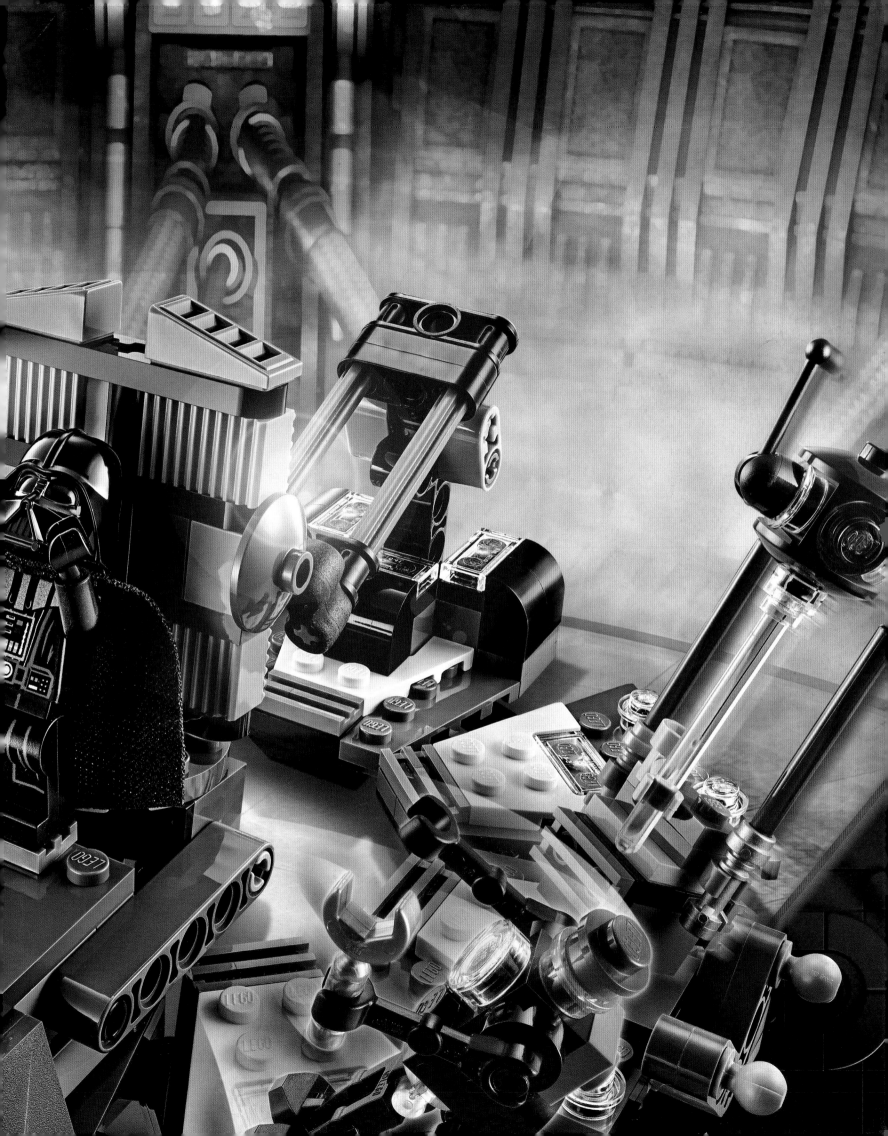

Anakin Skywalker

Anakin's journey from an enslaved boy to perhaps the most capable and ambitious Jedi ever is filled with action and danger. Anakin has always been an incredible pilot and has flown everything from "borrowed" speeders to custom-designed Jedi starfighters during the Clone Wars. But Anakin's daring has its price: the loss of his hand in battle with Count Dooku starts a process of dehumanization that will end in the full body armor of Darth Vader.

Anakin (Naboo Pilot)
Anakin's Naboo Starfighter Microfighter minifigure (set 75223) is ready for action in his peasant's tunic and helmet with flying goggles.

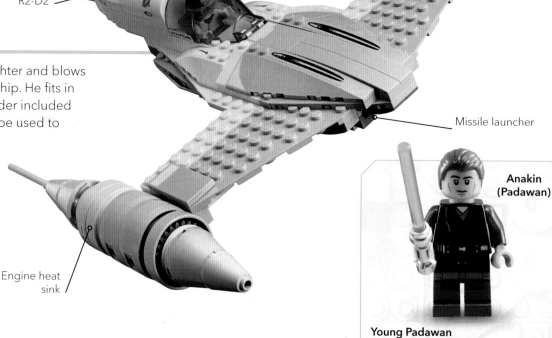

Cockpit holds a single pilot

R2-D2

Missile launcher

▶ Naboo Starfighter

As a boy, Anakin flies a Naboo N-1 starfighter and blows up the Trade Federation's Droid Control Ship. He fits in the cockpit, boarding the fighter via a ladder included with this set. Spring-loaded shooters can be used to fire at battle droids and destroyer droids, and a mechanism on the underside of the ship ejects R2-D2 from the droid socket in case of trouble.

Engine heat sink

Set name Naboo Starfighter	
Number 75092	**Pieces** 442
Year 2015	**Source** I

Anakin (Padawan)

Young Padawan
Protecting Padmé Amidala, Anakin falls in love with the brave senator. He briefly wields a green lightsaber on Geonosis. This minifigure came with the Republic Gunship (set 75021).

▶ Coruscant Airspeeder

Teenage Anakin is now a headstrong Padawan, training under Jedi Master Obi-Wan Kenobi. Anakin wears a Padawan braid (printed on his minifigure's shirt). He and Obi-Wan sit in this airspeeder with its exposed turbojets. The Jedi can store their lightsabers in a secret compartment. Can the Jedi catch up with assassin Zam Wesell's speeder as they weave through the skyscrapers of the city planet Coruscant?

Trunk is at back of speeder

Set name Bounty Hunter Pursuit	
Number 7133	**Pieces** 253
Year 2002	**Source** II

Turbojet engines

Headlights (used as cups in other LEGO® sets)

Padmé (Peasant Disguise)

Undercover Queen
When Anakin first meets his future wife, Padmé Naberrie is disguised as a peasant for her trip to Tatooine. This minifigure came with Darth Maul's Sith Infiltrator (set 7961).

▼ Swoop Bike

Padawan Anakin borrows Owen Lars' swoop bike to rescue his mother from the two Tuskens included with this set. The bike has an engine compartment behind the pilot seat. Watch out for that moisture vaporator, Anakin! (The vaporator comes with the set and opens to reveal secret controls.)

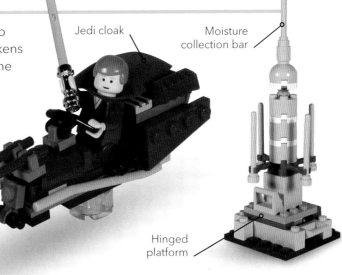

Jedi cloak

Moisture collection bar

Steering vane

Hinged platform

Moisture Vaporator

Set name	Tusken Raider Encounter	
Number 7113	Pieces 90	
Year 2002	Source II	

Large viewport

◀ Jedi Interceptor

Anakin is now a Jedi Knight, with a scarred face, pilot headset, cyborg hand, and black robe. He pilots a custom yellow starfighter (actually, an Eta-2 Actis interceptor) with movable wings and R2-D2's accompanying minifigure fully fixed in the astromech socket. The original version in 2005 featured only R2-D2's head piece.

Hinged radiator wing

Laser cannon

Ion cannon

Republic insignia

Set name	Anakin's Jedi Interceptor	
Number 75281	Pieces 248	
Year 2020	Source III	

Jedi Knight
After a lightsaber duel with Count Dooku, Anakin loses one of his hands, which is replaced with a cybernetic one. Turn Anakin's head to reveal an angry expression. This minifigure came with the 2018 Anakin's Jedi Starfighter (set 75214).

Anakin (Jedi)

▶ The *Twilight*

Anakin's personal starship in the Clone Wars is a battered Corellian G9 *Rigger*-class freighter, the *Twilight*. Anakin first "borrows" the damaged ship from a landing platform on Teth, when he and Ahsoka Tano are rescuing Jabba the Hutt's son, Rotta. Anakin has since repaired and upgraded its weapons and systems.

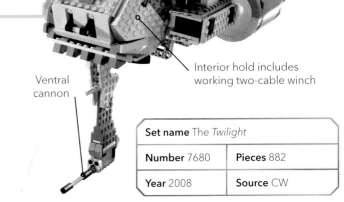

Laser turret

Deployable escape pod

Ventral cannon

Interior hold includes working two-cable winch

Set name	The *Twilight*	
Number 7680	Pieces 882	
Year 2008	Source CW	

Podracing

Ladies and gentlemen, Dugs and Hutts, please join us at the Boonta Eve Classic, the most keenly fought and downright dangerous podrace on Tatooine. Experienced racers Sebulba, Gasgano, and Aldar Beedo will power up their oversize podracers while the human newcomer, nine-year-old Anakin Skywalker, climbs aboard his self-made machine, watched nervously by his supporters. The tension here is electric!

▼ Starters' Box

The podrace starts and finishes at the starters' box, with shaded towers for race officials and the press.

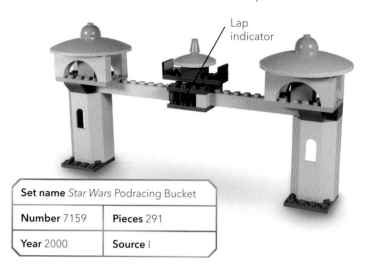

Lap indicator

Set name *Star Wars* Podracing Bucket	
Number 7159	Pieces 291
Year 2000	Source I

▶ Sebulba's Podracer

The dastardly Dug named Sebulba is determined to win the Boonta Eve Classic—and he doesn't care what dirty tricks he uses to do so. Sebulba's podracer includes secret flip-up saws that the Dug uses to cut through his rival racers' machines.

Sebulba

Set name Anakin & Sebulba's Podracers	
Number 7962	Pieces 810
Year 2011	Source I

Friendly Spectator
One of Anakin's friends, the Rodian Wald, cheers him on as he races in the Boonta Eve Classic. But Wald doubts Anakin can win the race—after all, he's never even managed to finish a competition before.

Wald

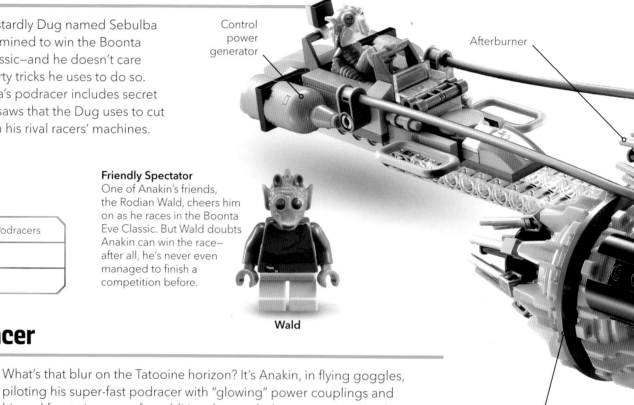

Control power generator

Afterburner

Combustion chamber

▼ Anakin's Podracer

What's that blur on the Tatooine horizon? It's Anakin, in flying goggles, piloting his super-fast podracer with "glowing" power couplings and hinged front air scoops for additional control when cornering. Anakin built the podracer himself, and relies on his Force-aided reflexes while racing. Padmé hopes Anakin will at least survive this dangerous enterprise.

Throttle lever

Control cable

Anakin's Podracer

Radon-Ulzer engines

Triple air scoops

Set name Anakin & Sebulba's Podracers	
Number 7962	Pieces 810
Year 2011	Source I

Watto

Junk Dealer
The Toydarian Watto is Anakin's master, and doesn't know that the boy has secretly built a podracer out of surplus parts. Watto loves to gamble, and usually bets heavily on the unscrupulous Sebulba.

▶ Boonta Eve Podracers

Tatooine podracer pilots such as Gasgano and Aldar Beedo rely on super-fast vehicles to stand a chance of winning the Boonta Eve Classic. Beedo looks for ways to make his Mark IV Flat-Twin Turbojet podracer even faster, while Gasgano fine-tunes his Ord Pedrovia podracer. Watto's junkyard is the place to find spare parts and custom accessories, or even to build a new craft. Perhaps parts from Mawhonic's GPE-3130 podracer might prove useful—but everyone knows that Watto drives a hard bargain.

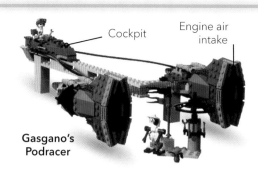

Cockpit
Engine air intake

Gasgano's Podracer

Set name	Mos Espa Podrace	
Number 7171		Pieces 894
Year 1999		Source I

Armored turbojet

Secondary thruster

Mawhonic's Podracer

Set name	Watto's Junkyard	
Number 7186		Pieces 446
Year 2001		Source I

Aldar Beedo's Podracer

Flip-up saw

Race decal

Repulsor generator housing

Air intake

Energy binder

Droid Mechanic
These pit droids are fast workers but quite accident-prone. They see by using a single photoreceptor. This droid belongs to Sebulba and appears in Mos Espa Podrace (set 7171).

Pit Droid

▶ Other Podracers

Lined up and ready to race, simplified versions of Anakin's and Aldar Beedo's podracers rev up alongside Neva Kee's experimental machine, with its cockpit placed in front of the massive engines (which could be dangerous). Clegg Holdfast's Voltec KT9 Wasp podracer has a winged protective canopy over the command chair.

Coolant radiators

Split-X stabilizing vane

Aldar Beedo's Podracer

Anakin's Podracer

Winged canopy

Neva Kee's Podracer

Clegg Holdfast's Podracer

Set name	Star Wars Podracing Bucket	
Number 7159		Pieces 291
Year 2000		Source I

Obi-Wan Kenobi

Padawan braid

Utility belt

Obi-Wan (Padawan)
In *Star Wars: The Phantom Menace*, Obi-Wan is Qui-Gon Jinn's Padawan, and he joins his master in trying to protect Queen Amidala from the Sith apprentice Darth Maul. Swivel Obi-Wan's 2017 head to reveal a face with a fierce look—ready to enter into battle against his Sith opponent.

For a Jedi who's not crazy about flying, Obi-Wan Kenobi pilots a starfighter a lot of the time—though he can't help losing them, too! Kenobi trains headstrong Anakin Skywalker, and goes on missions to far-flung planets including Utapau and Mustafar. Under the Empire, an exiled Obi-Wan meets Luke Skywalker and fights a final duel against his former Padawan, now known as Darth Vader.

Shield projector module

Docking mechanism

Rotating engine

Ion acceleration pod

Opening cockpit

▶ Jedi Starfighter

Obi-Wan wears a headset when piloting his Delta-7 *Aethersprite*-class light interceptor. Supported by his trusty astromech, R4-P17, Kenobi duels with Jango Fett's starship, blasting through the asteroids above rocky Geonosis. R4-P17 comes with the set, but only her head attaches to the craft, where it swivels on a turntable piece.

Deflector shield power hub

Storage area for lightsaber under wing

Stud shooters

R4-P17 astromech droid (dome only)

▲ Hyperdrive Booster Ring

Jedi interceptors do not carry their own drives for jumping into hyperspace. However, the original model of Obi-Wan's Jedi starfighter could easily make the leap thanks to a large external hyperdrive booster ring included in the set. For a big boost of speed, the ship docks with the ring, which is powered by two large engines.

Set name Obi-Wan Kenobi's Jedi Starfighter	
Number 75333	Pieces 282
Year 2022	Source II

Set name Jedi Starfighter with Hyperdrive	
Number 75191	Pieces 825
Year 2017	Source II

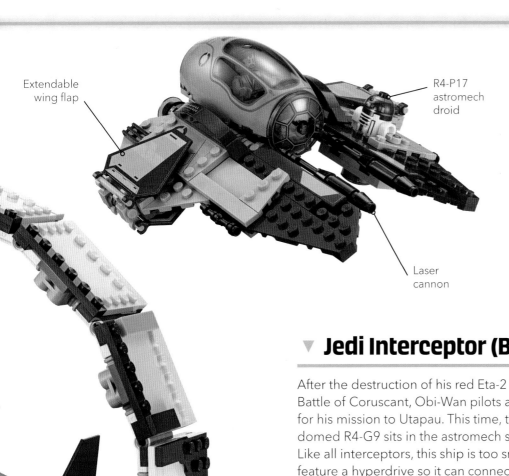

Extendable
wing flap

R4-P17
astromech
droid

Laser
cannon

◀ Jedi Interceptor (Red)

During the Battle of Coruscant, Obi-Wan Kenobi
pilots a red Eta-2 Actis interceptor. A full-bodied
R4-P17 can sit in the specially designed well
on the port wing. In the 2005 version of the
ship (set 7283), only R4-P17's dome piece
was attached to the wing.

Set name Obi-Wan's Jedi Interceptor	
Number 75135	Pieces 215
Year 2016	Source III

▼ Jedi Interceptor (Blue)

After the destruction of his red Eta-2 interceptor in the
Battle of Coruscant, Obi-Wan pilots a blue interceptor
for his mission to Utapau. This time, the bronze-
domed R4-G9 sits in the astromech socket.
Like all interceptors, this ship is too small to
feature a hyperdrive so it can connect
to an external hyperdrive booster ring.
Jedi Master Kit Fisto, also included
with the set, provides backup.

Transparisteel
viewport

Set name Jedi Starfighter with Hyperdrive Booster Ring	
Number 7661	Pieces 575
Year 2007	Source III

R4-G9 astromech
droid (dome only)

▼ Boga

On Utapau, Obi-Wan chases General
Grievous by riding a fast-moving reptilian
varactyl named Boga. The creature shares
her legs with the dewback from the 2004
Mos Eisley Cantina (set 4501).

Set name General Grievous Chase	
Number 7255	Pieces 111
Year 2005	Source III

Cloaked
Obi-Wan

Powerful
tail

Reins

Clawed
feet for
climbing

Obi-Wan (Jedi Master)
Now with the neat beard and short hair
of a disciplined veteran Jedi, Obi-Wan
hunts down General Grievous and
confronts Anakin after he falls to the
dark side.

Jedi Order

For millennia, the Jedi have been the guardians of peace and justice in the galaxy. Within their massive Temple on Coruscant, they train children strong in the Force to become new generations of Padawans, Jedi Knights, and eventually Jedi Masters. During the Clone Wars, the Jedi become military leaders, fighting alongside clone troopers—but in vain. The Sith emerge victorious and destroy the Jedi ranks as darkness engulfs the galaxy.

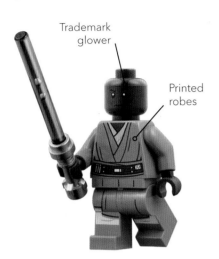

Trademark glower

Printed robes

Sensitive ears

Yoda
The title of Grand Master is given to the oldest and wisest member of the Jedi Order. Grand Master Yoda helped train Count Dooku before the Count abandoned the Jedi Order and joined the Sith. This 2019 minifigure, with its animation-style eye printing and head mold, looks like it could have jumped straight off the cinema screen.

▲ Mace Windu

A member of the Jedi Council, Mace is renowned for his skill with a lightsaber and his stern manner. His minifigure's saber blade is a unique purple. As a senior member of the Council, Mace commands great respect from younger Jedi, who rarely risk his wrath. Other minifigures with "bald" head pieces include Lobot, Asajj Ventress, Sugi, and Turk Falso.

▼ Jedi Masters

The greatest of the Jedi Knights attain the rank of Jedi Master, and the most revered among them are invited to serve on the Jedi Council, which makes decisions for the entire Order. The many species who make up the Jedi have expanded the varied collection of LEGO minifigures with weird and wonderful new head pieces.

Same leg piece as young Obi-Wan in set 75169

Obi-Wan Kenobi
Once Qui-Gon's Padawan, Obi-Wan is promoted to Jedi Knight. He takes on Anakin Skywalker as his apprentice.

Hair element unique to Qui-Gon

Qui-Gon Jinn
The esteemed Jedi Master has seven minifigure versions. This 2017 version includes gray hair details in the aging Jedi's beard.

Mirialan initiate's tattoos

Cape of rich fabric

▲ Barriss Offee

When she starts training, Barriss is a by-the-book Padawan. Her 2018 minifigure features a black skirt piece instead of legs, and a long cape. Her face has blue tattoos and comes with two expressions—calm and angry.

Outfit has just one sleeve

Aayla Secura
A Twi'lek Jedi Knight, Aayla Secura's 2017 minifigure appears in set 75182. Her legs show a printed rycrit-hide belt.

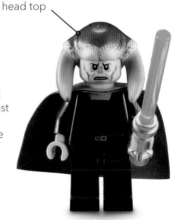

Unique horned head top

Saesee Tiin
Saesee Tiin's second minifigure, from Palpatine's Arrest (set 9526) in 2012, has teeth bared for combat.

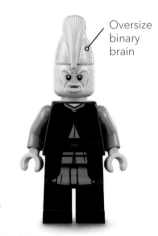

Oversize binary brain

Ki-Adi-Mundi
The Cerean Jedi Ki-Adi-Mundi's minifigure has a cone head top detailed with creases and a ponytail.

Tenoo Jedi Temple
Back when Master Yoda was only 660 years old, he taught younglings in the animated *Star Wars: Young Jedi Adventures*. In Tenoo Jedi Temple (set 75358), he puts Lys Solay and Kai Brightstar through their paces with a Force-suspended rock and an astromech training droid.

Head-tails are called "lekku"

Ahsoka wields two lightsabers

Mystery Jedi
The end of the Clone Wars sees most Jedi killed and the Jedi Temple ransacked, with many records lost. All we know about this Jedi (whose name may have been Bob) is that he once flew on a Republic gunship (set 7163).

Gray tunic

Jedi Bob

▲ Ahsoka Tano

Ahsoka Tano trains as Anakin Skywalker's Jedi Padawan during the Clone Wars. She is a Togruta—a species with colorful skin and long head-tails. Her 2023 minifigure shows her as a grown adult after the fall of the Empire.

Head top made of rubber

Agen Kolar
An Iridonian Zabrak, Agen Kolar's 2012 minifigure shares a head-top design with fellow Zabrak Eeth Koth.

Tholothian tendrils

Stass Allie
This Tholothian Jedi appears in Homing Spider Droid (set 75016), in 2013. Her head piece is unique.

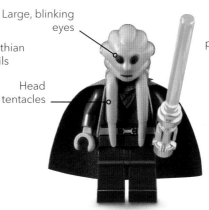

Large, blinking eyes

Head tentacles

Kit Fisto
In 2007, Nautolan Jedi Kit Fisto was the first minifigure to have a rubber head piece. His 2012 variant gained a cape.

Headdress piece is also found on the Jedi Consular minifigure

Luminara Unduli
The Mirialan Jedi is one of the survivors of Order 66. This 2016 version of her minifigure wears dark-brown Jedi robes.

Full-grown head-tails

Shaak Ti
Shaak Ti's 2011 minifigure comes with a unique rubber head piece with head-tails at front and back.

Eye lost in combat

Even Piell
A scarred Lannik Jedi, Even Piell appears with his friend Master Saesee Tiin's Jedi fighter in 2012.

Head crest

Coleman Trebor
A hulking Vurk Jedi, Coleman Trebor fights alongside Mace Windu in the 2013 AT-TE set (75019).

Fighting expression

Quinlan Vos
Unconventional Jedi Quinlan Vos' 2016 minifigure has a big hair piece to represent his long locks.

Jedi Fleet

The Jedi Knights' many missions on behalf of the Republic take them across the galaxy in a variety of transports, including the diplomatic cruisers known as "Coruscant reds" and agile shuttles such as the T-6. During the Clone Wars, the Jedi take to the spacelanes in specially made starfighters, proving their ace piloting skills in dogfights against Separatist droid fighters and other enemies.

▶ Yoda's Jedi Starfighter

Jedi Master Yoda uses a modified Jedi starfighter on a mission to the mysterious planet of Dagobah. The 2023 LEGO set, like the 2017 one, includes R2-D2, who accompanies Yoda. The fighter features Yoda's personal crest and spring-loaded shooters for fending off enemy ships during flight.

Set name Yoda's Jedi Starfighter	
Number 75360	Pieces 253
Year 2023	Source CW

▼ Republic Cruiser

The red Republic Cruiser *Radiant VII* transports Qui-Gon Jinn and Obi-Wan Kenobi to their diplomatic mission on Naboo. The ship can also accommodate the Republic captain and pilot minifigures, with seats for the Jedi in the detachable salon pod. The ship has hidden blaster cannons, detachable landing gear, storage for guns and electrobinoculars, and a space speeder mini-vehicle. An R2-R7 droid provides inflight backup.

Set name Republic Cruiser	
Number 7665	Pieces 919
Year 2007	Source I

▼ T-6 Jedi Shuttle

The T-6 shuttle's cockpit remains upright during flight while the wings rotate around it. Thanks to LEGO designers, the cockpit can be detached from the shuttle and used as an escape pod by the Jedi fighting in the Clone Wars. Years later, during the rule of the Empire, Ahsoka Tano flies a T-6 Jedi shuttle with Sabine Wren.

Set name Ahsoka Tano's T-6 Jedi Shuttle	
Number 75362	Pieces 601
Year 2023	Source AH

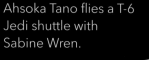

Hatch lifts off

Laser cannon

Folding wing

Wings pivot in flight mode

Deflector shield generator

Attachment point

Salon Pod
An oversize escape pod below the Republic Cruiser's bridge allows Qui-Gon and Obi-Wan to flee and activate a beacon to summon help.

Pod sensors

Transmissions mast

Rotating sensor dish

Space speeder under flap

Laser cannon hatch (closed)

Hinged cockpit roof

Sublight engine

Republic pilot

Switch activates hidden blaster cannon

Detachable salon pod

► Jedi Starfighters

During the Clone Wars, the Jedi train on Delta-7B *Aethersprite*-class light interceptors. These are innovative strike fighters built to respond to the lightning-fast reflexes of Force-wielding Jedi. In the galaxy far, far away, each fighter is tailored to suit its pilot. In the LEGO world, Anakin's fighter has retractable landing gear, Ahsoka Tano's and Mace Windu's ships can fire multiple missiles, Plo Koon's cockpit has a ejection seat, and Saesee Tiin's cockpit breaks away as a separate escape pod.

Radar eye

R7-D4

R3-D5

Hologram projector

R8-B7

R4-P44

Linkage/ repair arms

R4-P17

R7-A7

Astromechs

Astromech droids help the Jedi plot safe courses through hyperspace, repair damage to their fighters, and handle the routine aspects of spaceflight. Some astromechs develop personalities and a rapport with their Jedi partners. Most astromechs are variants of the same standard mold, but their varied color schemes and printed details make them individuals.

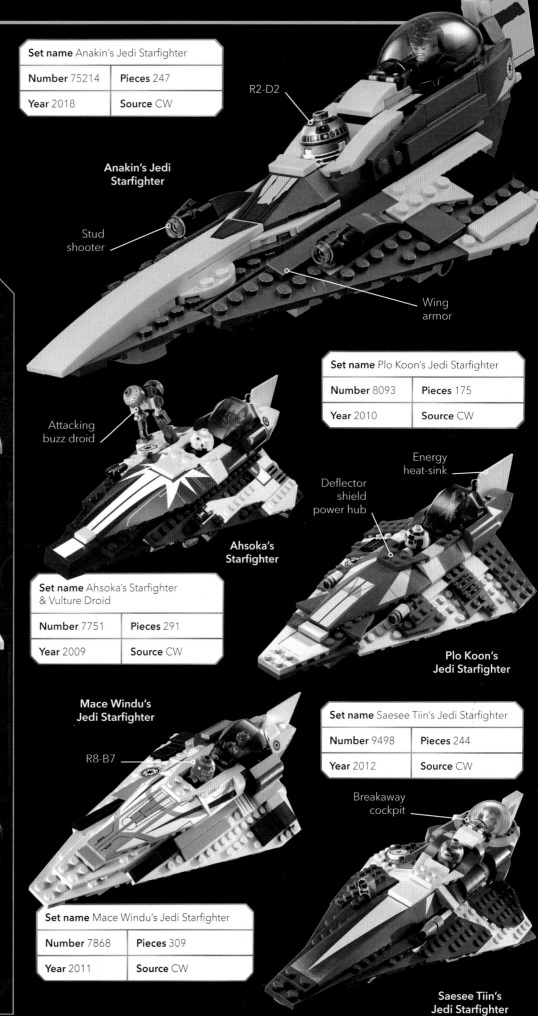

Set name Anakin's Jedi Starfighter	
Number 75214	**Pieces** 247
Year 2018	**Source** CW

R2-D2

Anakin's Jedi Starfighter

Stud shooter

Wing armor

Set name Plo Koon's Jedi Starfighter	
Number 8093	**Pieces** 175
Year 2010	**Source** CW

Attacking buzz droid

Ahsoka's Starfighter

Set name Ahsoka's Starfighter & Vulture Droid	
Number 7751	**Pieces** 291
Year 2009	**Source** CW

Energy heat-sink

Deflector shield power hub

Plo Koon's Jedi Starfighter

Mace Windu's Jedi Starfighter

R8-B7

Set name Saesee Tiin's Jedi Starfighter	
Number 9498	**Pieces** 244
Year 2012	**Source** CW

Breakaway cockpit

Set name Mace Windu's Jedi Starfighter	
Number 7868	**Pieces** 309
Year 2011	**Source** CW

Saesee Tiin's Jedi Starfighter

Chancellor Palpatine

Once a senator from remote Naboo, Palpatine has cunningly risen to become supreme chancellor of the Republic. He has agreed to stay in office while the Republic battles the Separatists in the Clone Wars. What no one knows is that he secretly leads both sides in the conflict, and he is the hidden mastermind of the war. His true identity is Darth Sidious, the Sith Lord who seeks to destroy the Jedi and control the galaxy.

▼ *Venator*-Class Republic Attack Cruiser

The precursor to the Imperial Star Destroyer, the *Venator*-class attack cruiser has enough firepower to blast through Separatist battleships with ease. The interior hangar carries Chancellor Palpatine and two Senate commandos, while the crew comprises a clone pilot and a clone gunner.

There are two minifigures of Palpatine in his red chancellor robes. This 2012 version has him brandishing a secret Sith lightsaber that he uses when the Jedi arrive in his office in Palpatine's Arrest (set 9526).

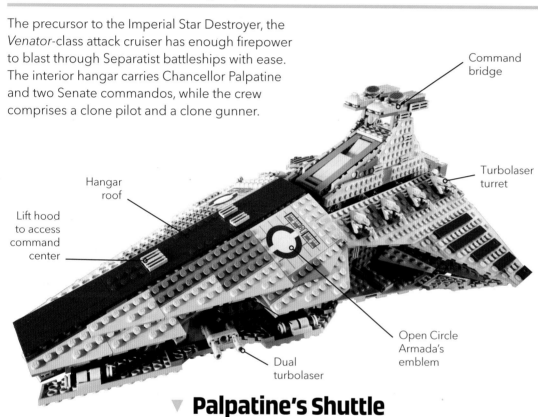

Command bridge

Hangar roof

Lift hood to access command center

Turbolaser turret

Open Circle Armada's emblem

Dual turbolaser

Set name *Venator*-Class Republic Attack Cruiser	
Number 8039	**Pieces** 1,170
Year 2009	**Source** CW

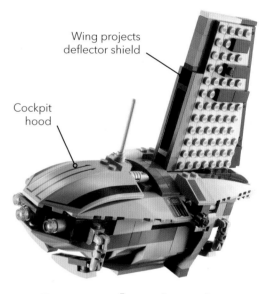

Wing projects deflector shield

Cockpit hood

▼ Palpatine's Shuttle

Captive Leader
It appears that General Grievous has raided Coruscant and captured Palpatine, carrying him off to his Separatist flagship.

Palpatine (Kidnapped)

Now Emperor, Palpatine races across the galaxy in his speedy *Theta*-class shuttle to rescue a badly injured Anakin following Anakin's duel with Obi-Wan Kenobi on Mustafar. A clone pilot accompanies the Emperor, while a 2-1B medical droid stands ready to transform Anakin into Darth Vader.

Set name Emperor Palpatine's Shuttle	
Number 8096	**Pieces** 592
Year 2010	**Source** III

▲ Separatist Shuttle

Palpatine secretly commands the wealthy Trade Federation. Neimoidian puppet leader Nute Gunray travels in a *Sheathipede*-class shuttle flown by a battle-droid pilot, with two battle droids for security. (Neimoidians are cowardly.)

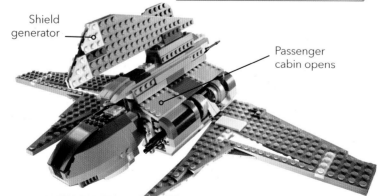

Shield generator

Passenger cabin opens

Set name Separatist Shuttle	
Number 8036	**Pieces** 259
Year 2009	**Source** CW

Count Dooku

The lethal Sith Lord Count Dooku was once a Jedi, but he lost his faith in the Jedi Order and abandoned it, eventually becoming the political leader of the Separatists. In secret, Dooku is the apprentice of Darth Sidious, and is called Darth Tyranus. He works to advance Sidious' plot to defeat the Jedi, not suspecting that his master plans to replace him with a younger, more powerful apprentice.

Sith Lord
A noble by birth, Dooku wears an elegant cape with a silver clasp. This version of the Count from the 2013 set Duel on Geonosis (75017) carries a lightsaber with a curved hilt.

▼ Duel on Geonosis

Dooku flees the fight on Geonosis, seeking to escape with the secret plans for the Death Star. He duels Yoda in an abandoned factory that serves as a hangar for the Count's Solar Sailer. Connected to a LEGO® Technic pole, Yoda's minifigure proves a nimble and acrobatic opponent— just watch out for falling columns!

Set name Duel on Geonosis	
Number 75017	**Pieces** 391
Year 2013	**Source** II

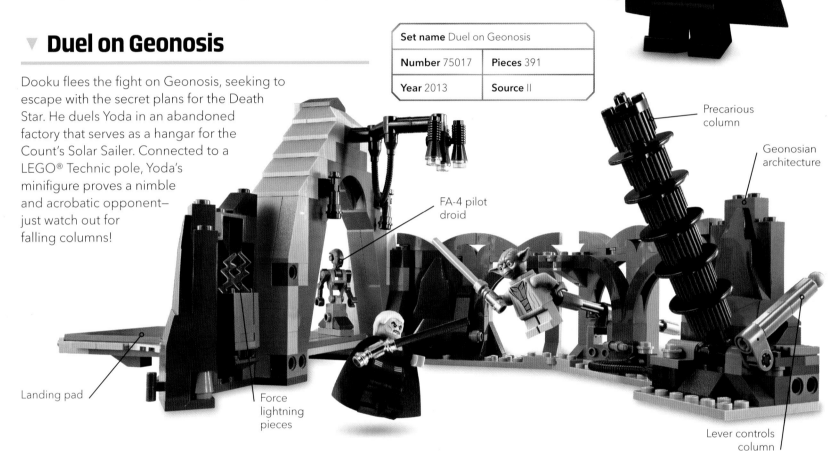

Precarious column

Geonosian architecture

FA-4 pilot droid

Landing pad

Force lightning pieces

Lever controls column

▼ Dooku's Speeder Bike

Dooku's open-cockpit Flitknot speeder bike enables the Sith Lord to escape the Republic's forces on Geonosis. He flees Yoda on a blue version in 2002, and later on a brown, more streamlined, version.

Set name Duel on Geonosis	
Number 75017	**Pieces** 391
Year 2013	**Source** II

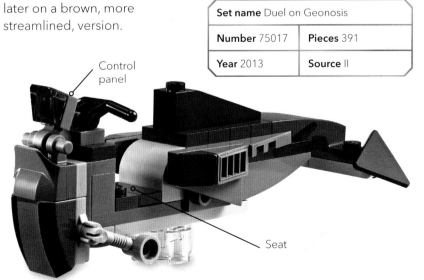

Control panel

Seat

▼ Solar Sailer

Count Dooku's personal starship is an elegant Geonosian solar sailer, piloted by an FA-4 droid. Dooku and two MagnaGuards travel to the battlefield, where Dooku uses his speeder bike to meet Separatist leaders.

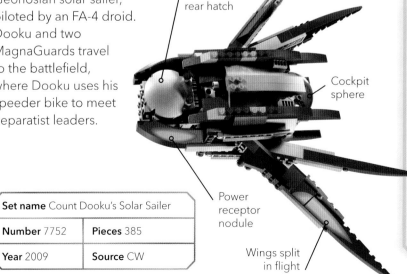

Opening rear hatch

Cockpit sphere

Power receptor nodule

Wings split in flight

Set name Count Dooku's Solar Sailer	
Number 7752	**Pieces** 385
Year 2009	**Source** CW

Sith Followers

"Always two there are. A master and an apprentice." Yoda explains that, for millennia, the secret Sith Order has preserved itself by passing down teachings while waiting for the right time to overthrow the Jedi and seize galactic control. But the Sith are deceitful by nature, and apprentices always end up plotting against their masters. And masters recruit beyond their apprentice to find other followers to do their bidding.

▼ Sith Infiltrator

Darth Maul is Darth Sidious' apprentice. His Sith Infiltrator appears for the first time on Tatooine in search of Padmé Amidala. There are four versions of the ship, each with its own version of Maul's speeder bike. This model has a large compartment in the center for the bike, and storage for Maul's probe droids.

Set name	Sith Infiltrator		
Number	75096	Pieces	662
Year	2015	Source	I

Storage compartment for speeder bike

Cockpit roof

Folding radiator wing

Cloak field generator

Folding landing gear

Darth Maul
For DK's LEGO® Star Wars™: Visual Dictionary: Updated Edition, the LEGO Group produced an exclusive Darth Maul minifigure.

Deadly double-bladed lightsaber

Control linkages

Hand grips

Open hatch

Cargo hold

Rear View

Sith Speeder Bike
In this 2015 set, Darth Maul rides an open-cockpit speeder after his ship lands on Tatooine. It is a super-fast vehicle with a powerful repulsor engine and the agility to maneuver around obstacles with ease. Maul carries a lightsaber to fight Qui-Gon Jinn, who also comes in the set, accompanied by a young Anakin Skywalker.

▼ Sith Nightspeeder

Asajj Ventress is on a mission for the Nightsisters, a clan of witches who rule her homeworld, Dathomir. She rides a fearsome speeder bike with a spiked hull. In battle, Asajj's bike and its sidecar can split off from the hulking portside engine pod, which launches missiles at enemies. She returns from her mission with Savage Opress on board, too—a warrior who will serve Count Dooku, but secretly remains loyal to the Nightsisters.

Set name	Sith Nightspeeder	
Number 7957		Pieces 214
Year 2011		Source CW

Sith Apprentice
Darth Sidious trained Maul from infancy, using cruelty and trickery to turn the young Zabrak into a ruthless warrior. This minifigure, with a Zabrak horns piece and a tattooed face and torso, was released with the Sith Infiltrator Microfighter (set 75224) in 2019.

Darth Maul (Apprentice)

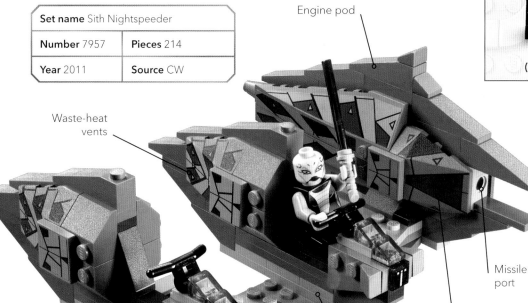

Engine pod

Waste-heat vents

Missile port

Nightsister design

Turbojet pod

Control linkages

Sidecar

▼ Maul Survives

Maul somehow survives being cut in half by Obi-Wan Kenobi on Naboo. He flees to the Outer Rim, but loses his sanity in exile. After Savage Opress finds him, the Nightsisters' magic heals Maul's mind and creates cybernetic legs for him. This intimidating 2013 minifigure with unique leg pieces is from the Mandalorian Speeder (set 75022).

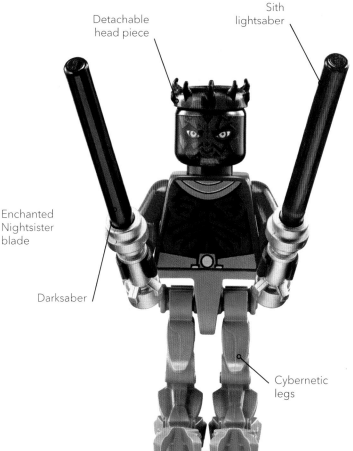

Detachable head piece

Sith lightsaber

Darksaber

Cybernetic legs

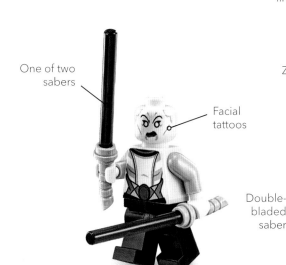

One of two sabers

Facial tattoos

Double-bladed saber

Asajj Ventress
A Force user, Asajj once trained as a Jedi, but turns to the dark side after the death of her master, becoming a servant to Count Dooku. She fights using twin lightsabers. Her 2015 minifigure depicts her looks from the original Star Wars: *Clone Wars* animated TV series (2003).

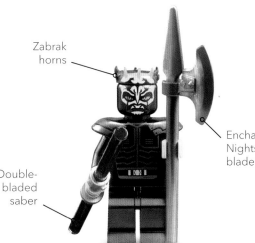

Zabrak horns

Enchanted Nightsister blade

Savage Opress
A Nightbrother from Dathomir, Savage is transformed into a deadly warrior by dark-side magic. Infuriated by Dooku's training and the Nightsisters' scheming, he flees in search of his lost brother, Maul, who becomes his new teacher.

Republic Army

For generations, the Republic had no army, relying instead on the Jedi Knights to maintain peace and justice in the galaxy. But the vast Separatist droid army forces Republic leaders to take decisive action. The Republic quickly amasses one of the largest armies ever seen, with millions of clone troopers led by Jedi generals and diverse, specialized vehicles designed for missions on the ground.

▼ AT-RT Walker

The All Terrain Recon Transport (AT-RT), or scout walker, is an open-cockpit recon vehicle. Heavily armed, it's also a swift opponent for the clones of the 501st Legion. The 2013 set has a swiveling laser cannon, whereas the 2020 one has a stud shooter front and center.

Set name	501st Legion Clone Troopers	
Number	75280	Pieces 285
Year	2020	Source CW

▼ AT-AP Walker

The All Terrain Attack Pod (AT-AP) is a two-legged walker. Like the previous two LEGO AT-APs, this version has a retractable third stabilizer leg. It is equipped with a massive blaster cannon, and the roof and side doors open to reveal an interior cabin.

Printed tile with Republic Navy emblem

Elevating cannon

Set name	AT-AP Walker	
Number	75234	Pieces 689
Year	2019	Source III

Stabilizer leg

▼ AV-7 Anti-Vehicle Cannon

These artillery units reposition themselves by shuffling on their four heavy legs, then spreading their feet to take the shock of blasts from the cannon barrel. They are effective against both enemy ground units and aircraft.

Power leads

Feet allow repositioning

Set name	Republic AV-7 Anti-Vehicle Cannon	
Number	75045	Pieces 434
Year	2014	Source CW

► AT-TE Walker

The six-legged All Terrain Tactical Enforcer, or AT-TE Walker, blasts ground or air targets with its massive cannon, while six laser cannon turrets focus on smaller targets. This set features a 212th Battalion clone gunner to sit on the top of the walker, Clone Commander Cody with his orange visor, three 212th Battalion clone troopers, and three battle droids to fight against.

Heavy projectile cannon

Gunner's station

Laser cannon turret

Bar step access to cabin

Cabin slides out

Terrain sensors

Servomotor disk

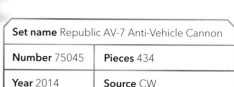

Set name	AT-TE Walker	
Number	75337	Pieces 1,082
Year	2022	Source III

◄ Clone Turbo Tank

Stud shooters

Sides fold down to release AT-RT

The Clone Turbo Tank, officially called the HAV A6 Juggernaut, or more simply the "rolling slab," is the stuff of legend. Its armor is nearly impenetrable, its weapons are devastating, and its 10 wheels crush droids beneath them. A folded AT-RT walker and extra ammo are stored in the cargo bay.

Sturdy wheel suspension

Huge rolling wheel

Set name Clone Turbo Tank	
Number 75151	**Pieces** 903
Year 2016	**Source** III

► BARC Speeder

This one-person Biker Advanced Recon Commando (BARC) speeder often escorts other ships but is also used for scouting missions. Clone troopers ride it during the Battle of Saleucami. The 75037 model includes a spring-loaded shooter.

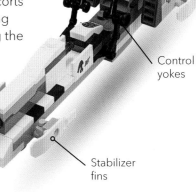

Control yokes

Stabilizer fins

Set name Battle on Saleucami	
Number 75037	**Pieces** 178
Year 2014	**Source** III

Space for 16 troops

Pilot and Gunner
A 2013 variant model of the BARC speeder includes a sidecar, allowing a gunner to shoot down enemies while the pilot flies (set 75012).

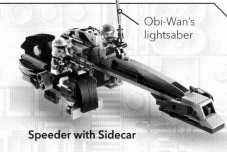

Obi-Wan's lightsaber

Speeder with Sidecar

Foot armor

Cabin splits open

▲ AT-OT Walker

Open-topped All Terrain Open Transports (AT-OTs) are not designed to be tanks, but to transport troops and cargo within safe zones.

Set name Republic Dropship with AT-OT Walker	
Number 10195	**Pieces** 1,758
Year 2009	**Source** III

▼ Swamp Speeder

Formally known as an Infantry Support Platform, or ISP, the Swamp Speeder uses its giant turbofan and repulsorlifts to race through marshy terrain.

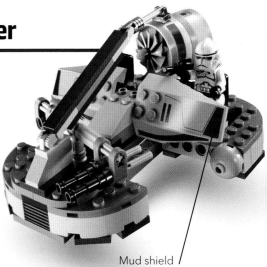

Set name Republic Swamp Speeder	
Number 8091	**Pieces** 176
Year 2010	**Source** III

Mud shield

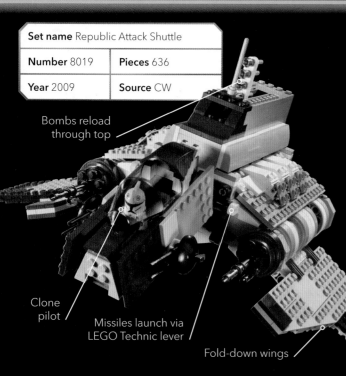

Set name	Republic Attack Shuttle	
Number 8019	Pieces 636	
Year 2009	Source CW	

Bombs reload through top

Clone pilot

Missiles launch via LEGO Technic lever

Fold-down wings

Republic Navy

The Republic defends its spacelanes and millions of worlds with a massive navy composed of giant warships; smaller transports and gunships; and sleek, speedy starfighters. Navy personnel include both clone officers and non-clones of many species. These brave beings clash with Count Dooku's Separatist starships above countless planets as the Clone Wars rage.

▲ Republic Attack Shuttle

The *Nu*-class attack shuttle is a fast, long-range gunship with heavy armor, powerful shields, and a range of laser weaponry, though this model is also equipped to drop missiles from a bomb hatch on the underside. A clone pilot flies the ship, which carries Mace Windu and a clone trooper into battle.

▼ Z-95 Headhunter

Clones serving Jedi General Pong Krell pilot Z-95s during the Battle of Umbara. The LEGO version flies into battle with retractable landing gear, a weapons locker, and a LEGO Technic missile.

Sensor suite

Set name Z-95 Headhunter	
Number 75004	Pieces 373
Year 2013	Source CW

Maneuvering fins

Set name Coruscant Police Gunship	
Number 75046	Pieces 481
Year 2014	Source CW

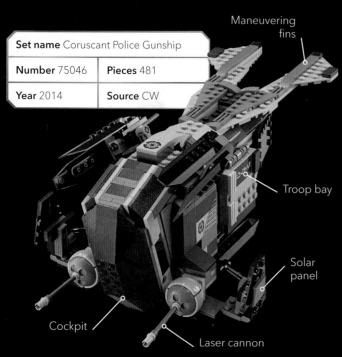

Troop bay

Solar panel

Cockpit

Laser cannon

▲ Police Gunship

Fast and maneuverable, police gunships respond to trouble on the Republic capital of Coruscant. They are less heavily armed than attack gunships, since avoiding damage to crowded city blocks is more important than the ability to unleash a heavy bombardment. Clone troopers sometimes command these craft for military missions.

▼ Republic Frigate

Most Republic frigates were originally consular ships used by ambassadors and diplomats for galaxy-wide missions. With the galaxy torn apart by war, the Republic upgrades these vessels for battle. This ship comes with flick-fire missiles, a mechanism for dropping three further missiles in bombing raids, gun turrets, and a detachable escape pod.

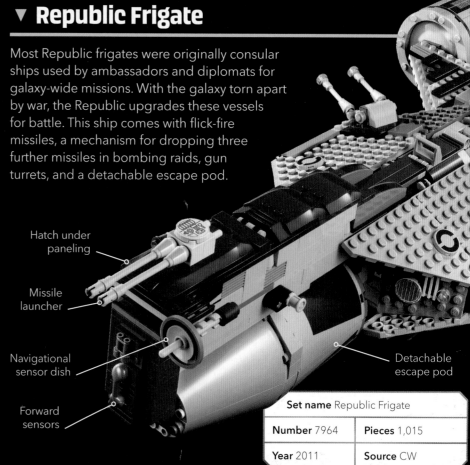

Hatch under paneling

Missile launcher

Navigational sensor dish

Forward sensors

Detachable escape pod

Set name Republic Frigate	
Number 7964	Pieces 1,015
Year 2011	Source CW

▶ ARC-170 Starfighter

The Aggressive ReConnaissance (ARC-170) fighter is hyperdrive-equipped for long-range missions. The 2010 ship's crew consists of Kit Fisto, Captain Jag, a clone pilot, and an R4 astromech. The ship's wings unfold when in flight, while mines can be dropped from the underside.

Wing-mounted laser cannon

Red styling

Heat sinks and cooling radiator panels on split wings

Captain Jag
Clone pilots such as Jag are chosen early in the clone training cycle after demonstrating superior eyesight, reflexes, and spatial awareness. Jag serves Jedi Plo Koon as a wingman.

Set name	ARC-170 Starfighter	
Number 8088	**Pieces** 396	
Year 2010	**Source** III	

Turbine

◀ Dropship

Low Altitude Assault Transport/carriers (LAAT/c or dropships) carry tanks into battle zones. This 2009 ship can lift and carry the AT-OT (see p.27) from this set with the use of LEGO Technic mechanisms.

Nose art (choice of stickers)

Communications antenna

Set name	Republic Dropship with AT-OT
Number 10195	**Pieces** 1,758
Year 2009	**Source** CW

Concussion missile launcher

Powerful thruster

Ventral airfoil

Laser cannon

Radiator panel wing

Sublight engine

▶ V-19 Torrent Starfighter

This fast, agile assault fighter features wing-mounted laser cannons and concussion missile launchers. The wings extend in flight and close for landing, allowing the clone pilot access to the cockpit via a sliding hatch.

Set name	V-19 Torrent
Number 7674	**Pieces** 471
Year 2008	**Source** CW

Ignition chamber

Portside guns

Bomb chamber

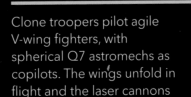

Eeth Koth
Eeth Koth (set 7964) is a Zabrak Jedi Master and member of the Jedi High Council during the final years of the Galactic Republic.

▶ V-Wing Starfighter

Clone troopers pilot agile V-wing fighters, with spherical Q7 astromechs as copilots. The wings unfold in flight and the laser cannons are powerful and deadly.

Swiveling laser cannon

Forward sensors

Wings in flying mode

Set name	V-Wing Starfighter	
Number 75039	**Pieces** 201	
Year 2014	**Source** III	

Republic Gunship

Formally known as the Low Altitude Assault Transport/infantry (LAAT/i), the Republic gunship ferries clone troopers into battle and provides deadly air-to-air and air-to-ground support, raking targets with missiles and blaster fire. The red 2023 model is based on the colors of the Coruscant Guard who protect the Republic capital, the Senate, and its leader, Supreme Chancellor Palpatine.

Wing Power

Three previous versions of the LEGO Republic gunship had ball turrets on their wings for gunners. This model allows for real LEGO battle action with two stud shooters on each wing.

Set name	Coruscant Guard Gunship	
Number 75354		**Pieces** 1,083
Year 2023		**Source** CW
Dimensions Length more than 37 cm (15 in); width more than 41 cm (16 in); height more than 15 cm (6 in)		
Minifigures 5—Supreme Chancellor Palpatine, Padmé Amidala, Clone Commander Fox, and 2 Imperial Shock Troopers		

Hinged panel lifts up

Twin stud shooters

Brick Facts

The 2013 Republic Gunship (set 75021) has the same colors in reverse: white with dark-red details. The Republic first used these attack craft at the Battle of Geonosis, where they deployed a surprise delivery of clone troopers, turning the tide of the battle.

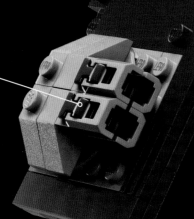

Engine pod

Rear View

Fox gives orders from the rear cockpit

Deployment ramp (closed during flight)

One of two shock troopers included in the set

Laser cannon

Anti-infantry nose turret

Ball joint rotates for maximum field of fire

Troop Deck

The side panels of the gunship hinge up to reveal a spacious troop deck. It has plenty of room for transporting clone troopers.

Supreme Chancellor
As senior leader of the Republic Senate, Sheev Palpatine enjoys the personal protection of the Coruscant Guard— no questions asked.

Padmé Amidala
During the Clone Wars, Padmé moves from having a purely political role to taking up arms to protect the Republic on the frontlines.

Clone Commander Fox
Clone officer CC-1010 (better known as "Fox") commands the Coruscant Guard. This is his first minifigure since 2008.

Imperial Shock Trooper
These elite clone troopers, also known as Coruscant shock troopers, form the bulk of the Coruscant Guard under Fox's command.

Clone Troopers

Rangefinder

Visor

Phase II helmet

Determined expression

Backpack mount

Pauldron armor

Ammo pouch

DC-17 commando blasters

Backpack

Kama (a flexible, anti-blast belt-cape)

Unique printed legs

Elite ARC Trooper

At the start of the Clone Wars, clone troopers wear Phase I armor, which is loosely based on Jango Fett's Mandalorian shock trooper armor. Informally called "the body bucket," this armor is heavy and often uncomfortable. Colored stripes denote rank. During the later part of the Clone Wars, Phase II armor mainly replaces Phase I armor. Phase II armor is stronger, lighter, and more adaptable than the earlier type, with many specialized variations. Color now denotes unit affiliation rather than rank.

"T" visor derived from Mandalorian design

Printed minifigure legs

Clone Trooper (Phase I)
Phase I clone trooper minifigures wear basic white armor with white helmets. The printed legs are new for 2018.

▼ Phase I Clone Troopers

Early Phase I clone minifigures had a faceless black head piece and carried a LEGO bullhorn piece for a weapon. In 2008, a new version of the Phase I clone minifigure gave them realistic skin-tone heads and bespoke blasters.

DC-15 rifle

Yellow pilot stripes

Clone Pilot

Clone Captain

Specially reinforced helmet

Bomb Squad Trooper

Dots indicate rank

Clone Sergeant

Blue markings denote lieutenant rank

Clone Lieutenant

▼ Phase I Clone Commanders

Promising clones are discovered early on in their production and are given special training, with more individuality than the troops they command. Commanders such as Wolffe, Fox, and Cody work closely with Jedi generals in the fight against the Separatists.

Commander (Horn Company)

Rangefinder

Commander Wolffe

Commander Fox

Visor shield unique to LEGO commanders

Commander Cody

Phase II Clone Commanders

By the end of the Clone Wars, many clone commanders are veterans of years of battle and have formed close relationships with their Jedi generals. When Chancellor Palpatine issues Order 66, these friendships mean nothing: obeying their insidious conditioning and training, clone commanders turn their guns on the Jedi they have served on so many missions.

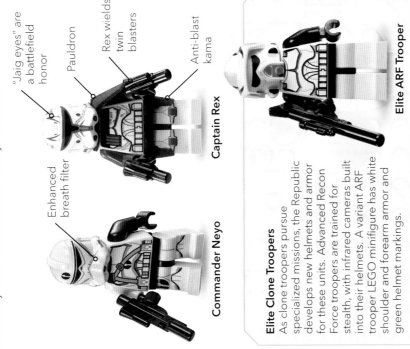

"Jaig eyes" are a battlefield honor

Pauldron

Rex wields twin blasters

Anti-blast kama

Captain Rex

Enhanced breath filter

Commander Neyo

Elite Clone Troopers
As clone troopers pursue specialized missions, the Republic develops new helmets and armor for these units. Advanced Recon Force troopers are trained for stealth, with infrared cameras built into their helmets. A variant ARF trooper LEGO minifigure has white shoulder and forearm armor and green helmet markings.

Elite ARF Trooper

Taun We
Long-necked Kaminoans, including Taun We, create the clone army.

Eyes see in the ultraviolet spectrum

Phase II Clone Troopers

Later in the Clone Wars, the Republic creates more sophisticated Phase II armor. As well as improved breath filters, it allows for greater agility in combat situations. Camouflage is also sometimes used on Phase II armor.

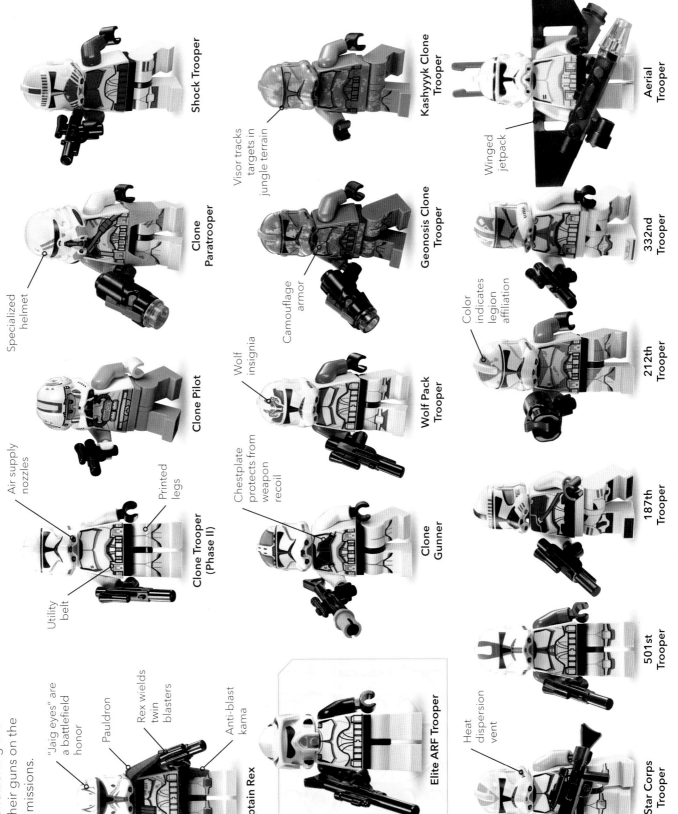

Shock Trooper

Clone Paratrooper

Specialized helmet

Clone Pilot

Air supply nozzles

Printed legs

Utility belt

Clone Trooper (Phase II)

Visor tracks targets in jungle terrain

Kashyyyk Clone Trooper

Geonosis Clone Trooper

Camouflage armor

Wolf insignia

Wolf Pack Trooper

Chestplate protects from weapon recoil

Clone Gunner

Aerial Trooper

Winged jetpack

332nd Trooper

Color indicates legion affiliation

212th Trooper

187th Trooper

501st Trooper

Heat dispersion vent

Star Corps Trooper

Separatist Army

Although mass armies are illegal at the start of the Clone Wars, many wealthy organizations use private forces to enforce payments and collect debts. These forces are pooled to create the Separatist war machine, under the command of Count Dooku. Consisting of huge numbers of deadly droids backed by attack vehicles, the Separatist Army assaults Republic worlds from one side of the galaxy to the other.

▼ Droid Speeder

The commando droid on this speeder chases Obi-Wan Kenobi and Captain Rex in 2013. The earlier 2011 version of the bike is used by a TX-20 tactical droid to ambush Mace Windu's Jedi starfighter.

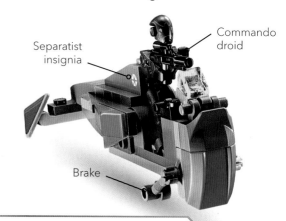

Separatist insignia

Commando droid

Brake

▼ Armored AAT

The 2015 AAT glides into battle armed with laser weapons and two battle droids, which can fit inside the opening cockpit. Jar Jar Binks and his fellow Gungans do everything they can to stop the Trade Federation's battle tanks from taking control of their homeworld, Naboo.

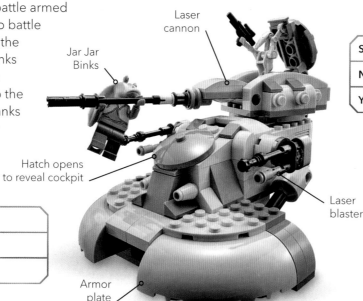

Laser cannon

Jar Jar Binks

Hatch opens to reveal cockpit

Laser blaster

Armor plate

Set name AAT	
Number 75080	Pieces 251
Year 2015	Source I

Set name BARC Speeder with Sidecar	
Number 75012	Pieces 226
Year 2013	Source CW

Mechanical Marvel
Programmed to think up ideal strategies for the battlefield, tactical droids assist the flesh-and-blood generals of the Separatist cause.

Tactical Droid

▼ MTT

The updated Multi-Troop Transport (MTT) carries eight battle droids. Turning the side gear deploys the droid storage rack, while various exterior panels are hinged to allow access to the interior. Hidden wheels allow the set to roll smoothly for the rapid transport of battle-ready droids. The set includes seven battle droids, one battle-droid pilot, a PK-4 droid, a Naboo security guard, Obi-Wan Kenobi, and Qui-Gon Jinn.

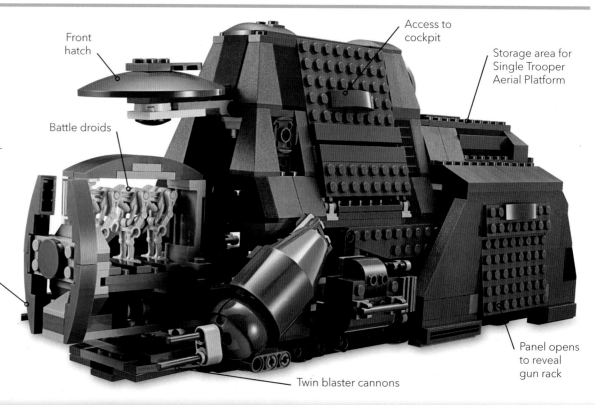

Front hatch

Access to cockpit

Storage area for Single Trooper Aerial Platform

Battle droids

Troop deployment rack

Twin blaster cannons

Panel opens to reveal gun rack

Set name MTT	
Number 75058	Pieces 954
Year 2014	Source I

Infantry Battle Droid

Infantry battle droids make up the majority of the Separatist land troops. Early versions of the minifigure have two identical hands. From 2007 onward, battle-droid minifigures have had a turned hand in order to properly hold a blaster.

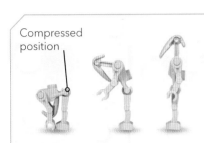

Compressed position

Collapsible Soldiers
Battle-droid minifigures fold up for efficient storage on deployment racks in MTTs and other carriers.

Droid Transports

Separatist troop carriers ferry battle droids to the battlefield more quickly than bulky MTTs. Two battle-droid pilots control the troop carrier, deploying 12 battle droids. This model of troop carrier can carry weapons but is unarmed, relying on its speed to escape Gungan warriors and other enemies.

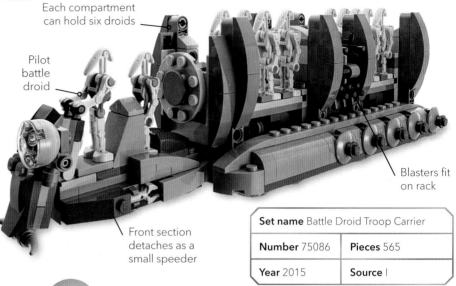

Each compartment can hold six droids

Pilot battle droid

Blasters fit on rack

Front section detaches as a small speeder

Set name	Battle Droid Troop Carrier	
Number 75086	**Pieces** 565	
Year 2015	**Source** I	

STAP

Battle droids pilot repulsorlift gun platforms called STAPs (Single Trooper Aerial Platforms). Brown and blue LEGO versions of the vehicles have been created.

One of two blasters

Power cell housing

Clear piece makes the STAP appear to hover

Set name	Battle on Saleucami	
Number 75037	**Pieces** 178	
Year 2014	**Source** III	

Octuptarra Droid

Missile

Multiple photoreceptors and blasters give these stilt-legged droids the ability to detect and target enemies in all directions, making them tough opponents. Octuptarras defend General Grievous' headquarters on Utapau against the Republic's clone troopers.

Hydraulic limb

Set name	Utapau Troopers	
Number 75036	**Pieces** 83	
Year 2014	**Source** III	

Super Battle Droids

Super battle droids are larger, stronger versions of regular battle droids. They are also equipped with tougher armor. There are three versions of the minifigure in different colors, one with a specially molded blaster arm.

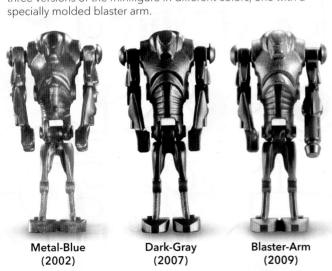

Metal-Blue (2002)   **Dark-Gray (2007)**   **Blaster-Arm (2009)**

Separatist Cannon

Proton cannons use their powerful legs to shift position on the battlefield. Controlled by a battle-droid gunner, they launch powerful explosive shells that are a threat to far-off transports and airborne Republic gunships. The cannon's bright red eyes are made from a versatile LEGO piece that has served as a headlight, a spotlight, and a segment of a medical droid!

High-velocity muzzle

Operator's station

Set name	Battle for Geonosis	
Number 7869	**Pieces** 331	
Year 2011	**Source** CW	

Droideka

Destroyer droids, or droidekas, roll into battle, uncurl, and then deploy built-in blasters to deadly effect. So far, droideka models have battled clones in eight LEGO sets, with the droids looking more and more like their on-screen counterparts.

Set name	Naboo Starfighter	
Number 75092		Pieces 442
Year 2015		Source I

Battlefield Droids

For years, the galaxy's wealthy, unsavory corporations enforced their will on customers using menacing weaponized droids designed to collect debts, force labor settlements, and eliminate rivals. When those corporations join together to form the Separatist Alliance, their droids become the muscle of the armies sent to invade Republic worlds, with Separatist factories working overtime to produce new models.

Dwarf Spider Droid

Dwarf spider droids are mobile laser cannons that walk into battle in advance of battle droids. While not very smart, these droids sometimes refuse to advance when badly outnumbered by enemies.

Set name	Homing Spider Droid	
Number 75142		Pieces 310
Year 2016		Source III

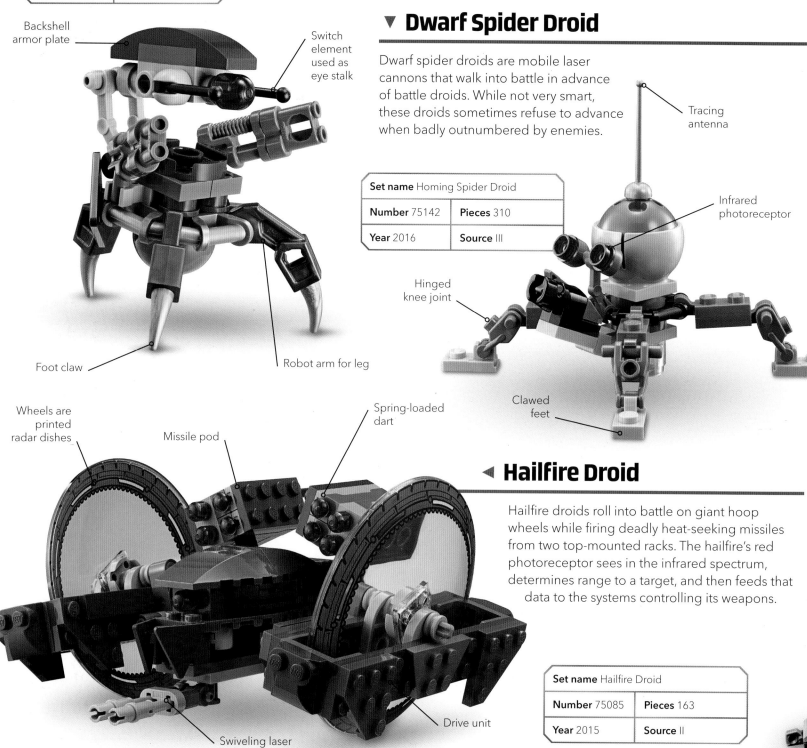

Backshell armor plate

Switch element used as eye stalk

Foot claw

Robot arm for leg

Tracing antenna

Infrared photoreceptor

Hinged knee joint

Clawed feet

Wheels are printed radar dishes

Missile pod

Spring-loaded dart

◄ Hailfire Droid

Hailfire droids roll into battle on giant hoop wheels while firing deadly heat-seeking missiles from two top-mounted racks. The hailfire's red photoreceptor sees in the infrared spectrum, determines range to a target, and then feeds that data to the systems controlling its weapons.

Drive unit

Swiveling laser blasters

Set name	Hailfire Droid	
Number 75085		Pieces 163
Year 2015		Source II

▼ Tank Droid

Amphibious NR-N99 tank droids roll into battle on high-traction caterpillar treads. Three LEGO versions of the tank have been deployed: on Kashyyyk in 2005, one for the new *Clone Wars* movie in 2009, and this one on Geonosis in 2013. Deployed side by side, they form an unstoppable wall of armor, obliterating everything in their path.

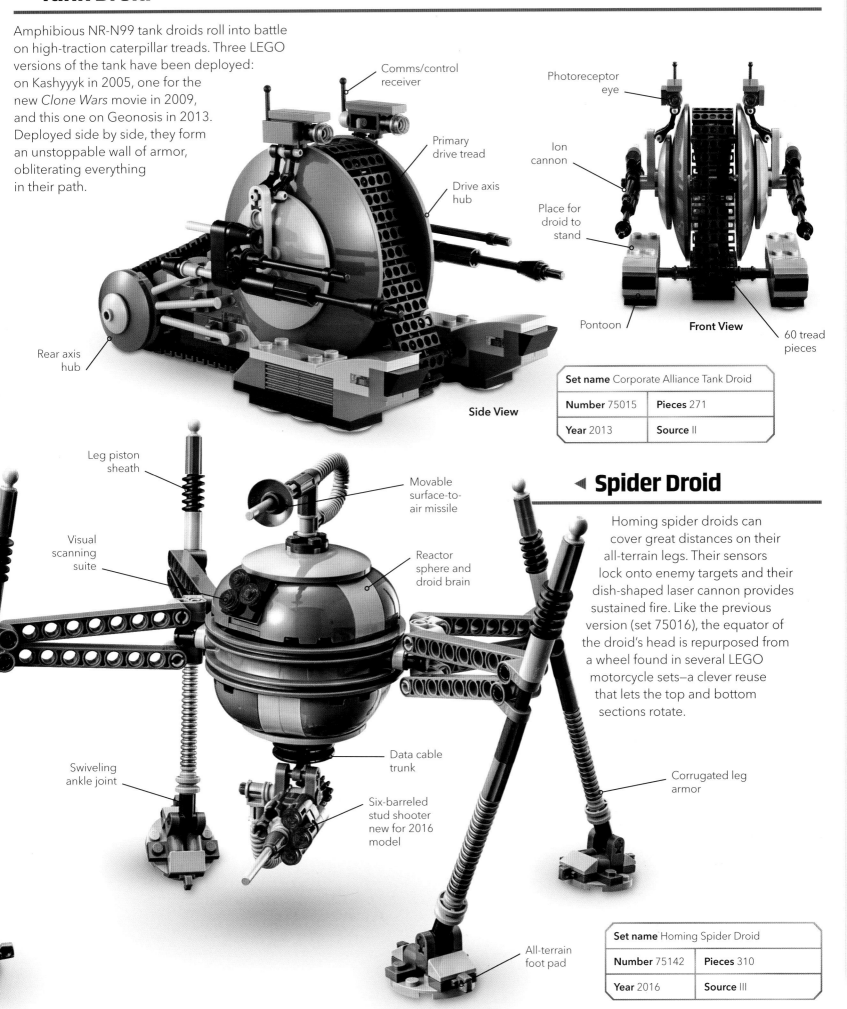

Comms/control receiver

Primary drive tread

Drive axis hub

Rear axis hub

Side View

Photoreceptor eye

Ion cannon

Place for droid to stand

Pontoon

Front View

60 tread pieces

Set name	Corporate Alliance Tank Droid	
Number 75015	Pieces 271	
Year 2013	Source II	

Leg piston sheath

Visual scanning suite

Movable surface-to-air missile

Reactor sphere and droid brain

Swiveling ankle joint

Data cable trunk

Six-barreled stud shooter new for 2016 model

Corrugated leg armor

All-terrain foot pad

◀ Spider Droid

Homing spider droids can cover great distances on their all-terrain legs. Their sensors lock onto enemy targets and their dish-shaped laser cannon provides sustained fire. Like the previous version (set 75016), the equator of the droid's head is repurposed from a wheel found in several LEGO motorcycle sets—a clever reuse that lets the top and bottom sections rotate.

Set name	Homing Spider Droid	
Number 75142	Pieces 310	
Year 2016	Source III	

Separatist Navy

Following their first success at the Battle of Geonosis, Separatist leaders plot and scheme even greater exploits. A space battle rages above Coruscant after General Grievous kidnaps Supreme Chancellor Palpatine. It sees the use of a deadly range of specialized droid fighters. Other Separatist units batter ground forces and civilian targets on contested planets such as Kashyyyk and Ryloth.

▼ Droid Gunship

Droid gunships are well-shielded heavy missile platforms (HMPs) designed for suborbital air strikes. They are relatively slow to maneuver, but their firepower is devastating. Droid brains usually control the gunships, but some modified versions include a cockpit for a battle-droid pilot.

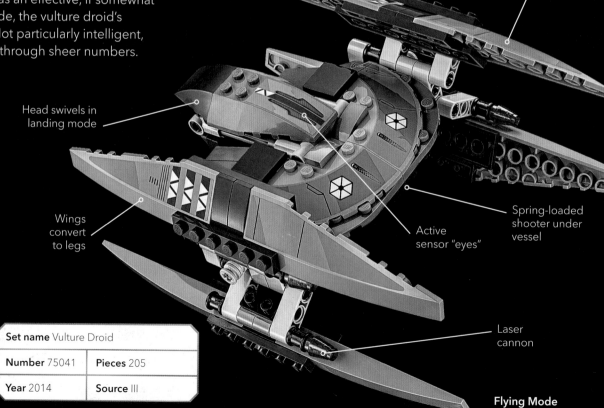

Reactor core

Medium laser cannon

Set name Droid Gunship	
Number 75233	Pieces 389
Year 2019	Source III

Wing pod with spring-loaded dart

Cockpit turns into an escape pod

Rotating laser cannon turret

Long-range sensor ports

▼ Vulture Droid

The Trade Federation defends its battleships with swarms of these pilotless droid fighters. When the fighter lands, the droid reconfigures into walk mode. It reorients its head and walks on its wingtips, doing double duty as an effective, if somewhat ungainly, patrol unit. In walking mode, the vulture droid's wings expand to reveal weapons. Not particularly intelligent, vulture droids overwhelm enemies through sheer numbers.

Claw wing

Head swivels in landing mode

Wings convert to legs

Active sensor "eyes"

Spring-loaded shooter under vessel

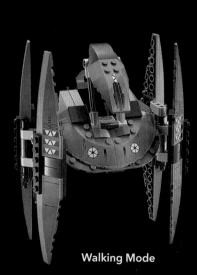

Walking Mode

Set name Vulture Droid	
Number 75041	Pieces 205
Year 2014	Source III

Laser cannon

Flying Mode

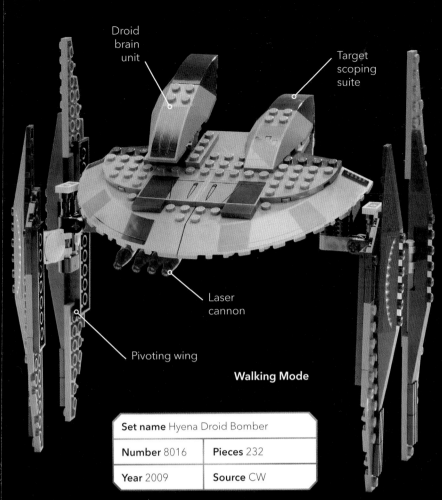

Droid brain unit

Target scoping suite

Laser cannon

Pivoting wing

Walking Mode

Set name Hyena Droid Bomber	
Number 8016	**Pieces** 232
Year 2009	**Source** CW

▼ Hyena Droid Bomber

Hyena-class droid bombers are modified vulture fighters, with a secondary cockpit sensor "head" for improved target scoping, and upgraded weapons systems, including concussion missile launchers. Notoriously, hyena droid bombers carry out a series of devastating raids on Twi'lek cities during the Battle of Ryloth.

Jetpack

Rocket Battle Droid

Torpedo channel

Concussion missiles drop from underneath

Flying Mode

Swiveling wing blaster

▼ Droid Tri-Fighter

With a nose-mounted laser cannon and three light laser cannons, droid tri-fighters are deadlier than vulture droids. These fast, agile fighters excel against Republic starfighters. Some modified tri-fighters are piloted by battle droids that sit in their central spheres.

Cockpit

Nose laser cannon

Set name Droid Tri-Fighter	
Number 75044	**Pieces** 262
Year 2014	**Source** III

Pivoting wings

Rocket Battle Droids
These modified B1 battle droids are designed for scouting missions in deep space. They hunt down and destroy enemies fleeing in escape pods. Commanders are recognizable by a yellow marking on their head.

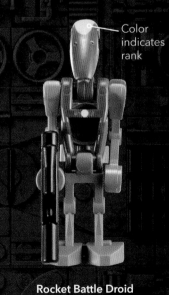

Color indicates rank

Rocket Battle Droid Commander

Spring-Loaded Missile Launcher

Buzz Droid
Separatist fighters launch swarms of buzz droids as guided missiles. They hunt for enemy ships, slip through shields, and wreak havoc with their saws and graspers.

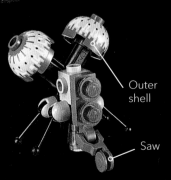

Outer shell

Saw

General Grievous

The Supreme Commander of the Droid Armies is a villainous cyborg called General Grievous. Grievous does not consider himself a droid, however—and reacts savagely to anyone who calls him one. His hatred of the Jedi Knights in particular is long-standing and all-consuming. His only pleasure comes from defeating Jedi in battle and collecting their lightsabers as trophies.

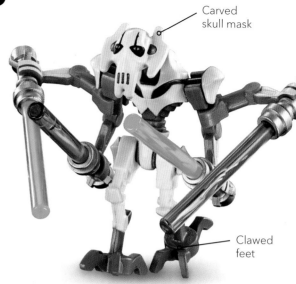

Carved skull mask

Clawed feet

General Grievous
The first two Grievous minifigures used mostly battle-droid parts. In 2010, a more specialized minifigure was created in tan, which was then released in white in 2014.

▼ Malevolence

General Grievous' flagship, the *Malevolence*, is one of the largest warships ever built. It strikes terror into Republic worlds, with no fleet able to stand up to its massive twin ion cannons, backed up with turbolasers. The *Subjugator*-class heavy cruiser has an internal transport train and the top of the LEGO model lifts off to reveal the inner ship.

Set name *Malevolence*	
Number 9515	**Pieces** 1,094
Year 2012	**Source** CW

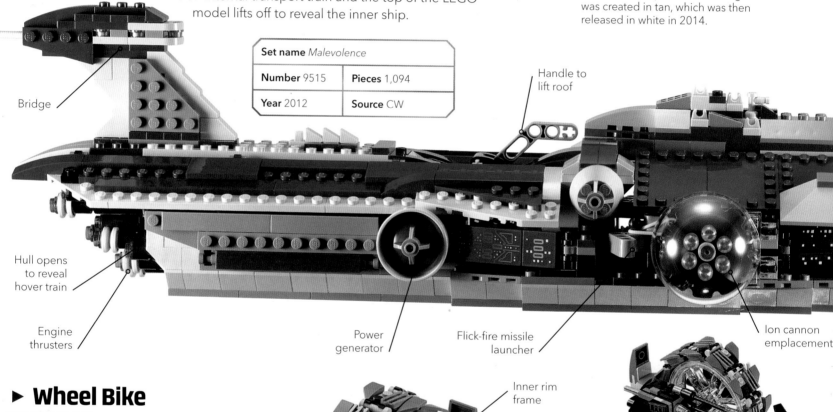

Bridge

Hull opens to reveal hover train

Engine thrusters

Power generator

Flick-fire missile launcher

Handle to lift roof

Ion cannon emplacement

▶ Wheel Bike

On Utapau, General Grievous rides a wheel bike, designed to achieve intimidatingly high speeds across hard terrain. If obstacles block its path, no problem—its two pairs of legs just walk over them! When Grievous flees clone troops on Utapau, Obi-Wan Kenobi gives chase on Boga, a brave varactyl.

Inner rim frame

Walking Mode

Drive wheel

Wheel Mode

Legs folded in wheel mode

Set name General Grievous' Wheel Bike	
Number 75040	**Pieces** 261
Year 2014	**Source** III

▶ General Grievous' Starfighter

General Grievous' battle-worn Belbullab-22 fighter is hyperdrive-capable and features a sliding cockpit, folding tail landing gear, and flip-up laser cannon. Missile launchers hidden inside the wings flip open during combat. When not aboard his fighter, Grievous directs operations from his command chair, keeping his lightsabers close at hand.

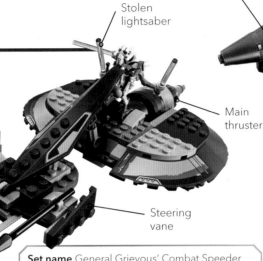

Cockpit slides open

Forward scanner

Plating hides missile launcher

Set name	General Grievous's Starfighter	
Number 75286	Pieces 487	
Year 2020	Source III	

▼ Grievous' Speeder

This super-fast repulsorlift speeder is used by Grievous when he tries to conquer the planet Florrum. The craft is armed with twin laser cannons and rocket launchers (hidden beneath the speeder), and its thruster exhaust is harmless to battle droids. It is the first time the rarely seen vehicle has appeared in LEGO form.

Stolen lightsaber

Main thruster

Steering vane

Laser cannon

Set name	General Grievous' Combat Speeder	
Number 75199	Pieces 157	
Year 2018	Source CW	

Surgical laser

Droid Doctor
A chatty surgical droid with a printed sticker for a face, A4-D tends to Grievous in his lair on Vassek, using medical tools to repair damage done to the cyborg in battles with the Republic.

A4-D

Command center beneath prow

Crew levels

▼ MagnaGuard Starfighter

The Separatists purchased the *Rogue*-class starfighter from the Baktoid Armor Workshop, adapting the tough little fighter's systems for larger pilots such as the MagnaGuards. This fighter has a hyperdrive, superior sensors, and a bevy of weapons, including laser cannons and missile launchers on elite models. The bounty hunter Cad Bane has been known to fly one of these on at least one of his missions.

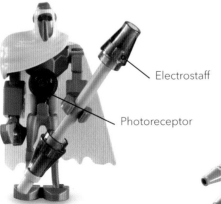

Electrostaff

Photoreceptor

MagnaGuard
These feared droids guard Separatist leaders such as Grievous. A photoreceptor in their chests lets them fight on even without their heads.

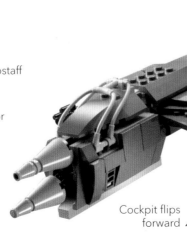

Thruster branch vents

Concealed missile launcher

Cockpit flips forward

Cockpit release lever

Forward scanners

Swiveling laser cannon

Set name	MagnaGuard Starfighter	
Number 7673	Pieces 431	
Year 2008	Source CW	

Geonosians

During the Clone Wars, the hive-dwelling Geonosians are notorious for their huge factories that endlessly churn out battle droids for the Separatist Army. A winged elite class rules over this savage, caste-based society, with wingless drones doing all the work. Geonosian soldiers carry exotic sonic weapons and fly twin-pronged fighter ships.

Chin wattles grow with age

High-caste cranial ridges

Wings not used since youth

Jeweled armor

Poggle the Lesser
A key Separatist leader, Poggle the Lesser takes his orders from Karina the Great, the hidden Queen of Geonosis, who dwells in a subterranean lair. Poggle's minifigure, with its impressive quadruple wings, appears in the Duel on Geonosis (set 75017) from 2013.

▼ Geonosian Cannon

Geonosian soldiers deploy both handheld sonic blasters and platform-mounted LR1K sonic cannons, which fire balls of high-impact concussive energy. The LR1K cannon is a scaled-up artillery version of the handheld sonic blaster. The cannon fires a sphere of sonic energy contained by a plasma charge. When the sphere hits its target, the plasma charge dissipates, releasing a devastating wave of sound. The cannon's platform can tilt up and down.

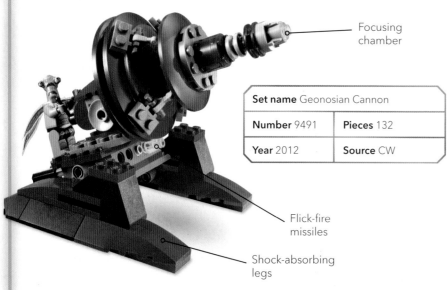

Focusing chamber

Set name	Geonosian Cannon	
Number	9491	Pieces 132
Year	2012	Source CW

Flick-fire missiles

Shock-absorbing legs

Cockpit hatch opens for pilot access

Set name	Geonosian Starfighter	
Number	7959	Pieces 155
Year	2011	Source CW

Dorsal capacitor housing

Dorsal prong

Engine orb can rotate

Torpedo bay underneath

Gun-turret housing

▲ Geonosian Fighter

Thousands of deadly *Nantex*-class starfighters are launched against Republic forces at the Battle of Geonosis. These ships are specially designed to accommodate the anatomy of Geonosian pilots, and include a lifting cockpit hatch, a swiveling laser cannon, and a hidden proton torpedo.

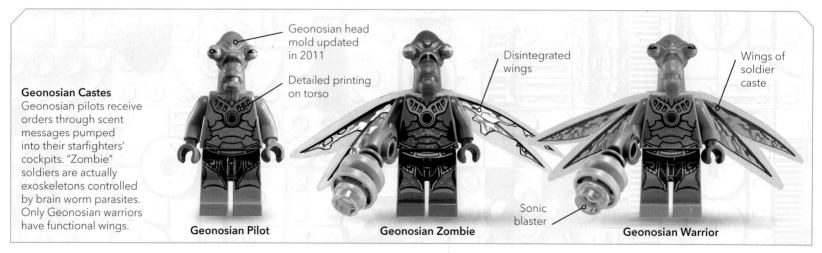

Geonosian Castes
Geonosian pilots receive orders through scent messages pumped into their starfighters' cockpits. "Zombie" soldiers are actually exoskeletons controlled by brain worm parasites. Only Geonosian warriors have functional wings.

Geonosian head mold updated in 2011

Detailed printing on torso

Disintegrated wings

Wings of soldier caste

Sonic blaster

Geonosian Pilot

Geonosian Zombie

Geonosian Warrior

Naboo and Gungans

It takes an invasion by the villainous Trade Federation to propel peaceful Naboo to consider war. Its inhabitants—human Naboo and amphibious Gungans—must band together and work with their Jedi protectors to repel the hordes of merciless battle droids.

Set name Gungan Patrol	
Number 7115	Pieces 77
Year 2000	Source I

Feathers indicate status

Energy shield

Jar Jar Binks

Battle wagon

Billed snout

Saddle made of fambaa skin

Energy ball

▼ Naboo Swamp

Jedi Qui-Gon Jinn and Obi-Wan Kenobi land on Naboo to help its inhabitants. In the Naboo swamp, Qui-Gon uses his lightsaber to deflect blaster fire from battle droids on STAPs (Single Trooper Aerial Platforms) and shield his Gungan guide, Jar Jar Binks. The STAPs come with "invisible" stands to make them hover.

Set name Naboo Swamp	
Number 7121	Pieces 81
Year 1999	Source I

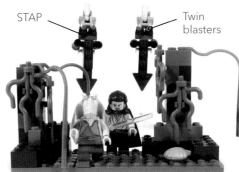

STAP

Twin blasters

▲ Gungan Patrol

Gungans ride large, flightless kaadu. These amphibious animals are fast and agile. Many kaadu are used as beasts of burden, though larger four-legged falumpasets are also popular. One of these kaadu is ridden by a Gungan soldier and is pulling a wagon carrying energy-ball ammunition into battle against the droid army. The energy balls roll out of the back of the wagon.

▼ Flash Speeder

Repulsorlift Flash speeders are normally piloted by Naboo security officers. They are used for patrols in peacetime, but employed in the defense of Theed Palace during the invasion of Naboo.

Set name Gungan Sub	
Number 9499	Pieces 465
Year 2012	Source I

Underwater mine

Forward cockpit bubble

Rotating drive fins

Detachable mini-sub

Cargo container

Forward diving plane

Set name Flash Speeder	
Number 75091	Pieces 312
Year 2015	Source I

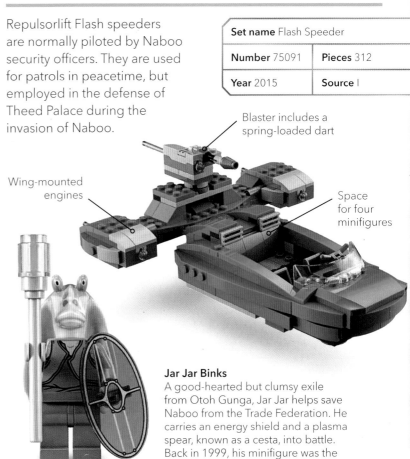

Blaster includes a spring-loaded dart

Wing-mounted engines

Space for four minifigures

▲ Gungan Sub

Qui-Gon, Obi-Wan, and Jar Jar travel to Theed from the underwater city of Otoh Gunga in a bongo, or Gungan sub. Naboo's watery depths are home to dangerous monsters. The 2012 set has bongo defenses not shown on-screen: a mine to scare off attackers, flick-fire missiles, and a detachable mini-sub for a quick getaway. It was also the first LEGO set to include a Queen Amidala minifigure dressed in all her royal garb.

Jar Jar Binks
A good-hearted but clumsy exile from Otoh Gunga, Jar Jar helps save Naboo from the Trade Federation. He carries an energy shield and a plasma spear, known as a cesta, into battle. Back in 1999, his minifigure was the first to have a unique head sculpt.

Umbarans and Mandalorians

The Republic faces many perils in the Outer Rim during the Clone Wars. The shadowy world of Umbara is home to Separatist-allied soldiers whose technology rivals anything in the Republic. Mandalore is a neutral world, officially choosing no side. However, ruthless Death Watch warriors will stop at nothing to overthrow its ruler, the pacifist Duchess Satine.

▼ The Death Watch

Duchess Satine insists Mandalore has left its warlike past behind. But a secretive band of armored warriors, the Death Watch, has allied itself with the Separatists. Well-armed and deadly, they seek to take over the planet.

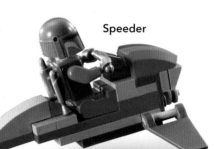

Speeder

Swiveling cannon

Gun Turret

Set name Mandalorian Battle Pack	
Number 7914	Pieces 68
Year 2011	Source CW

Electromagnetic pulse cannon

Rear Cockpit

Opening cockpit

Movable legs

◀ Umbaran Cannon

On Umbara, one of the toughest machines the clones face is the juggernaut, or Mobile Heavy Cannon. A blast from this six-legged tank can wipe out an entire Republic platoon. This 2013 Umbaran MHC comes with Ahsoka Tano, a 212th Attack Battalion clone trooper, and two Umbaran soldiers.

Set name Umbaran MHC	
Number 75013	Pieces 493
Year 2013	Source CW

Umbaran Soldier

Mandalorians

The Death Watch's Mandalorian super commandos are led by Pre Vizsla, who wields the Darksaber: an ancient lightsaber with a black blade. After Maul takes over the Death Watch, the super commandos repaint their armor red and black in his honor.

Maul's colors

Darksaber

Mandalorian Super Commando

Pre Vizsla

▼ Mandalorian Speeder

When Maul and the Death Watch take over Mandalore, they patrol its skies in these fast, powerful police speeders. The craft is full of surprises: its front hatch hides a missile emplacement, while its gun turret is built on top of a secret weapons locker.

Elevated cannon

Hidden weapons locker

Missiles hidden beneath hatch

Armored skirt

Set name Mandalorian Speeder	
Number 75022	Pieces 211
Year 2013	Source CW

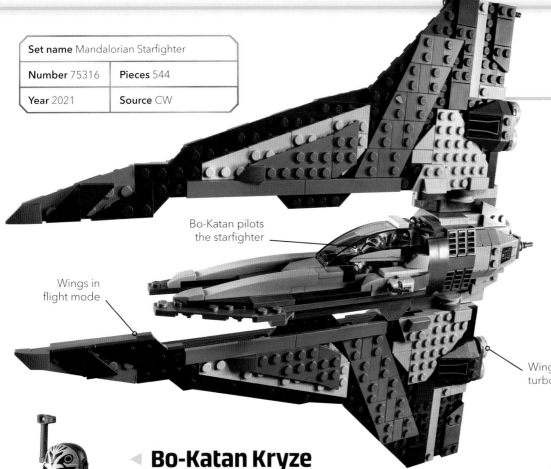

Set name	Mandalorian Starfighter	
Number 75316	Pieces 544	
Year 2021	Source CW	

◄ Mandalorian Starfighter

The aggressive Death Watch use *Kom'rk*-class Gauntlet starfighters in their takeover of Mandalore. Maul likes the design so much he adopts them for his Shadow Collective. The fuselage of this ship has LEGO Technic connections so it stays level while the wings swivel, giving the transport and combat craft maximum agility and precision.

Bo-Katan pilots the starfighter

Wings in flight mode

Wing-mounted turbo jets

Mandalorian Loyalist

Compact engine

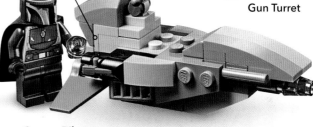

Swoop Bike

Gun Turret

◄ Bo-Katan Kryze

Bo-Katan of House Kryze is Duchess Satine's sister and the rightful leader of Mandalore. She leads an elite unit called the Nite Owls in a bid to reclaim her planet and her birthright. Two yellow stripes on her chestplate show her service in the Clone Wars, and her helmet can be swapped for a red hair piece.

► Gar Saxon

As a Mandalorian super commando, Gar Saxon joins Maul and his criminal group, the Shadow Collective. Saxon shows his loyalty to Maul with Zabrak-like horns on his helmet and armor decorations that echo Maul's markings. He is a sworn enemy of Bo-Katan, who wants her planet back.

Set name	Mandalorian Battle Pack	
Number 75267	Pieces 102	
Year 2020	Source M	

▲ Life in Exile

The Empire leaves Mandalore all but destroyed. Citizens flee their uninhabitable planet and scatter across the galaxy, settling where they can. One such clan finds refuge on a planet with a recently discovered Mandalorian settlement, and makes the most of their basic surroundings. The LEGO battle pack of multicolor Mandalorian warriors includes a battered old Balutar swoop bike and a gun turret assembled from rocks.

Hidden Covert
A clan of exiled Mandalorians keeps its traditions by following an ancient creed called "the Way." Each minifigure has its own color of armor.

Mandalorian (Gray)

Mandalorian (Green)

Mandalorian (Orange)

Mandalorian (Blue)

Bounty Hunters

Bounty hunters track down and capture people in order to collect a fee, or bounty. Generally, they will work for whoever pays the most credits. These ruthless, capable hunters prefer to work alone, but occasionally hire fellow professionals to aid on their mission.

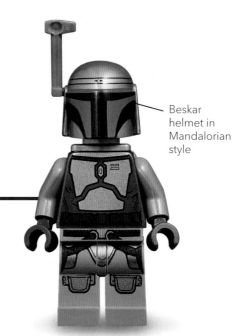

Beskar helmet in Mandalorian style

Jango Fett

▶ Jango Fett

One of the most legendary bounty hunters of all time, Jango Fett is known across the galaxy. When the Kaminoans create the clone army, they use Jango's DNA as the template for the clone troopers. Jango raises one of these clones, Boba Fett, as his son. Jango wears beskar Mandalorian armor and flies a modified pursuit ship that he has upgraded so it positively bristles with weapons. He later passes the ship to Boba.

Young Boba
Jango Fett treats an unaltered clone as his son and teaches him to be a bounty hunter. The 2013 Advent Calendar (set 75023) introduces the first young Boba Fett minifigure to have non-yellow skin tones.

▼ Hutt Starhopper

HH-87 Starhoppers are tough little gunships favored by several lawless organizations that operate from shadowy corners of the galaxy, including Zygerrian gangs, pirates, and the Hutt clans. On the Hutt homeworld, Nal Hutta, Hutt servants fly HH-87s to hunt down the bounty hunter Cad Bane, who has fled to the planet with a disguised Obi-Wan.

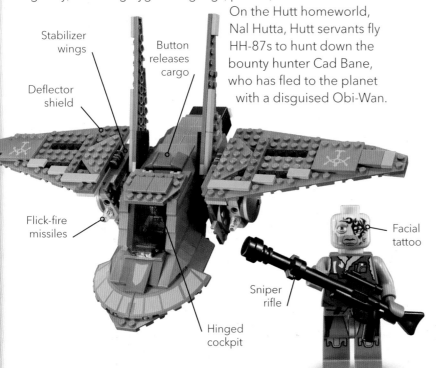

Stabilizer wings

Button releases cargo

Deflector shield

Flick-fire missiles

Sniper rifle

Facial tattoo

Hinged cockpit

▼ Zam Wesell

Assassin Zam Wesell is hired to track down Padmé Amidala. She flies a sleek airspeeder that is perfect for quick getaways on risky missions. This makes it difficult for Anakin and Obi-Wan to give chase in their borrowed airspeeder through the towering spires of Coruscant. Wesell's cockpit screen is hinged, and a hidden mechanism makes the wings fall off, re-creating the crash-landing at the end of the high-speed chase in the movie.

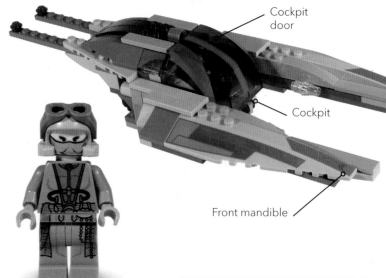

Cockpit door

Cockpit

Front mandible

Set name HH-87 Starhopper	
Number 75024	**Pieces** 362
Year 2013	**Source** CW

Rako Hardeen
This is actually Obi-Wan Kenobi in disguise! The Jedi Master assumes the identity of a bounty hunter to go undercover with a gang and uncover its plot to assassinate Chancellor Palpatine.

Zam Wesell
A shapeshifting Clawdite, Wesell's minifigure has a double-sided head that reveals her natural face as well as the human face she adopts to pass unnoticed through Coruscant.

Set name Bounty Hunter Pursuit	
Number 7133	**Pieces** 253
Year 2002	**Source** II

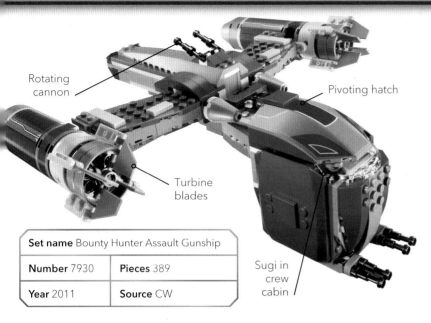

Rotating cannon

Turbine blades

Pivoting hatch

Sugi in crew cabin

Set name	Bounty Hunter Assault Gunship	
Number 7930	Pieces 389	
Year 2011	Source CW	

▲ Sugi's Gunship

During the Clone Wars, the Zabrak bounty hunter Sugi is captain of a gunship called the *Halo*. The craft was originally built for military strikes, but Sugi refitted it with a crew cabin and hold, making it suitable for longer-term missions. Sliding the top of the hull pivots the wings and allows access to a hidden compartment for stashing valuable cargo. The set comes with three exclusive bounty hunter minifigures—Sugi, Embo, and Aurra Sing.

Sugi   Embo   Aurra Sing

▼ Pirate Tank

Led by Hondo Ohnaka, Weequay pirates on the planet Florrum use starships, speeder bikes, and tanks to defend their base. For ground operations, Hondo depends on his WLO-5 tanks, which boast thick armor and heavy guns.

Turk Falso

Antipersonnel armor

Ancient pistols

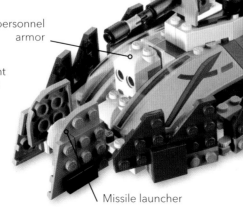

Missile launcher

▼ Cad Bane's Speeder

Cad Bane and his crew favor these repulsorlift vehicles for their high speeds and agility. In one of his most daring raids, Bane and a gang of hired thugs attack the Senate building in the heart of Coruscant, taking a group of senators hostage and demanding that the Republic free crime lord Ziro the Hutt in exchange for the captives. Bane and his hunters, including Shahan Alama and an assassin droid, then flee the Senate.

Beloved fedora

Set name	Cad Bane's Speeder	
Number 8128	Pieces 318	
Year 2010	Source CW	

Cad Bane
A Duros bounty hunter, Cad Bane is infamous across the galaxy for his ruthlessness and successful methods. He often works for the Sith Lord Darth Sidious.

Bow hatch

Headlights hide missiles

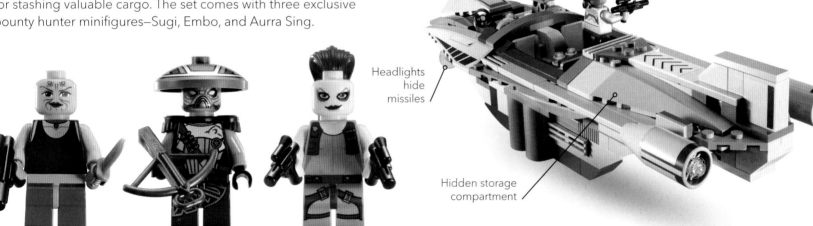

Hidden storage compartment

Turbine engine

Steering vane

Fancy stolen coat

Hondo Ohnaka
Hondo Ohnaka believes in grog, loot, and good times, though he is not without a sense of honor. He shares his black epaulet piece with the bounty hunter Embo and a LEGO space officer.

Set name	Pirate Tank	
Number 7753	Pieces 372	
Year 2009	Source CW	

Fallen Jedi

Tormented by visions of his wife, Padmé Amidala, coming to harm, Anakin turns to Chancellor Palpatine, who hints that there is more to the Force than Jedi teachings. He also reveals his true identity: he is the Sith Lord Darth Sidious! Desperate to save Padmé, Anakin falls to the dark side, leading Sidious' assault on the Jedi and crossing lightsabers with his old master Obi-Wan Kenobi on the lava planet Mustafar.

▼ Palpatine's Arrest

Mace Windu assembles a party of Jedi to arrest Chancellor Palpatine, but the Sith Lord is full of tricks and his office holds many surprises. Will Mace fall victim to the hidden locker of dark-side weapons, or get flung out of the set's breakaway window? Anakin docks his airspeeder and rushes into the fray, where he must choose between his loyalty to the Jedi and his hunger to learn the dark side's secrets.

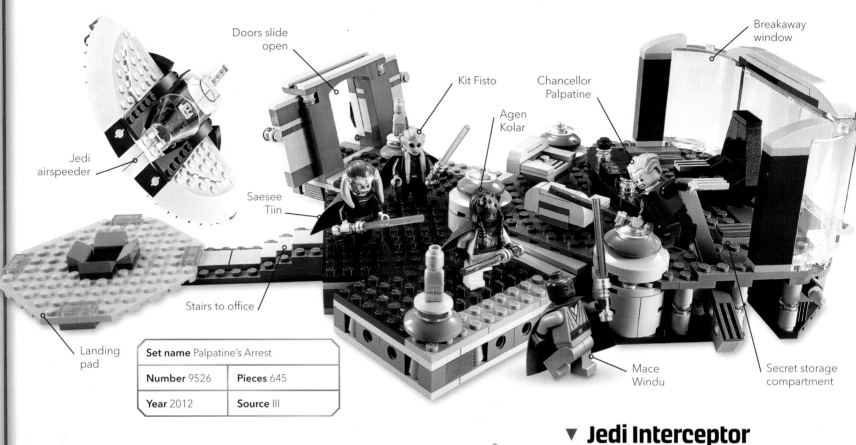

Doors slide open

Breakaway window

Kit Fisto

Chancellor Palpatine

Agen Kolar

Jedi airspeeder

Saesee Tiin

Stairs to office

Landing pad

Mace Windu

Secret storage compartment

Set name Palpatine's Arrest	
Number 9526	**Pieces** 645
Year 2012	**Source** III

▼ Jedi Interceptor

After swearing allegiance to Darth Sidious, Anakin becomes his Sith apprentice. He attacks the Jedi Temple and says goodbye to Padmé. Boarding his Jedi interceptor, Anakin travels to Mustafar to eliminate the Separatist leaders. But Padmé and Obi-Wan follow him, leading to a fateful duel and tragic consequences. This 2012 set comes with five minifigures, including Nute Gunray and a battle droid.

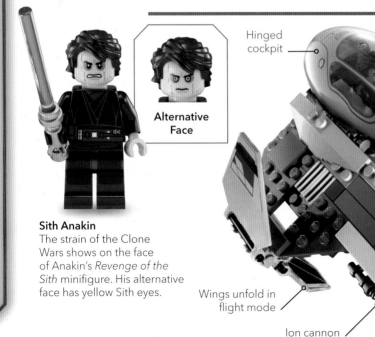

Hinged cockpit

R2-D2

Alternative Face

Sith Anakin
The strain of the Clone Wars shows on the face of Anakin's *Revenge of the Sith* minifigure. His alternative face has yellow Sith eyes.

Wings unfold in flight mode

Ion cannon

Laser cannon

Set name Anakin's Jedi Interceptor	
Number 9494	**Pieces** 300
Year 2012	**Source** III

▶ Duel on Mustafar

Teetering on service platforms above the red-hot lava of Mustafar, Obi-Wan fights his former Padawan, Anakin, now renamed Darth Vader after being recruited to the Sith. They are moved on long rods and their lightsabers glow. Meanwhile, the pillars could come crashing down at any time!

Lava load spills from container

Orange transparent brick for fiery effect

Pillars collapse when pushed

Pole for moving minifigures

Bubbling red-hot lava fountains

Set name	Ultimate Lightsaber Duel	
Number 7257	Pieces 282	
Year 2005	Source III	

Duel on Mapuzo
Obi-Wan Kenobi vs. Darth Vader (set 75334) re-creates the duel from the live-action series *Star Wars: Obi-Wan Kenobi*. The set features revolving platforms and a pop-up flame barrier. Obi-Wan is aided by Imperial officer Tala Durith and an NED-B loader droid.

Mechanism attaches Vader's helmet

First LEGO version of DD-13 medical assistant droid

Seeker droid

FX-9 surgical droid

▶ Rehabilitation Center

After his battle with Obi-Wan on Mustafar, Vader would have died had Palpatine not found him and taken him to Coruscant. A medical droid stabilizes Vader's burned body and organs, then encases him in a life-supporting black suit of armor.

Arise Darth Vader
Darth Sidious oversees Anakin's transformation into a ruthless cyborg. Now known as Sith Lord Darth Vader, he is more dangerous than ever before.

Set name	Darth Vader Transformation	
Number 75183	Pieces 282	
Year 2017	Source III	

Handle lowers and flips operating table to change Anakin into Vader

Wookiees

During the Clone Wars, an epic battle takes place on Kashyyyk, home planet of the Wookiees. Droid armies face fierce resistance from proud, well-armed Wookiee warriors, including the chieftain, Tarfful, and Chewbacca. Wookiees use traditional wood-framed vehicles, and their knowledge of the swamps and forests of their planet gives them an advantage over the ruthless droids.

On Kashyyyk, Separatist battle droids, spider droids, and tank droids launch a massive attack. The Wookiees fight bravely in their ornithopters, catamarans, and other vehicles, supported by Republic clone troops led by Jedi generals.

◀ Ornithopter

Wookiee ornithopters, also known as fluttercraft, are lightweight, two-seater fliers used to patrol the swamps of Kashyyyk. During the Battle of Kashyyyk, Wookiee pilots and gunners fly these open-cockpit craft, many retrofitted with tail-mounted laser cannons, relying on speed and agility to avoid incoming fire.

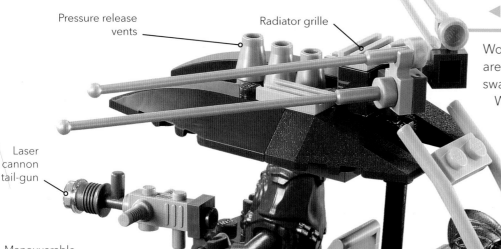

Pressure release vents

Radiator grille

Laser cannon tail-gun

Maneuverable flight wings

Power generator

Wooden frame

Primary control nexus

Steering vanes

Stabilizing flaps

Set name Wookiee Attack	
Number 7258	Pieces 366
Year 2005	Source III

Clone Leader
Like the 41st Elite Corps troopers he commands, Commander Gree's 2014 minifigure is dirty and battle-scarred. This seasoned clone leader carries a blaster and specialized macrobinoculars.

Clone Commander Gree

▶ Kashyyyk Troopers

Camouflaged to blend in on lush, jungle planets, the 41st Elite Corps come to the Wookiees' defense on Kashyyyk. The troopers' minifigure armor is printed to look scratched and battle-worn after lengthy duty in hostile terrains.

Stud is propelled by blaster

Phase II helmet

Kashyyyk Clone Trooper

Scout trooper helmet

41st Elite Corps Trooper

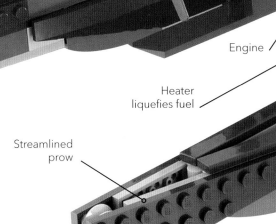

Chief Tarfful

Kashyyyk long-gun

Clan emblem

Wookiee Warrior
An old friend of Chewbacca's, the clan chieftain, Tarfful, fights alongside the Republic's clones on Kashyyyk. He later helps rescue Yoda when the clone troopers mysteriously turn their guns on their own Jedi generals. Tarfful fights with a long-barreled rifle and wears a bandolier displaying his clan emblem.

▼ Catamaran

Slim, twin-hulled Wookiee catamarans skim over the waters of Kashyyyk at great speeds. During the Battle of Kashyyyk, Chewbacca joins forces with Yoda and Luminara Unduli on board a catamaran to make a raid on Separatist lines. Usually unarmed, this catamaran has been retrofitted with a centrally mounted heavy missile cannon and several bombs (dropped from each hull). Catamarans are lifted by repulsors and propelled by jet engines or, as here, a propeller pod.

Set name Wookiee Catamaran	
Number 7260	**Pieces** 376
Year 2005	**Source** III

Propeller pod

Propeller

Exhaust vent

Stabilizing spar

Engine

Rudder

Heater liquefies fuel

Wookiee warrior

Streamlined prow

Wooden hull

Luminara Unduli

► Chewbacca

BRICK FACTS
Reddish-brown Chewbacca appears in several Imperial-era sets, including Death Star (set 10188), the Ultimate Collector *Millennium Falcon* (set 10179), and X-Wing Fighter (set 6212). A brown Chewbacca appears in Imperial AT-ST (set 7127), *Millennium Falcon* (set 7190), and the minifigure pack *Star Wars* #3 (set 3342).

Chewbacca (Reddish-Brown)

Small and skinny for a Wookiee, Chewbacca fights against the Separatist battle droids on Kashyyyk, firing energy bolts from his sturdy bowcaster. This 2014 version of Chewie's minifigure has a new mold, with visible teeth and new details in his multicolor fur and eyes. His bowcaster is now black. He's found in Droid Gunship (set 75042).

Teeth bared

Bowcaster

Bandolier

The Bad Batch

Clone Force 99—nicknamed the Bad Batch—are a special forces squad of experimental clones, with a difference. Genetic variations make them less obedient, so when the Empire takes control of the clone army they break away and set out on their own.

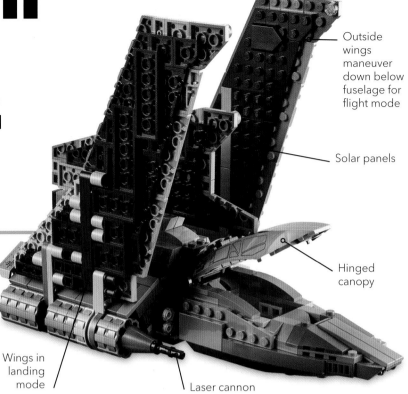

Outside wings maneuver down below fuselage for flight mode

Solar panels

Hinged canopy

▶ The *Marauder*

A modified *Omicron*-class attack shuttle, the *Marauder* serves the Bad Batch on undercover missions during the Clone Wars, and they flee in it when they escape from the Empire. The ship, with many rare sand-blue LEGO pieces, becomes the crew's mobile base as they travel the galaxy.

Set name The Bad Batch Attack Shuttle	
Number 75314	Pieces 969
Year 2021	Source BB

Gonk Droid

Wings in landing mode

Laser cannon

▼ Imperial Speeder Bike

Being on the run is not easy when the Empire has agents everywhere. Imperial troops patrol planets on speeder bikes. These transports are very similar to the BARC speeders that the Bad Batch's clone colleagues used to ride—except they are now Imperial gray.

Recessed vent

Set name The Bad Batch Attack Shuttle	
Number 75314	Pieces 969
Year 2021	Source BB

Airscoop

▼ Civilian Speeder Bike

Team leader Hunter grabs a Rawlings TK5 speeder bike from the roadside on Pantora. He leaps aboard for a high-speed chase through the city streets to save his teammate Omega from being kidnapped. Her Kaminoan employers want her back, so they've hired bounty hunters to catch her.

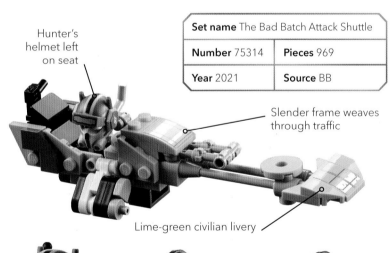

Hunter's helmet left on seat

Set name The Bad Batch Attack Shuttle	
Number 75314	Pieces 969
Year 2021	Source BB

Slender frame weaves through traffic

Lime-green civilian livery

Fugitives
Each Bad Batch member has genetic mutations that give him unique skills as well as an independent streak—as expressed in their personalized armor. Clone Sergeant Hunter is their leader.

Hunter **Wrecker** **Tech** **Echo** **Crosshair**

Cad Bane

Gun-toting, blue-skinned Cad Bane is a deadly bounty hunter whose favorite pastime is hunting Jedi. There aren't many of them left under the Empire, but there is still plenty of chaos for him to profit from. Bane clashes with the Bad Batch when he's hired to kidnap one of their own.

Bane's trademark wide-brimmed hat

Breathing tubes

▶ Fearsome Duros

Having appeared as two Clone Wars–era minifigures, Cad Bane makes a return in LEGO bricks as part of *The Bad Batch* storyline. The notorious blaster-for-hire has updated prints, new breathing tubes, and a new hat—but still the same fearsome reputation.

Glowing eyes

Head can be loaded with security chips

Feet have boosters for flying

◀ Todo 360

Techno-service droid Todo 360 is Cad Bane's loyal sidekick in a single LEGO piece. Despite not being treated well, he assists Bane with whatever's required: technical tasks, kidnapping, stealing, and even being exploded in the name of earning credits.

Adjustable pillar contains four engines

Landing skid for alternate mode

Spring-loaded shooter

Pair of laser cannons

Landing Mode

▶ The *Justifier*

A powerful ship for a powerful bounty hunter, the *Justifier* is Bane's personal starship. He flies it through hyperspace, chasing quarries and high-credit jobs. The LEGO thruster pillar at the rear of the ship rotates 90 degrees to switch between flying and landing modes. The roomy model has plenty of space for carrying stolen goods, and there's even a prison cell with a red transparent laser door to keep Bane's prisoners right where he wants them.

Large, tinted viewport

Extra storage under wing panels

Omega
A clone, Omega escapes her job at the cloning facility and joins the Bad Batch. But the Kaminoans want her back, so they send Bane after her.

Set name The *Justifier*	
Number 75323	**Pieces** 1,022
Year 2022	**Source** BB

Chapter 2
The Galactic Civil War

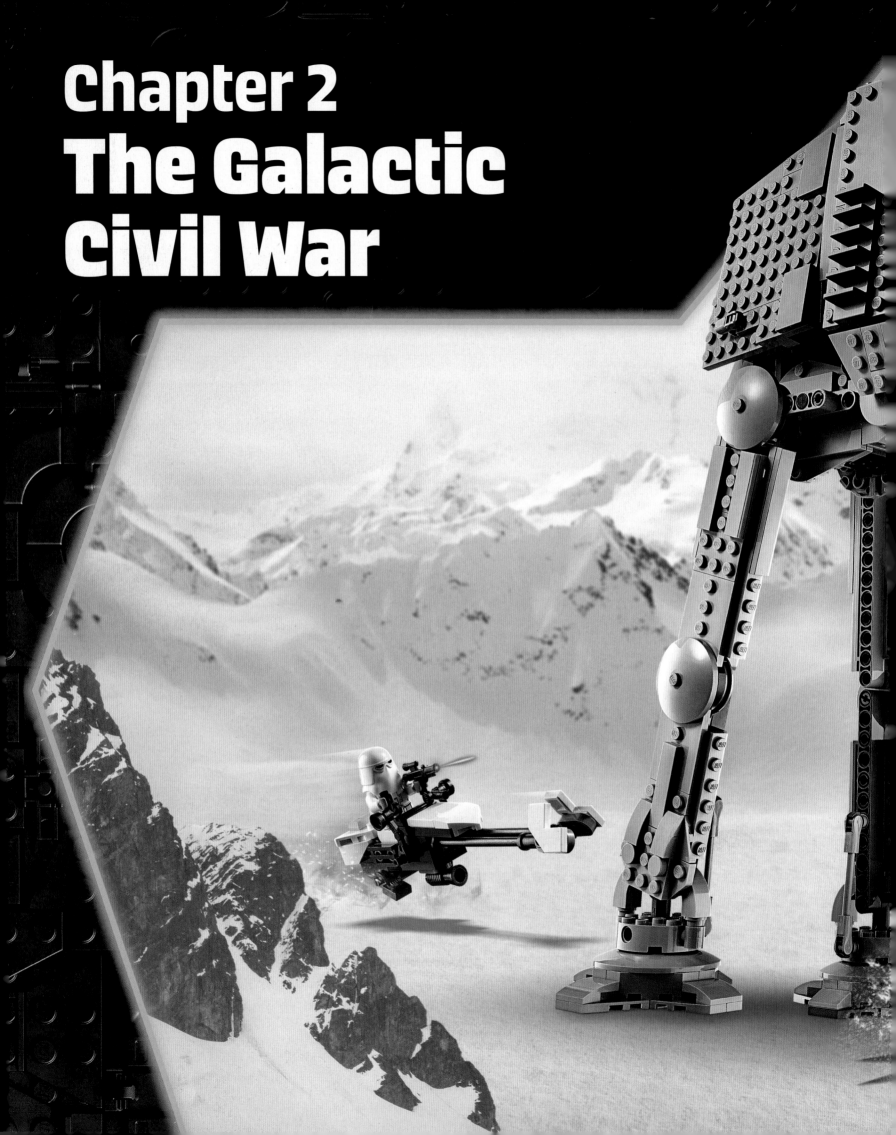

Han Solo

Han Solo is a hero of the Rebellion, but at one point he worked for the Empire! He didn't make a very good Imperial soldier, though, so he became a smuggler instead. The key to his success is down to two things: his super-fast ship, the *Millennium Falcon*, and his brave copilot and best friend, Chewbacca. Han and Chewie are happy being small-time crooks, but fate has a way of involving them in the galaxy's greatest struggles.

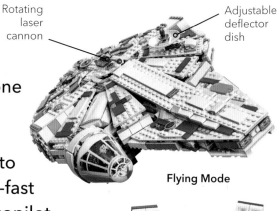

Rotating laser cannon

Adjustable deflector dish

Flying Mode

Gunslinging Han
In this 2018 minifigure, Han wears a gunslinger's belt and a holster that allows for a quick draw.

▶ *Millennium Falcon*

When Han Solo first flies the *Millennium Falcon*, it belongs to another smuggler, Lando Calrissian. Lando has turned the cargo freighter into a gleaming white sports ship, and Han pushes it to its limits by piloting it through the hazardous Kessel Run in just over 12 parsecs. Later, he challenges Lando to a card game for ownership of the vessel, and Han wins the *Falcon* fair and square.

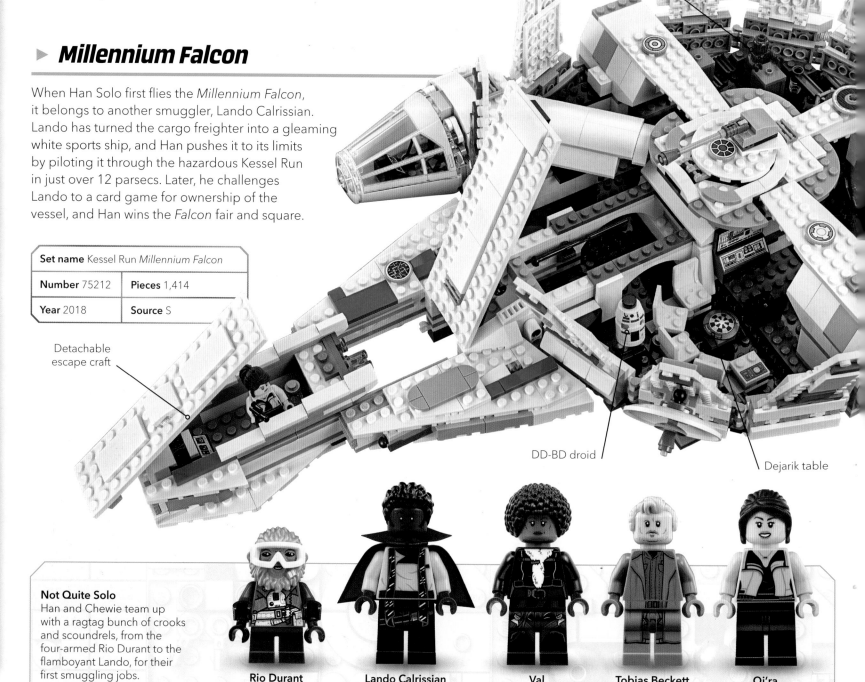

Kessel operations droid

Detachable escape craft

DD-BD droid

Dejarik table

Set name	Kessel Run *Millennium Falcon*	
Number 75212	Pieces	1,414
Year 2018	Source	S

Not Quite Solo
Han and Chewie team up with a ragtag bunch of crooks and scoundrels, from the four-armed Rio Durant to the flamboyant Lando, for their first smuggling jobs.

Rio Durant

Lando Calrissian

Val

Tobias Beckett

Qi'ra

Faithful Furball

The Wookiee Chewbacca swears his loyalty to Han after they team up to escape an Imperial prison cell. A veteran of the Clone Wars, Chewie is an expert shot with a bowcaster and wears ammunition across his huge, hairy chest.

Chewbacca

▶ Han and Qi'ra

Han was born on Corellia, and grew up wishing he could get away from its Imperial factories and criminal gangs. He eventually steals an M-68 landspeeder in the hope of escaping the planet with his girlfriend, Qi'ra.

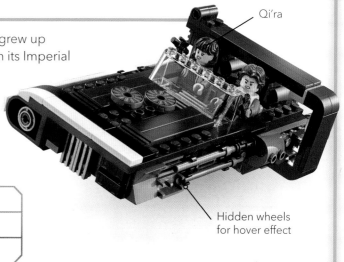

Qi'ra

Hidden wheels for hover effect

Set name Han Solo's Landspeeder	
Number 75209	**Pieces** 345
Year 2018	**Source** S

▼ Moloch and the White Worms

Hinged hull section

Moloch

On Corellia, Han and Qi'ra work for the criminal gang called the White Worms. Its other members include a wormlike Grindalid named Moloch who chases the pair when they try to escape. His A-A4B speeder is bigger and more powerful than Han's.

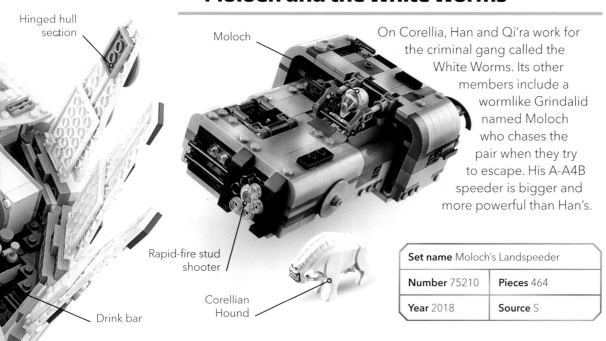

Rapid-fire stud shooter

Corellian Hound

Drink bar

Set name Moloch's Landspeeder	
Number 75210	**Pieces** 464
Year 2018	**Source** S

Brick Facts

DK's LEGO® *Star Wars™ Character Encyclopedia* (2011) included this exclusive Han minifigure. He wears the medal he earned by helping to destroy the first Death Star.

Celebration Han

Solidified Solo

A Han Solo minifigure fits inside this special piece, which has appeared in four sets to date. It depicts Han after he was frozen in carbonite and given to Jabba the Hutt as a gift!

Carry handles

Panel swings open to reveal space inside

Han Solo in Carbonite

Full disguise includes a helmet

Helping Han

Han dons a stormtrooper disguise to help rescue rebel leader Leia from the Death Star. He likes Leia so much that he swiftly joins the Rebellion!

Head has a smiling face printed on reverse side

Standard blaster

Hoth Han

Han wears cold-weather gear on the icy world of Hoth when he ventures out to find Luke Skywalker, who has gone missing in the snow.

Classic LEGO hair piece

Camouflage coat

Han with a Plan

General Solo is a vital part of the plan to destroy the second Death Star, and his efforts on Endor help bring an end to the Empire once and for all.

Millennium Falcon

According to its captain, Han Solo, the *Millennium Falcon* "may not look like much, but she's got it where it counts." It's a fast and well-equipped craft, though prone to malfunctions. Han and its previous captains have tinkered with its systems over the years, adding Imperial military-grade armor, quad laser cannons, an outsize sensor dish, and many other customized features—all of which require frequent repairs!

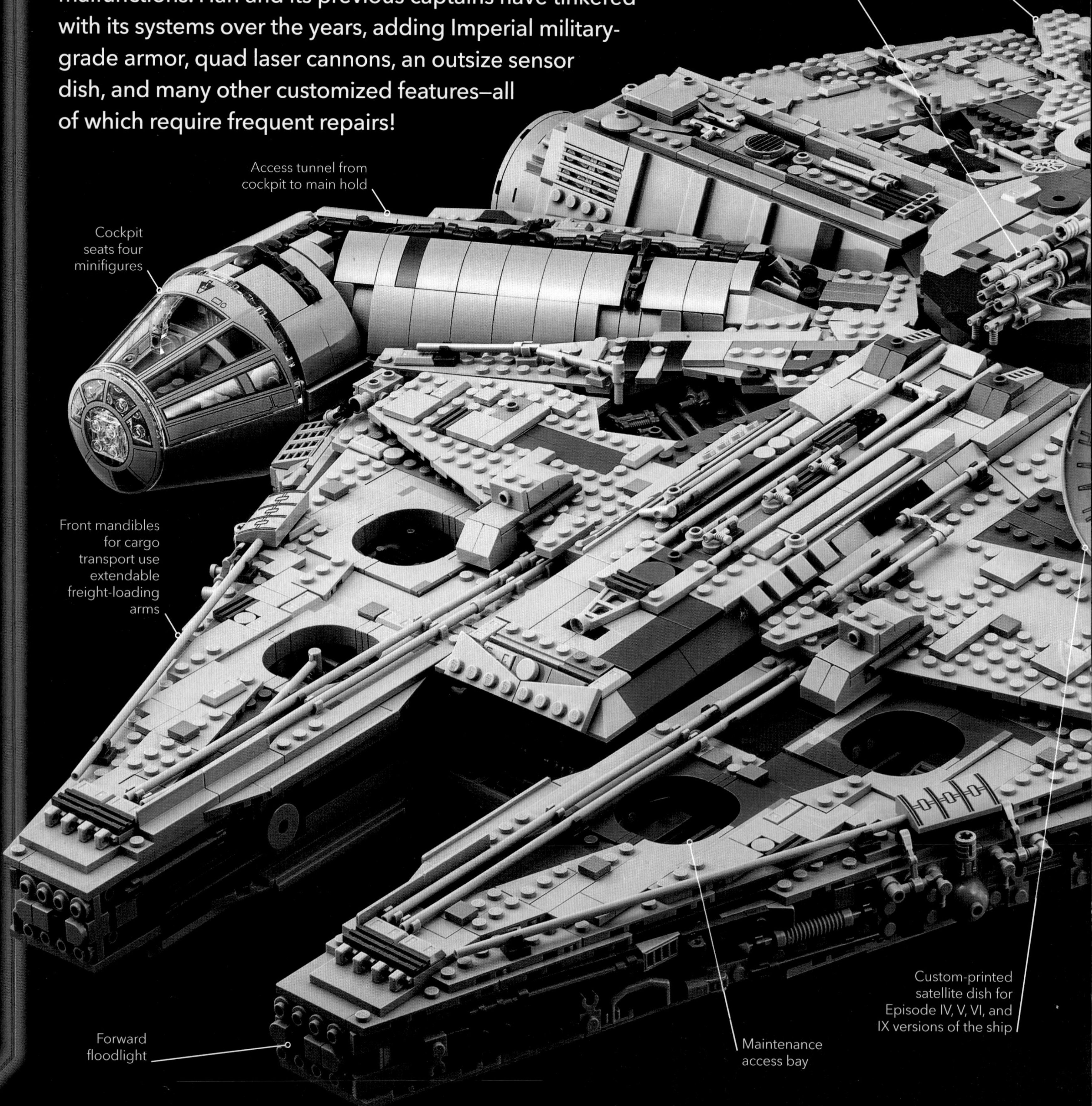

Upper quad laser cannon

Armor plating

Access tunnel from cockpit to main hold

Cockpit seats four minifigures

Front mandibles for cargo transport use extendable freight-loading arms

Forward floodlight

Maintenance access bay

Custom-printed satellite dish for Episode IV, V, VI, and IX versions of the ship

Engines

Moving at sublight speed, the *Falcon* relies on two heavily modified Girodyne SRB42 engines that emit glowing blue exhaust gases when fired up. Sublight drives propel starships within star systems or far enough away from planets so they can safely jump to hyperspace.

Heat exhaust vent

Rear view

Engine exhausts

Port docking ring

Brick Facts

On its release in 2017, the Ultimate Collector Series *Millennium Falcon* (set 75192) was the largest LEGO set ever, with more than 7,500 bricks and a 494-page instruction manual. The set includes an interchangeable satellite that allows builders to convert the original ship into the version flown in the Sequel Trilogy.

Set name *Millennium Falcon*	
Number 75192	**Pieces** 7,541
Year 2017	**Source** IV–IX
Dimensions Length more than 84 cm (33 in); width more than 22 cm (8½ in); height more than 21 cm (8 in)	
Minifigures 7–C-3PO, Chewbacca, Finn, Han Solo (young), Han Solo (older), Princess Leia, and Rey, plus BB-8	

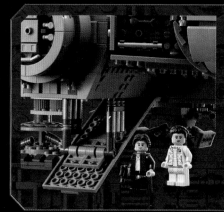

Boarding Ramp

The *Falcon*'s crew enter the ship via a retractable boarding ramp that lowers from behind the starboard docking ring. Han and Leia are all set to board!

Luke Skywalker

Yearning for adventure, farm boy Luke Skywalker grows up on a remote planet named Tatooine. When he meets Obi-Wan Kenobi, Luke begins to learn the truth of his origins as the secret son of Anakin Skywalker. Luke's journey transforms him into a pilot for the Rebel Alliance and a Jedi Knight—and leads to a reconciliation with his father and freedom from Imperial rule for the galaxy.

Luke on Tatooine
On the desolate planet Tatooine, Luke wears a simple farm tunic, a utility belt for his tools, and leg bindings to keep out the planet's sand. He drinks bantha milk—which is blue!

Brick Facts

In 2009, the LEGO Group made an exclusive Luke Skywalker minifigure for DK's LEGO® *Star Wars*™: *The Visual Dictionary*. Because the 2009 edition of the book celebrates 10 years of LEGO *Star Wars*, Luke is dressed for the celebration scene at the end of *Star Wars: A New Hope*.

Celebration Luke

▶ T-16 Skyhopper

Thrill-seeking teenagers on Tatooine take to racing skyhoppers through narrow ravines, blasting womp rats with front-mounted rifles. Luke owns an Incom T-16 skyhopper (though his Uncle Owen disapproves of it). The 2003 variant featured an open cockpit, but the 2015 model has been upgraded with an angled cockpit canopy. Both models feature an unnamed pilot—they are two of just a few sets that feature an unnamed main minifigure.

Set name	T-16 Skyhopper		
Number 75081		**Pieces** 247	
Year 2015		**Source** IV	

Upper airfoil

Cockpit

Movable lower airfoil

Navigation light

Spring-loaded missiles under wing

Primary laser cannon

Dorsal turbine hides secret compartment

◀ Luke's Landspeeder

Luke and his new friends, Obi-Wan Kenobi, R2-D2, and C-3PO, travel around the desert terrain of his homeworld in his battered X-34 landspeeder. Its low-power repulsors make it hover off the ground, while triple turbines provide thrust. Speeders are a common sight on Tatooine, though heat and sand make maintenance a constant headache.

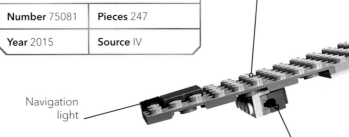

Communications receiver

Turbine engine

Repulsor vent

Battered front

Set name	Luke's Landspeeder	
Number 75173		**Pieces** 149
Year 2017		**Source** IV

▼ X-Wing Starfighter

Luke flies an X-wing as "Red Five" in the rebel attack on the first Death Star. This 2021 fighter has a hinged cockpit canopy, an astromech droid socket, functional landing gear with LEGO ski pieces, and a push lever to open the S-foil wings into attack position. The wings can be pushed to close them back together. The set includes minifigures of Luke, Princess Leia, General Jan Dodonna, and R2-D2.

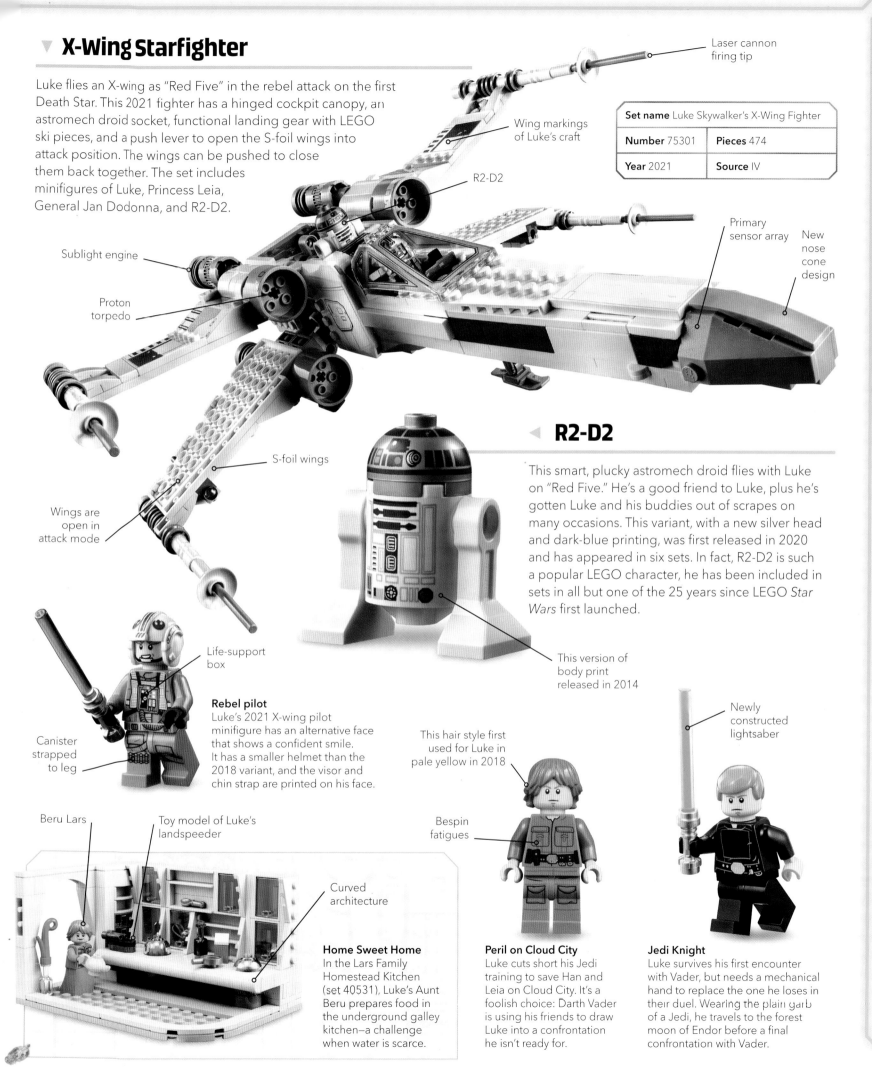

Laser cannon firing tip

Wing markings of Luke's craft

R2-D2

Set name	Luke Skywalker's X-Wing Fighter	
Number 75301		Pieces 474
Year 2021		Source IV

Primary sensor array

New nose cone design

Sublight engine

Proton torpedo

S-foil wings

Wings are open in attack mode

Life-support box

Canister strapped to leg

Rebel pilot
Luke's 2021 X-wing pilot minifigure has an alternative face that shows a confident smile. It has a smaller helmet than the 2018 variant, and the visor and chin strap are printed on his face.

◄ R2-D2

This smart, plucky astromech droid flies with Luke on "Red Five." He's a good friend to Luke, plus he's gotten Luke and his buddies out of scrapes on many occasions. This variant, with a new silver head and dark-blue printing, was first released in 2020 and has appeared in six sets. In fact, R2-D2 is such a popular LEGO character, he has been included in sets in all but one of the 25 years since LEGO *Star Wars* first launched.

This version of body print released in 2014

Newly constructed lightsaber

This hair style first used for Luke in pale yellow in 2018

Bespin fatigues

Beru Lars

Toy model of Luke's landspeeder

Curved architecture

Home Sweet Home
In the Lars Family Homestead Kitchen (set 40531), Luke's Aunt Beru prepares food in the underground galley kitchen—a challenge when water is scarce.

Peril on Cloud City
Luke cuts short his Jedi training to save Han and Leia on Cloud City. It's a foolish choice: Darth Vader is using his friends to draw Luke into a confrontation he isn't ready for.

Jedi Knight
Luke survives his first encounter with Vader, but needs a mechanical hand to replace the one he loses in their duel. Wearing the plain garb of a Jedi, he travels to the forest moon of Endor before a final confrontation with Vader.

▼ Escape Pod

C-3PO and R2-D2 slip into a small escape pod to avoid being caught by Darth Vader when he seizes the rebel blockade runner. After the droids crash-land on Tatooine, Jawas capture them and sell them to Owen Lars.

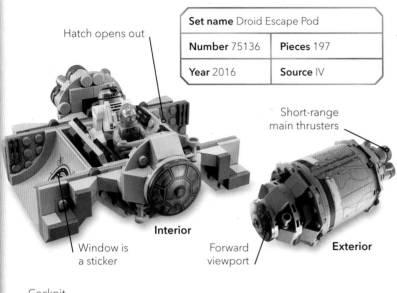

Hatch opens out

Set name	Droid Escape Pod	
Number 75136		Pieces 197
Year 2016		Source IV

Short-range main thrusters

Interior

Window is a sticker

Forward viewport

Exterior

Tatooine

The barren desert planet of Tatooine is a dangerous, lawless world. The galaxy's most wretched hive of villainy has become a port of call for smugglers, pirates, and gangsters. Life is tough for its inhabitants, who face water shortages, ferocious sandstorms, and extreme heat. Fierce Tuskens and scavenging Jawas have found ways to survive by living in temporary settlements or patrolling the deserts and wastelands in search of scrap metal.

▼ Sandcrawler

Jawas have repurposed these old mining vehicles to round up stray droids, junked vehicles, scrap metal, or minerals that can be used or sold. Each sandcrawler is home to an entire clan of Jawas, and serves as transport, workshop, traveling store—and protection from predators, such as rampaging Tuskens.

Set name	Sandcrawler	
Number 75220		Pieces 1,239
Year 2018		Source IV

Open Cockpit

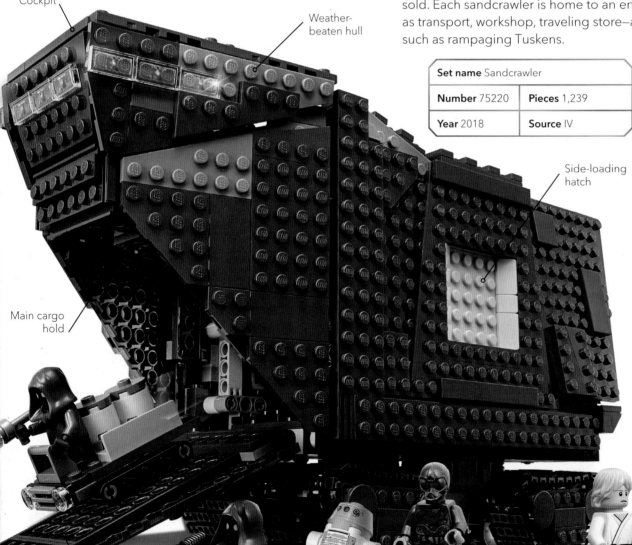

Cockpit

Weather-beaten hull

Main cargo hold

Side-loading hatch

Jawa
The small, hooded Jawas use scrap parts from crashed starships to mend broken equipment or droids. After a sale, they move on quickly, as their patched-up goods rarely remain working for long.

Ramp opens to deploy vehicles and cargo

R5-A2

Steerable treads

Medical droid

▼ Tusken Encampments

In the inhospitable wastes of Tatooine, Tuskens—also known as Sand People—shelter in nomadic tents called urtya. They also build ballistae—wooden missile launchers that are like huge crossbows. The Sand People use their ballistae to fire bolts attached to ropes to restrain a huge krayt dragon that is terrorizing the settlement, but they prove too weak.

Tap piece connects to top of droid

Articulated crane

Set name	Tatooine Battle Pack	
Number 75198	Pieces 97	
Year 2018	Source IV	

Animal hide stretched over wooden poles

Rope binds wood together to construct ballista

Gaffi stick

Reel of wound rope

Winch for pulling bow strings

Set name	Trouble on Tatooine	
Number 75299	Pieces 276	
Year 2021	Source M	

▲ Tusken Attack

Tuskens attack Jawas and other settlers on Tatooine. The Jawas defend themselves and their service vehicle with ion blasters. The small vehicle cleverly uses LEGO® Technic beams as both a crane and as treads.

Water vaporator

Traditional Tatooine architecture

Droids are not welcome here

Kabe

Dr. Evazan

Ponda Baba

▶ Mos Eisley Cantina

The Cantina is a perilous den of smugglers, misfits, and renegade pilots. Han's tense encounter with a battle-ready Greedo can be re-created in this set, the fourth LEGO version of the raucous watering hole, with both seats featuring flipping mechanisms. The Master Builder Series set includes a V-35 Courier landspeeder, a Ubrikkian 9000 landspeeder, a dewback, two water vaporators, and 21 minifigures.

Set name	Mos Eisley Cantina	
Number 75290	Pieces 3,187	
Year 2020	Source IV	

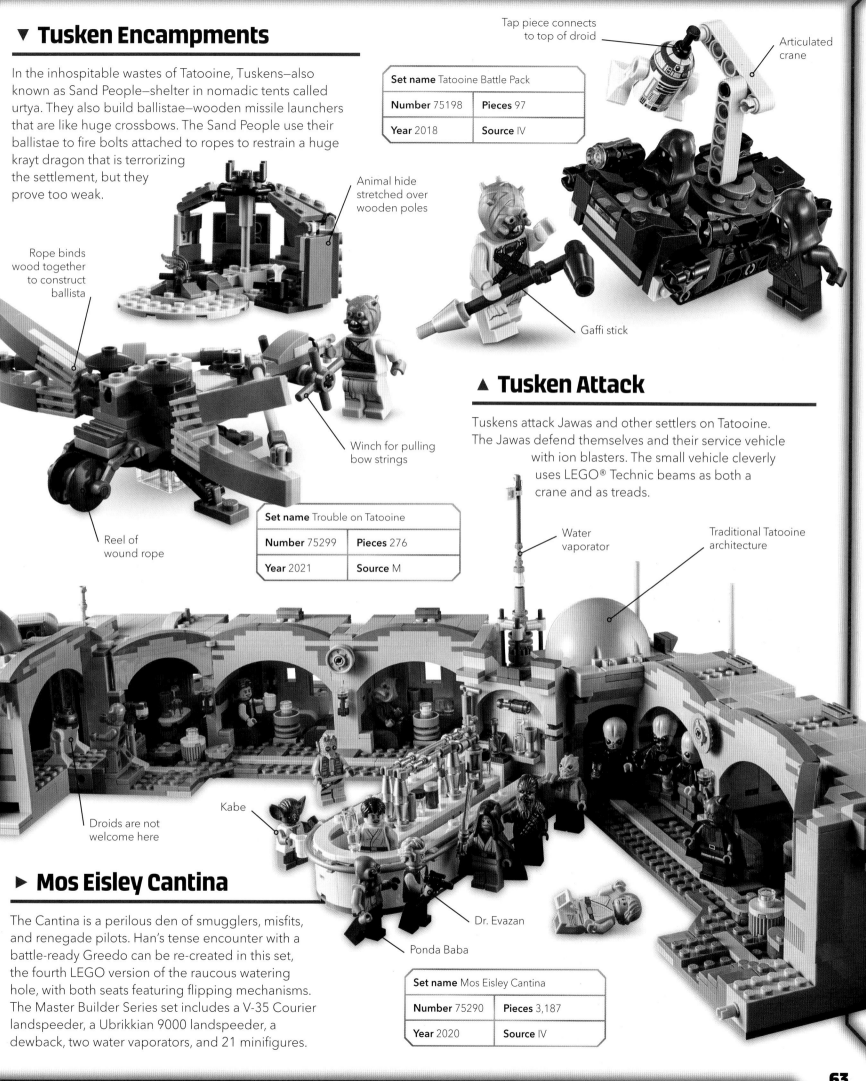

Imperial Leaders

Sith Lord Darth Sidious, better known as the feared dictator Emperor Palpatine, rules over the most oppressive regime the galaxy has ever known. His apprentice, once known as Anakin Skywalker, was one of the most celebrated Jedi before he fell to the dark side and became Darth Vader. Vader now travels the Empire to enforce his master's dark will. But Palpatine is never content with the extent of his rule. His focus turns to replacing his apprentice with Vader's own son, powerful Jedi Luke Skywalker.

Force lightning shoots from hands

Emperor Palpatine
Sith Lord Emperor Palpatine's face is distorted by dark-side energies and his sulfurous eyes betray his inner anger. Rarely seen even by his own officers, Palpatine wears a black robe with a hood to hide his face.

▼ Palpatine's Throne Room

On board the second Death Star, the Emperor rules from his throne room tower. It is here that Darth Vader steps in to save his son from the deadly Force lightning that the Emperor lashes out at Luke Skywalker.

Brick Facts

The Imperial Star Destroyer (set 6211), released in 2006, includes a room belowdecks where Vader communicates with a hologram of Emperor Palpatine. The holo effect is achieved by a sticker on a transparent brick.

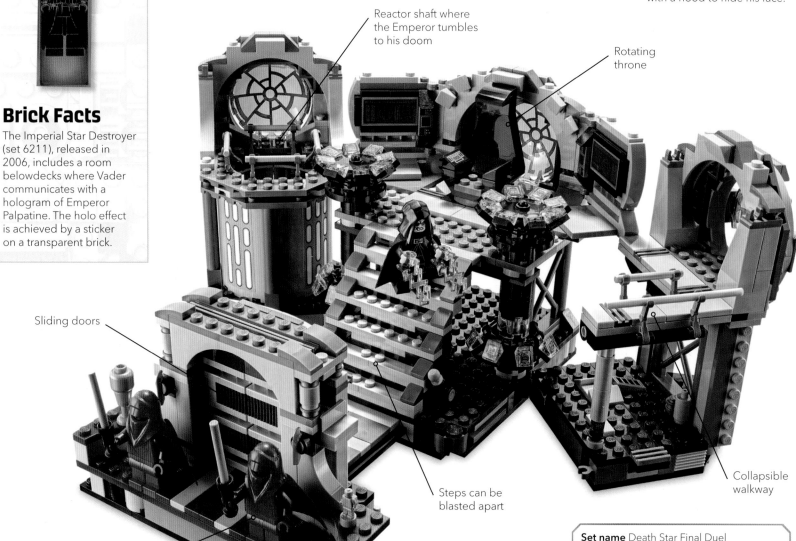

Reactor shaft where the Emperor tumbles to his doom

Rotating throne

Sliding doors

Collapsible walkway

Steps can be blasted apart

Royal Guard

Set name Death Star Final Duel	
Number 75291	**Pieces** 775
Year 2020	**Source** VI

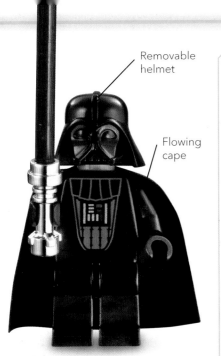

Removable helmet

Flowing cape

Evolution of an Icon
The original Darth Vader minifigure from 1999 has a simplified torso design compared with later versions, but the iconic black mask was there from the start.

Serving the Empire
The Emperor's will is enforced by a number of high-ranking officials who carry out his and Darth Vader's orders. Only the most cunning and ambitious can survive.

Tarkin
Grand Moff Wilhuff Tarkin is ruthless and intimidating in his role as Imperial Governor.

Krennic
Director Orson Krennic runs the Death Star—until Grand Moff Tarkin pulls rank.

Yularen
Admiral Wullf Yularen serves as a senior officer aboard the Death Star.

Thrawn
Thrawn is one of a few nonhuman officers to have risen through the Imperial ranks.

The Inquisitor
Taking his orders directly from Darth Vader, the Inquisitor hunts for Jedi in hiding.

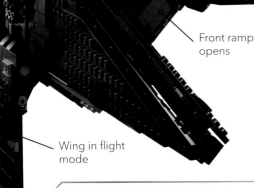

Laser cannon

Front ramp opens

Wing in flight mode

Set name Inquisitor Transport *Scythe*	
Number 75336	**Pieces** 924
Year 2022	**Source** ○

◀ The *Scythe*

A dreaded sight for any Jedi who survived Order 66, the *Scythe* is the transport of the Inquisitorius. It carries the Force-sensitive team of dark-side Jedi-hunters. The Imperial agents work for Darth Vader, prowling the galaxy in the *Scythe*, searching for Jedi to destroy and Force-sensitive younglings who could be recruited to serve the Empire.

▼ Darth Vader's TIE Advanced

Darth Vader is a gifted pilot, so he has his own high-tech starfighter called the TIE Advanced. The 2016 edition of the craft is the most detailed minifigure-scale model to date. The laser cannons beneath the cockpit are spring-loaded missiles operated by a trigger behind the top hatch.

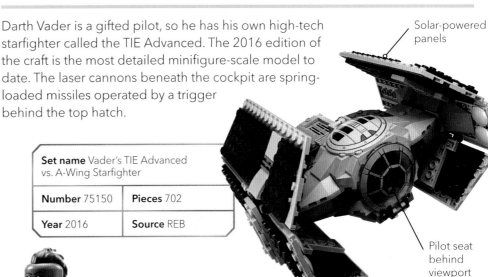

Solar-powered panels

Pilot seat behind viewport

Set name Vader's TIE Advanced vs. A-Wing Starfighter	
Number 75150	**Pieces** 702
Year 2016	**Source** REB

Grand Inquisitor

Fifth Brother

Third Sister

◀ Inquisitorius

The most senior Jedi-hunter, the Grand Inquisitor is a Pau'an with bright-white skin and face markings. Second-in-command, the Fifth Brother wears a large metallic hat with wide straps that protect much of his face. Darth Vader should keep an eye on Reva Sevander, better known as the Third Sister: her loyalty may waver. They all wield red double-bladed lightsabers with circular hilts.

Death Star

The Imperial battle station known as the Death Star is designed to quash potential dissent through displays of great force. The first Death Star uses its superweapon to obliterate Princess Leia's home planet, Alderaan. The second Death Star, though seemingly incomplete, is actually fully operational—and is intended to lure the rebels to their doom.

LEGO Leap
In Death Star Escape (set 75229), Luke and Leia are in trouble. The door has closed behind them and their walkway is retracting, so they grab ahold of a LEGO string and leap across a chasm!

Updated rotating turbolaser turret

Turbolaser turning mechanism

Emperor Palpatine's throne

Collapsing catwalk

Vader duels with Luke

Railing

Air duct

Air shaft

Luke and Leia swing across chasm

Mechanism controls central turbolift

Death Star droid on workbench

Imperial astromech

Stormtrooper helmet

TIE docking rack

TIE Advanced

Redesigned hangar bay elevator

Imperial Navy officer

Winch handle raises and lowers pilot lift

Loading bay

Cargo crane operated by stormtrooper

Cargo crate

Mouse droid in storage bay

Central turbolift shaft

Set name	Death Star	
Number 75159		**Pieces** 4,016
Year 2016		**Source** IV, VI

Dimensions Length more than 41 cm (16 in); width more than 41 cm (16 in); height more than 40 cm (15¾ in)

Minifigures 23—Luke Skywalker (regular outfit, stormtrooper disguise, and Jedi Knight outfit), Han Solo (regular outfit and stormtrooper disguise), Obi-Wan Kenobi, Princess Leia, Chewbacca, Darth Vader, Emperor Palpatine, Grand Moff Tarkin, Imperial Officer, 2 Royal Guards, 2 Stormtroopers, 2 Death Star Troopers, Death Star Droid, 2 Imperial Gunners, Imperial Navy Officer, and C-3PO, plus R2-D2, Imperial Astromech droid R3-M3, Dianoga, Interrogation Droid, and Mouse Droid

Movie Action
More than a dozen different scenes can be re-created within the playset, including the iconic duel between old enemies Obi-Wan and Vader.

Two Death Stars in One

The first LEGO Death Star (set 10188) was released in 2008. The 2016 set is an updated version with several new minifigures and extra details. The set combines features of the first and second movie Death Stars. Luke, for example, appears three times: in stormtrooper uniform to rescue Leia, in his regular outfit to swing across the air shaft, and as a Jedi Knight to battle Darth Vader.

Detention Cell
In her detention cell, Princess Leia refuses to give Vader the location of the rebel base. She even stands firm against the interrogator droid's electroshock devices. Finally Luke and Han arrive to rescue her—and they all dive into a filthy trash compactor!

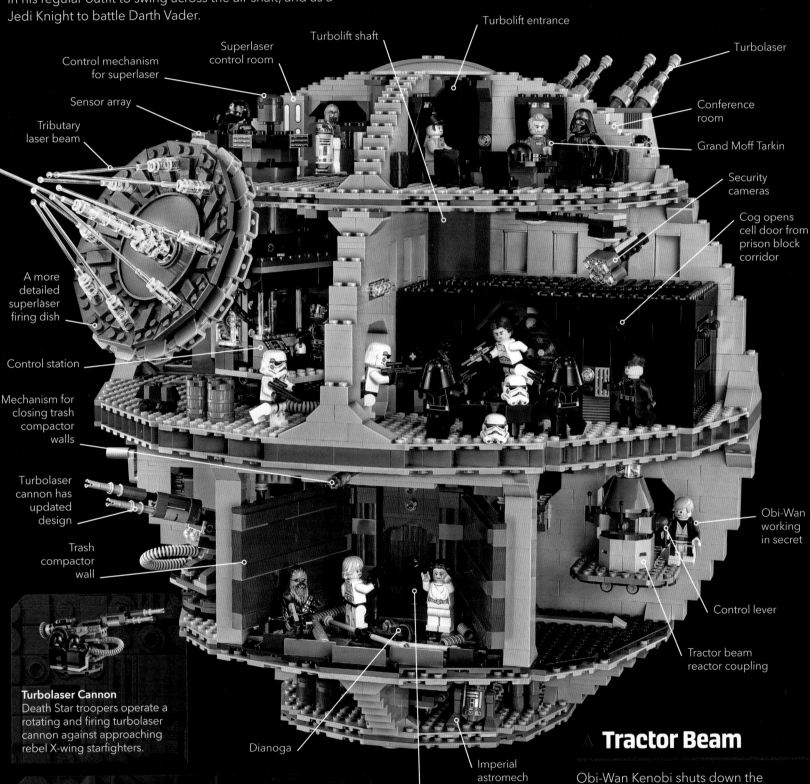

Control mechanism for superlaser

Sensor array

Tributary laser beam

Superlaser control room

Turbolift shaft

Turbolift entrance

Turbolaser

Conference room

Grand Moff Tarkin

Security cameras

Cog opens cell door from prison block corridor

A more detailed superlaser firing dish

Control station

Mechanism for closing trash compactor walls

Turbolaser cannon has updated design

Trash compactor wall

Obi-Wan working in secret

Control lever

Tractor beam reactor coupling

Dianoga

Imperial astromech occupies storage level

Trash compactor door

Turbolaser Cannon
Death Star troopers operate a rotating and firing turbolaser cannon against approaching rebel X-wing starfighters.

Eye stem

Tentacle

Garbage Squid
Dianogas, or garbage squids, live in trash compactors, garbage pits, and sewers across the galaxy. They feed on scraps of decaying organic matter.

Tractor Beam

Obi-Wan Kenobi shuts down the tractor beam (the projected force-field used to capture the *Millennium Falcon*) but Darth Vader then confronts him, leading to a lightsaber duel.

Darth Vader's Castle

Darth Vader's menacing castle is on the volcanic planet of Mustafar, the site of his worst defeat. It's here that his former self, Anakin Skywalker, lost his lightsaber duel with Obi-Wan Kenobi, cementing Vader's status as a Dark Lord. At his castle, Darth Vader meditates on the dark side of the Force and meets with his Imperial leaders.

Blaster pistol

Transport Pilots
Imperial transport pilots were first visualized in *Star Wars: Secrets of the Empire* in 2017. In this hyper-reality experience, players wear a virtual-reality headset and goggles and take on the role of rebels in a mission to steal a powerful weapon from an Imperial facility on Mustafar.

Castle sits on cliff edge

Exterior View

Transport pilot on lookout duty

Darth Vader in meditation chamber

Castle made of obsidian

Royal Guards
The Royal Guard is made up of the most skilled soldiers in the Imperial military. They are known for their strength, intelligence, and loyalty—and their sinister crimson uniforms. Royal Guard minifigures carry a baton and wear long robes with a special hood element.

Set name	Darth Vader's Castle	
Number 75251		Pieces 1,060
Year 2018		Source R1

Royal Guards vigilantly protect Darth Vader

Bacta Tank
Darth Vader's bacta tank allows him to relax without his life-support armor. The front of the LEGO tank opens and closes so Darth Vader's battle-scarred minifigure can be positioned in place.

Bacta Tank Vader
The set comes with two Darth Vader minifigures, including one for his bacta tank. It shows him without his armor, so the injuries from his near-fatal duel on Mustafar are visible. His body has burn scars, battle wounds, and prosthetic arm and legs.

TIE fighter in underground hanger

Interior View

Stairs down to underground level of the castle

▲ Interior Chambers

At the base of Darth Vader's castle is an underground hangar with a mouse droid and a docking station for a TIE Advanced fighter. Within the tower there is an ancient Sith shrine with a holocron, racks for ammunition, and a secret compartment for a lightsaber. There is also a bacta tank and a meditation chamber for Darth Vader, with a holographic communication unit.

Imperial Stormtroopers

The gleaming white ground troops of the Galactic Empire can be found on thousands of planets across the galaxy. Hidden behind imposing masks and blastproof armor, they present a unified show of strength that few would dare to challenge. Yet for all their seeming uniformity, there are many different kinds of stormtrooper, each specially trained for various duties and environments.

Stormtrooper
Nameless, faceless stormtroopers are utterly loyal to the Empire. The 2019 minifigure has a new updated helmet mold for the 20th anniversary that replaces a previous mold, in use since 2001.

Electric prod to control dewback

Snowtrooper
Trained and outfitted for survival in the coldest environments, snowtroopers wear less armor than other stormtroopers, but a lot more insulation. Battery packs on their backs serve as portable heating systems, while their legs are kept warm by distinctive belt-capes.

Sand-stained armor

Survival backpack

Heated mask

Kama belt-cape

E-Web heavy repeating blaster cannon

◀ Sandtrooper

With vital supplies of food and water strapped to their backs, sandtroopers are equipped to serve in dry, desert conditions. On the planet Tatooine, they often ride giant green lizards called dewbacks rather than rely on vehicles that can break down when clogged up with sand.

Set name	Mos Eisley Cantina	
Number 75052	Pieces 616	
Year 2014	Source IV	

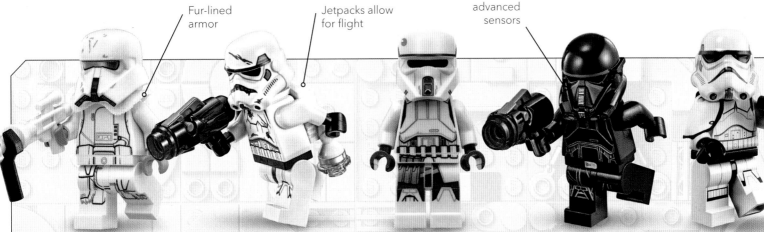

Fur-lined armor

Jetpacks allow for flight

Helmet has advanced sensors

Range Trooper
These tough troopers serve on the wildest fringes of Imperial space.

Jumptrooper
With jetpacks on their backs, these special troopers can actually fly.

Shoretrooper
Life's a beach for these sand-colored coastal defender stormtroopers.

Death Trooper
The grimly named death troopers are elite warriors in all-black armor.

Stormtrooper Sergeant
A white pauldron on the shoulder indicates the rank of sergeant.

Imperial Army

At the end of the Clone Wars, the Galactic Republic becomes an Empire and its military resources now serve the new regime. Clone troopers become stormtroopers, their ranks made up of clones and, now, human recruits. Stormtroopers have a huge arsenal of powerful ground vehicles to choose from, including giant armored walkers for smashing through enemy armies.

▼ Mobile Tac-Pod

Sturdy Mobile Tac-Pods transport the Pre-Mor Enforcement officers who protect their territory, especially places like mines that the Empire has an interest in. Three arrive on the planet Ferrix on a mission to arrest the rebel Cassian Andor.

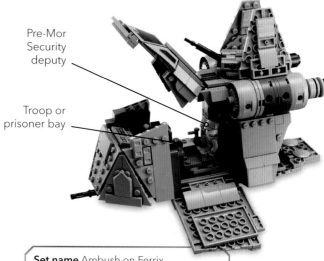

Pre-Mor Security deputy

Troop or prisoner bay

Set name	Ambush on Ferrix	
Number 75338		Pieces 679
Year 2022		Source AN

▼ Imperial Conveyex Transport

A long line of armored cargo cars that can travel on both the top and underside of the track is an imposing sight—even for daring smugglers! Range troopers walk up the sides of these fast-moving trains in their magnetic boots or using the studs on the sides of the LEGO conveyex.

Set name	Imperial Conveyex Transport	
Number 75217		Pieces 622
Year 2018		Source S

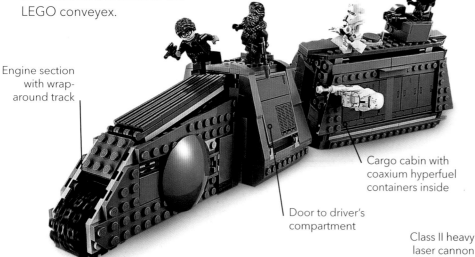

Engine section with wrap-around track

Cargo cabin with coaxium hyperfuel containers inside

Door to driver's compartment

Command cockpit

Class II heavy laser cannon

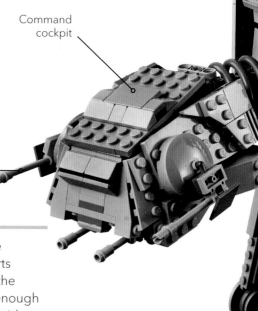

Knee joint

Ankle joint

▶ AT-AT Walker

During the Battle of Hoth, the Empire deploys All Terrain Armored Transports (AT-ATs) against the rebels, knowing the mere sight of these walking tanks is enough to scare off most soldiers. An AT-AT's side opens to reveal a staging platform for General Veers and two snowtrooper minifigures, who stand ready to attack the rebel artillery. One of two AT-AT drivers steers the walker from a cockpit in its head.

AT-AT Driver
Equipped with insulated jumpsuits and life-support packs, AT-AT drivers guide the huge walkers.

General Veers
General Veers masterminds the devastating assault on the rebel base on Hoth from the cockpit of the lead AT-AT.

Set name	AT-AT	
Number 75288		Pieces 1,267
Year 2020		Source V

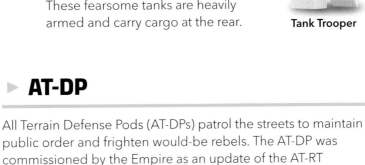

Front armor plate lifts to access cockpit

Rotating and elevating turret gun

Rotating laser cannon

◄ Imperial Assault Hovertank

This repulsorlift variant of the Imperial combat assault tank seen in *Rogue One* rolls along on four concealed transparent wheels to create the effect that it is hovering just above the ground. The movie features the primary model of the craft, which runs on heavy metal tracks. These fearsome tanks are heavily armed and carry cargo at the rear.

Tank Trooper

Set name Imperial Assault Hovertank	
Number 75152	Pieces 385
Year 2016	Source R1

Opening cockpit fits two minifigures inside

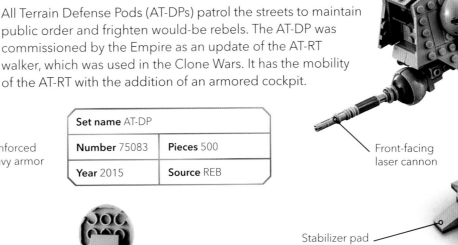

► AT-DP

Side panel opens up

All Terrain Defense Pods (AT-DPs) patrol the streets to maintain public order and frighten would-be rebels. The AT-DP was commissioned by the Empire as an update of the AT-RT walker, which was used in the Clone Wars. It has the mobility of the AT-RT with the addition of an armored cockpit.

Reinforced heavy armor

Set name AT-DP	
Number 75083	Pieces 500
Year 2015	Source REB

Front-facing laser cannon

Stabilizer pad

◄ AT-ST Walker

Imperial All Terrain Scout Transports (AT-STs) can run through rugged terrain on antipersonnel or reconnaissance missions. They are piloted from the cockpit in the walker's head and are armed with blaster and concussion weapons.

Twin blaster cannon

Polarized visor

Set name Hoth AT-ST	
Number 75322	Pieces 586
Year 2022	Source V

Footpad yaw strut

Footpad

Toe flap

Computer-controlled foot sensor

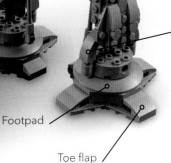

AT-ST Driver

TIE Variants

When Palpatine establishes the Empire, the Republic's navy is appropriated and put to brutal use. Jedi interceptors, with their solar wings, are reborn as aggressive TIE fighters. The Imperial fleet expands further with a variety of new, ever-deadlier models and the TIE fighter becomes a staple in the Imperial fleet.

R3-J2
This is the only LEGO astromech with a transparent dome.

TIE Fighter Pilot
Imperial fighter pilots are a specially trained elite flying corps.

▼ TIE Defender

A prototype starfighter developed in secret by the Empire, the TIE defender is agile and heavily armored to stand up to rebel fighters. The LEGO set has a unique rotating cockpit and is armed with six flick-fire missiles.

Set name	TIE Defender	
Number 8087	**Pieces** 304
Year 2010	**Source** L

Flick-fire missile

Solar panels

Gyroscopic cockpit lets pilot remain upright

Targeting sensors

▼ TIE Fighter

TIE fighters are armed with cannons and have no deflector shields or hyperdrives, making them light and agile in battle. These craft are mass-produced by the Empire and they swarm around an enemy to take them out. This 2018 set includes a highly detailed design with an opening cockpit and two spring-loaded shooters. Four minifigures are included: a TIE fighter pilot, an Imperial mudtrooper, Han Solo, and Tobias Beckett.

Set name	Imperial TIE Fighter	
Number 75211	**Pieces** 519
Year 2018	**Source** S

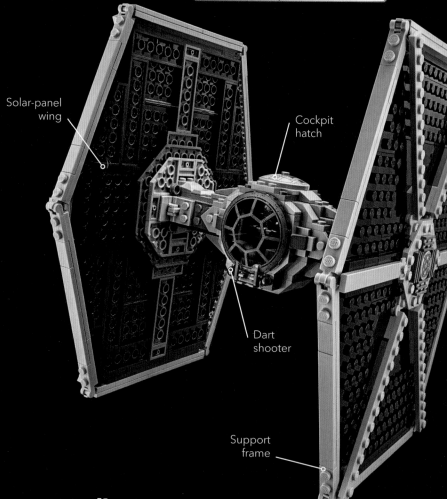

Solar-panel wing

Cockpit hatch

Dart shooter

Support frame

▶ TIE Striker

The TIE striker is deployed to defend the Imperial base on Scarif. Levers on the back of this model switch the wings from attack mode to cruising mode. Two spring-loaded darts are mounted below the pilot's canopy.

Set name	TIE Striker	
Number 75154	**Pieces** 543
Year 2016	**Source** R1

Wings in attack mode

TIE Interceptor

The TIE interceptor is one of the fastest, most maneuverable, and best-armed starfighters in the Imperial fleet. Its upgraded ion engines deliver immense power for dogfights, and each wingtip boasts a blaster cannon whose linked fire can rip through enemy fighters.

Set name	TIE Interceptor	
Number 6206	**Pieces** 212	
Year 2006	**Source** VI	

Wingtip blaster cannon

Cutaway wing profile

Advanced targeting sensors

Angled solar wing

TIE minifigure pilot in cockpit

TIE Advanced Prototype

The Grand Inquisitor flies a new TIE fighter prototype when Darth Vader assigns him a new mission. It's a smaller ship than the advanced fighter Darth Vader uses.

Set name	TIE Advanced Prototype	
Number 75082	**Pieces** 355	
Year 2015	**Source** REB	

Hatch is the same element as the canopy

Spring-loaded dart

Cockpit hatch

Inferno Squad Agent

Iden Versio

Inferno Squad
Led by the formidable Commander Iden Versio, Inferno Squad is an elite special forces unit. It is sent on the toughest missions by the Empire. Iden has unique printing to denote her military rank.

TIE Bomber

Single-pilot TIE bombers make precise "surgical strikes" that would be impractical for the Empire's capital ships. The bomber is armed with laser weapons and proton bombs that can be deployed against shielded targets, blasting open their hiding places.

Set name	TIE Bomber	
Number 75347	**Pieces** 625	
Year 2023	**Source** V	

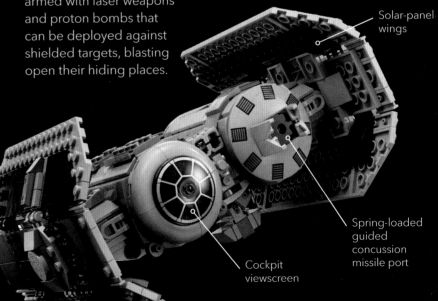

Solar-panel wings

Spring-loaded guided concussion missile port

Cockpit viewscreen

Imperial Transports

The Empire uses its distinctive tri-wing shuttles for ferrying troops, cargo, and important personnel. In most cases, the vessels have a fixed-position stabilizer wing on top and adjustable stabilizers on the sides. These side wings fold upward when a shuttle lands—not only to take up less space on the ground but also to provide a defensive shield for the central section.

Imperial Shuttle Pilot
These pilots are handpicked for their loyalty as many fly to the Empire's most secret bases.

White LEGO Technic beams provide stability

▶ *Tydirium*

More elegant-looking than most Imperial ships, *Lambda*-class T-4a shuttles are often used to transport dignitaries, including the Emperor himself. The T-4a shuttle *Tydirium* is stolen by the Rebel Alliance and used to mount a sneak attack on the second Death Star's shield generator on the forest moon of Endor.

Set name Imperial Shuttle *Tydirium*	
Number 75094	**Pieces** 937
Year 2015	**Source** VI

Side panel opens to reveal passenger area

Leia in Camouflage
In her camouflage cape, Leia is equipped for battle in the forests of the moon of Endor.

Wings are raised for landing

Landing Mode

Cockpit viewscreen

Missile shooter hidden under wing

Double laser cannon can be tilted

Wings constructed out of plates, tiles, and LEGO Technic beams

Folding wing

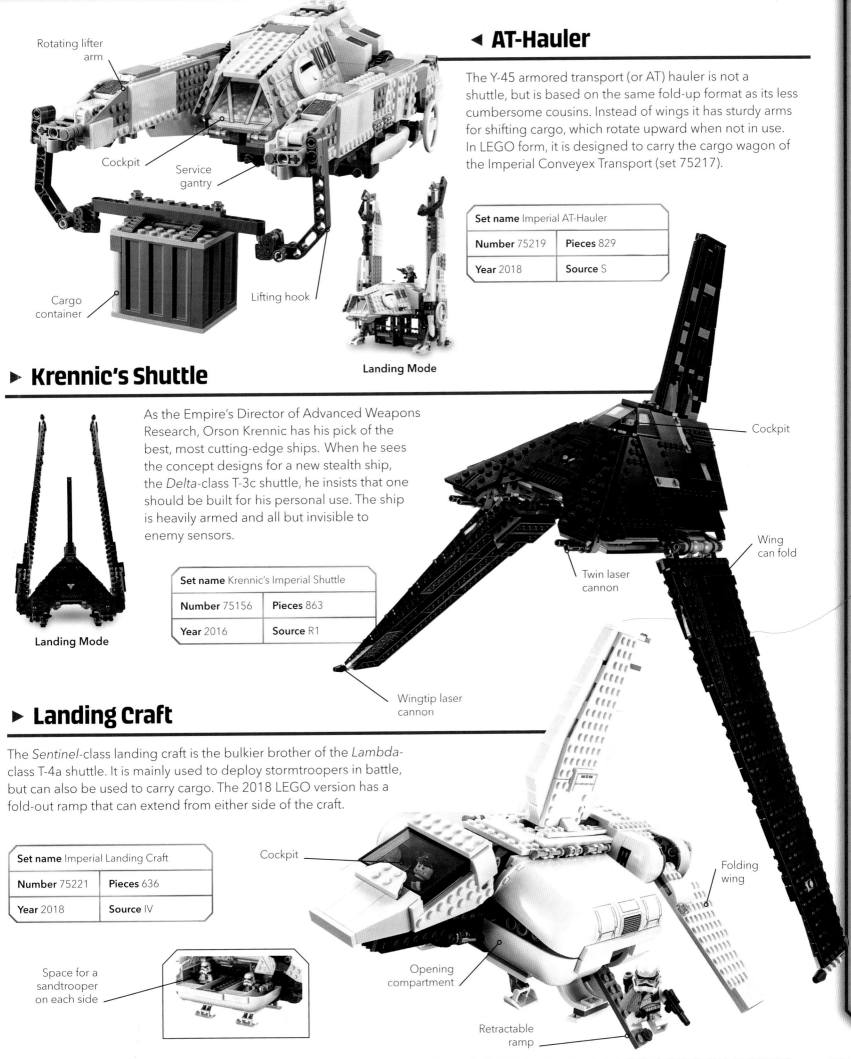

Rotating lifter arm

Cockpit

Service gantry

Cargo container

Lifting hook

◀ AT-Hauler

The Y-45 armored transport (or AT) hauler is not a shuttle, but is based on the same fold-up format as its less cumbersome cousins. Instead of wings it has sturdy arms for shifting cargo, which rotate upward when not in use. In LEGO form, it is designed to carry the cargo wagon of the Imperial Conveyex Transport (set 75217).

Set name Imperial AT-Hauler	
Number 75219	Pieces 829
Year 2018	Source S

Landing Mode

▶ Krennic's Shuttle

As the Empire's Director of Advanced Weapons Research, Orson Krennic has his pick of the best, most cutting-edge ships. When he sees the concept designs for a new stealth ship, the *Delta*-class T-3c shuttle, he insists that one should be built for his personal use. The ship is heavily armed and all but invisible to enemy sensors.

Landing Mode

Set name Krennic's Imperial Shuttle	
Number 75156	Pieces 863
Year 2016	Source R1

Cockpit

Wing can fold

Twin laser cannon

Wingtip laser cannon

▶ Landing Craft

The *Sentinel*-class landing craft is the bulkier brother of the *Lambda*-class T-4a shuttle. It is mainly used to deploy stormtroopers in battle, but can also be used to carry cargo. The 2018 LEGO version has a fold-out ramp that can extend from either side of the craft.

Set name Imperial Landing Craft	
Number 75221	Pieces 636
Year 2018	Source IV

Space for a sandtrooper on each side

Cockpit

Opening compartment

Folding wing

Retractable ramp

Star Destroyer

Dagger-shaped Star Destroyers are the most feared symbol of Imperial might, armed with incredible firepower and powerful scanner and tractor-beam arrays. In the final years of the Clone Wars, the Republic developed the *Venator*-class Star Destroyers, and the Emperor went on to expand the fleet with upgraded *Imperial*-class Star Destroyers, used to crush and subdue worlds.

Command Bridge
The bridge is situated at the center of the command tower, in view of any ship under attack. Grand Moff Tarkin and an Imperial officer stand at the flight consoles and tracking systems.

Meditation Chamber
On long space voyages, Darth Vader sits in his meditation chamber, or hyperbaric pod. The high-pressure air mix within the chamber means Vader can remove his helmet safely (using a lifting mechanism), revealing his horribly scarred face and head.

Defense turret

Escape Pod
The ship contains a life-support escape pod for emergency evacuations. Escape pods contain food and oxygen, as well as flares, a porta-shelter, and survival suits for passengers.

Mouse droid

Grand Moff Tarkin

R2-D5

Armored hull

Flight deck

Escape pod

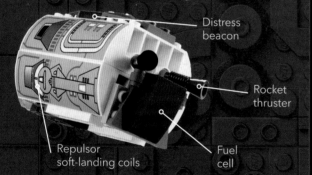

Distress beacon

Rocket thruster

Repulsor soft-landing coils

Fuel cell

▶ Forward Systems

A Star Destroyer's nose contains powerful pursuit tractor beams. The model contains a mechanism that, when pulled, ejects the escape pod through a hatch in the ship's underside.

Escape pod release mechanism

Entrance to escape pod hangar bay

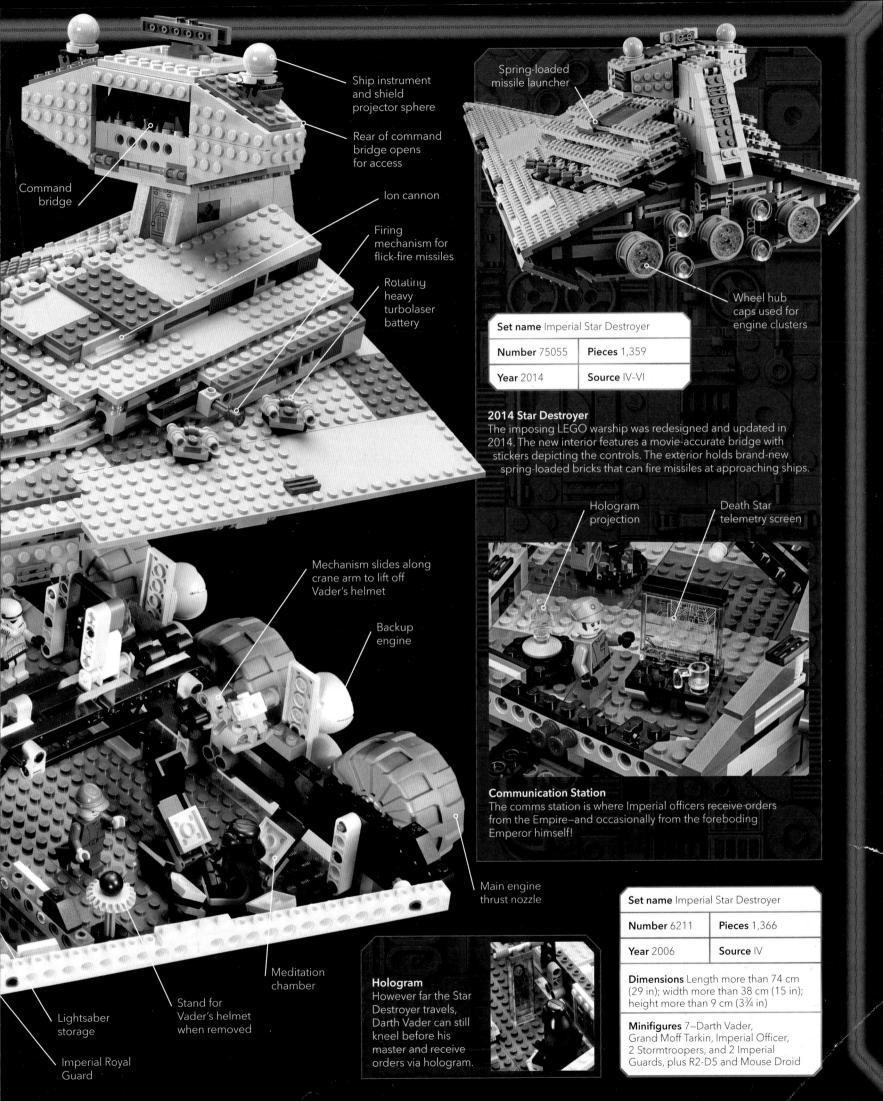

Ship instrument
and shield
projector sphere

Rear of command
bridge opens
for access

Command
bridge

Ion cannon

Firing
mechanism for
flick-fire missiles

Rotating
heavy
turbolaser
battery

Spring-loaded
missile launcher

Wheel hub
caps used for
engine clusters

Set name Imperial Star Destroyer	
Number 75055	Pieces 1,359
Year 2014	Source IV-VI

2014 Star Destroyer
The imposing LEGO warship was redesigned and updated in
2014. The new interior features a movie-accurate bridge with
stickers depicting the controls. The exterior holds brand-new
spring-loaded bricks that can fire missiles at approaching ships.

Hologram
projection

Death Star
telemetry screen

Mechanism slides along
crane arm to lift off
Vader's helmet

Backup
engine

Communication Station
The comms station is where Imperial officers receive orders
from the Empire—and occasionally from the foreboding
Emperor himself!

Main engine
thrust nozzle

Meditation
chamber

Stand for
Vader's helmet
when removed

Lightsaber
storage

Imperial Royal
Guard

Hologram
However far the Star
Destroyer travels,
Darth Vader can still
kneel before his
master and receive
orders via hologram.

Set name Imperial Star Destroyer	
Number 6211	Pieces 1,366
Year 2006	Source IV
Dimensions Length more than 74 cm (29 in); width more than 38 cm (15 in); height more than 9 cm (3¾ in)	
Minifigures 7—Darth Vader, Grand Moff Tarkin, Imperial Officer, 2 Stormtroopers, and 2 Imperial Guards, plus R2-D5 and Mouse Droid	

Early Rebel Craft

In the earliest days of the Empire, pockets of resistance give people hope that democracy might one day return to the galaxy. Slowly, these rebel groups gain in strength and number. They travel the galaxy in a host of crafts and vehicles, working to undermine the Empire.

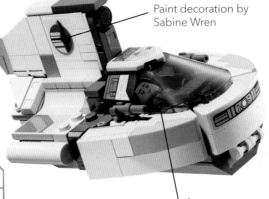

Dorsal laser cannon turret

Phantom II docks here

▶ The *Ghost*

The heavily modified VCX-100 light freighter the *Ghost* is home to the rebel group known as the Spectres. This model is the second LEGO version of the ship, from the time of the *Ahsoka* live-action series. Three rebels—Hera Syndulla, her son Jacen, and droid Chopper—reunite in the *Ghost*, along with First Officer Hawkins and Lieutenant Beyta.

Laser turret swivels

Set name *Ghost & Phantom II*	
Number 75357	**Pieces** 1,394
Year 2023	**Source** AH

▶ *Phantom II*

Paint decoration by Sabine Wren

The Spectres used a *Sheathipede*-class transport called *Phantom* until it was destroyed in the Galactic Civil War. It's later replaced by *Phantom II*. Both were designed to connect with the *Ghost*.

Set name *Ghost & Phantom II*	
Number 75357	**Pieces** 1,394
Year 2023	**Source** AH

Jacen Syndulla

▼ Wookiee Gunship

Most Wookiees are made to work without pay for the Empire, but some have escaped Imperial clutches and now fight for their species' freedom. Formerly enslaved Wookiees such as Wullffwarro assist other rebels in their *Auzituck*-class gunships.

Set name Wookiee Gunship	
Number 75084	**Pieces** 570
Year 2015	**Source** REB

Kanan Jarrus

Ezra Bridger

Hera Syndulla

Zeb Orrelios

The Spectres
The rebel cell known as the Spectres is made up of Jedi Kanan Jarrus, his apprentice Ezra Bridger, Hera Syndulla (captain of the *Ghost*), Lasat warrior Zeb Orrelios, graffiti artist Sabine Wren, and their droid, C1-10P.

Sabine Wren   **C1-10P (Chopper)**

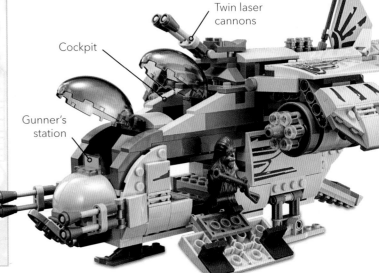

Twin laser cannons

Cockpit

Gunner's station

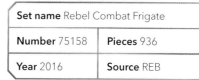

◁ *Phoenix Home*

The Phoenix cell is one of the largest early rebel groups, led by Commander Jun Sato and Anakin Skywalker's former Jedi Padawan, Ahsoka Tano. Their HQ is the *Pelta*-class frigate known as *Phoenix Home*.

Stud shooters

Fold-out wings

Retracted carry handle

Ahsoka Tano

Set name	Rebel Combat Frigate	
Number 75158		**Pieces** 936
Year 2016		**Source** REB

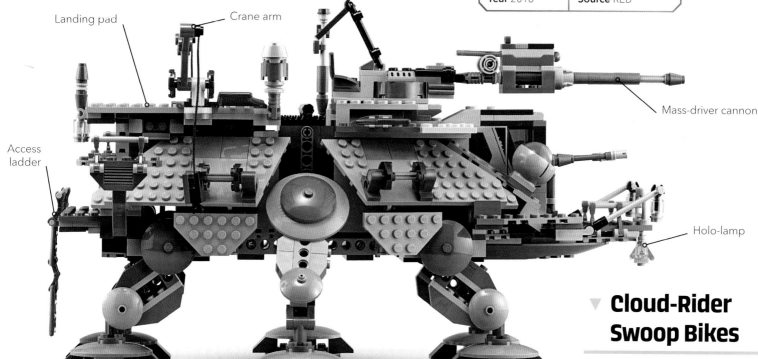

Landing pad

Crane arm

Mass-driver cannon

Access ladder

Holo-lamp

▲ Captain Rex's AT-TE

After the Clone Wars, three retired clone soldiers make their home in a battered old AT-TE on the planet Seelos. Captain Rex and his friends, Commander Wolffe and Commander Gregor, want no part in the Rebellion, but find themselves drawn into the fight against the Empire when they met the Spectres. Rex soon becomes a member of the Phoenix rebel cell.

Captain Rex   **Commander Wolffe**

Set name	Captain Rex's AT-TE	
Number 75157		**Pieces** 972
Year 2016		**Source** REB

▽ Cloud-Rider Swoop Bikes

The Cloud-Riders are a band of rebels and pirates who make raids against Imperial sympathizers on fast and dangerous swoop bikes. Their leader, Enfys Nest, pilots a Skyblade-330 swoop, while her sidekick Weazel rides a larger 221 model with a sidecar.

Enfys Nest

Set name	Cloud Rider Swoop Bikes	
Number 75215		**Pieces** 355
Year 2018		**Source** S

Weazel

Steering vanes

Rebel Alliance

Courageous freedom fighters have banded together to bring down the Empire. They are known as the Rebel Alliance. Some rebels are deserters from the Imperial forces, but many are untrained volunteers. With skillful leaders and a ragtag assortment of ships and weapons, the rebels prove a serious threat to Emperor Palpatine's tyrannical rule.

Princess Leia
A bold leader of the Rebellion, Leia Organa is kidnapped by the Empire and taken to the Death Star. She and Luke Skywalker try to outwit the battle station's crew in the LEGO set Death Star Escape (75229).

Leia Organa

▼ Y-Wing Fighter

BTL-A4 Y-wings are old but tough workhorses of the rebel fleet, famously employed in the attacks on both Death Stars. They have hyperdrives, ion fission engines, and massive firepower. This trusty fighter was also used during the Battle of Scarif to retrieve the plans for the Death Star. LEGO Technic gears open the bottom of the ship to deploy bombs.

Set name Y-Wing Starfighter	
Number 75172	Pieces 691
Year 2017	Source R1

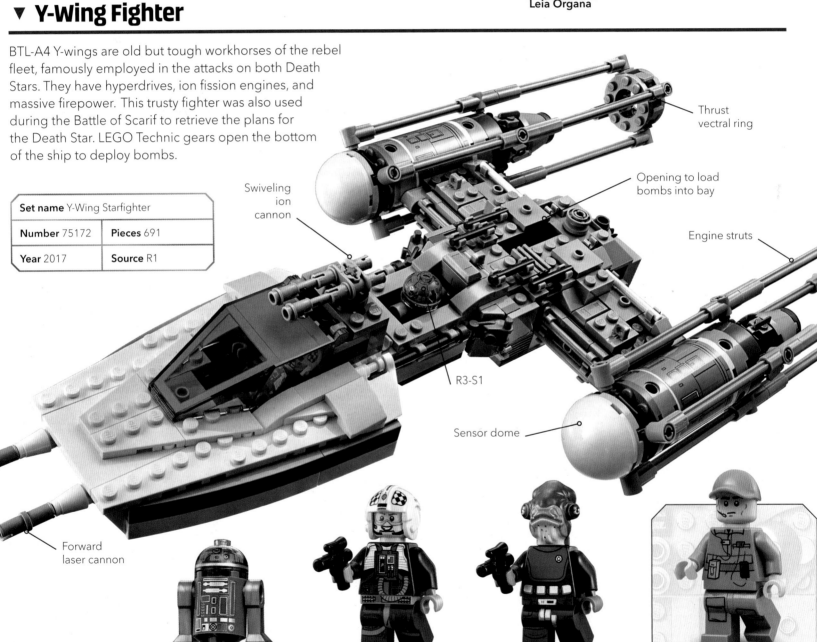

Swiveling ion cannon

Thrust vectral ring

Opening to load bombs into bay

Engine struts

R3-S1

Sensor dome

Forward laser cannon

R3-S1
This astromech droid is unusually vain, even though the silver design on her torso is a standard astromech droid print pattern.

Y-Wing Pilot
This rebel pilot's torso has detailed printing, depicting a Guidenhauser ejection harness and a life-support unit.

Admiral Raddus
Strategic and bold, Raddus is in charge of the rebel fleet. He perishes, along with his flagship, *Profundity*, at the Battle of Scarif.

Rebel Technician

Engineer Corps
Rebel engineers and technicians maintain and repair spaceships and vehicles, among other tasks.

The *Tantive IV*

As a senator for Alderaan, Princess Leia Organa travels in a diplomatic starship, the *Tantive IV*. The ship also carries out covert missions for the Rebel Alliance—until Darth Vader catches up to it and storms aboard.

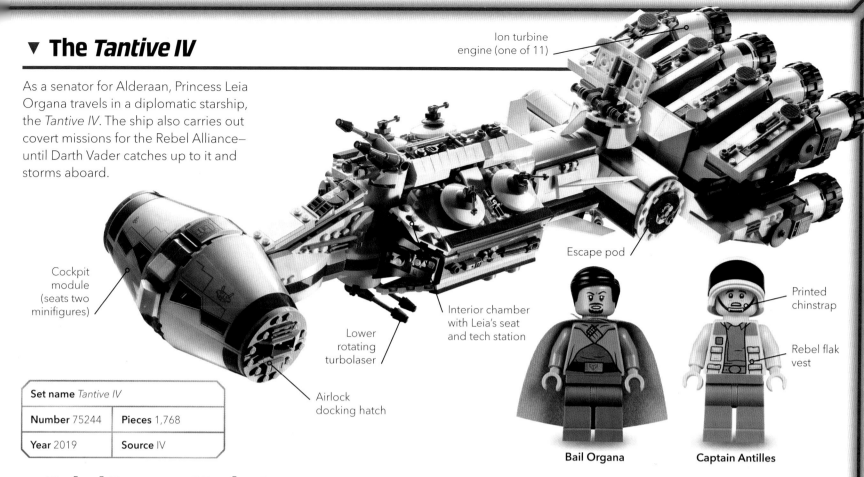

Ion turbine engine (one of 11)

Escape pod

Interior chamber with Leia's seat and tech station

Cockpit module (seats two minifigures)

Lower rotating turbolaser

Airlock docking hatch

Printed chinstrap

Rebel flak vest

Bail Organa

Captain Antilles

Set name *Tantive IV*	
Number 75244	**Pieces** 1,768
Year 2019	**Source** IV

Rebel Base on Yavin 4

Hidden in the jungle on the moon Yavin 4 is the Rebel Alliance's headquarters. The set features a command room, a pilot briefing room, a watchtower, and a stage for presenting Luke and Han's minifigures with medals after their success at the Battle of Yavin. A Y-wing provides air cover.

Watchtower moves up and down

Rotating stud shooters

Set name Yavin 4 Rebel Base	
Number 75365	**Pieces** 1,066
Year 2023	**Source** IV

Home One

Giant Mon Calamari star cruisers are the largest ships of the rebel fleet. At the Battle of Endor, Admiral Ackbar leads the rebels from his flagship, *Home One*. The LEGO cruiser features the bridge, the command center, and a hangar for an A-wing.

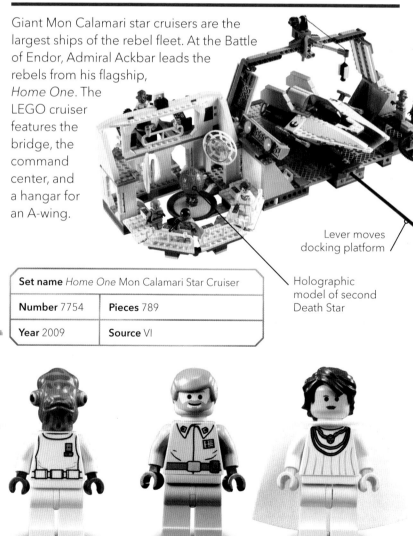

Lever moves docking platform

Holographic model of second Death Star

Set name *Home One* Mon Calamari Star Cruiser	
Number 7754	**Pieces** 789
Year 2009	**Source** VI

Admiral Ackbar

Crix Madine

Mon Mothma

Rogue Heroes

When Jyn Erso finds out about a new Imperial superweapon, she realizes that the fate of the galaxy lies with whoever knows its secrets. She commits herself to the rebel cause and convinces a ragtag band of heroes to join her on a mission to steal the Death Star plans. Calling their ship *Rogue One*, Jyn, Captain Cassian Andor, the droid K-2SO, and the rest of the team set course for the Imperial archive on the planet Scarif.

Always Prepared
Jyn Erso's practical, protective clothes are suitable for the harsh environments in which she has often found herself. Her warm poncho comes in handy on the rain-soaked world of Eadu.

Jyn Erso

▼ Speeder Bike Escape

Cassian Andor is drawn into the Rebellion after meeting the rebel coordinator Luthen Rael. Pre-Mor Enforcement military forces, who are aligned with the Empire, corner Cassian on the planet Ferrix. Luthen saves Cassian's life and helps him escape on a repulsorlift speeder bike.

Repulsorlift engine

Set name Ambush on Ferrix	
Number 75338	**Pieces** 679
Year 2022	**Source** AN

Steering vane

Outrigger

Empire State of Mind
A reprogrammed rebel droid, K-2SO was loyal to the Empire—until Cassian Andor got inside his head! He's much happier as a rebel, though he hates to let it show. He is found in just one LEGO set: Krennic's Imperial Shuttle (set 75156).

K-2SO

Cassian Andor
Although initially reluctant to join the Rebellion, Cassian will become one of its most dedicated fighters.

Luthen Rael
Luthen Rael deals antiques, but he is also a rebel spymaster. He risks his life to run networks of agents for the Rebellion.

◀ U-Wing

Cockpit

The U-wing is a starfighter large enough to carry troops—deploying them in battle before providing covering fire. When the Rebel Alliance hears that *Rogue One* has landed on Scarif, it sends U-wings to help Cassian and company complete their mission.

Rebel soldier Bistan

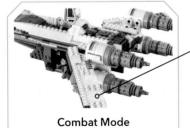

Pronglike wings fold backward for combat mode

Combat Mode

Set name Rebel U-Wing Fighter	
Number 75155	**Pieces** 659
Year 2016	**Source** R1

Laser cannon

A280-CFE convertible blaster

Fur-lined jacket worn on Jedha

Cassian Andor

82

Rogue's Gallery
Joining Jyn, Cassian, and K-2SO on the *Rogue One* mission are blind warrior monk Chirrut Îmwe and his best friend Baze Malbus, former Imperial pilot Bodhi Rook, and Drabatan commando Pao. Pao's full name is Paodok'Draba'Takat Sap'De'Rekti Nik'Linke'Ti'Ki'Vef'Nik'NeSevef'Li'Kek!

Walking staff is also a weapon

Lightbow

Repeating blaster

Generator for blaster

Backpack antenna

Chirrut Îmwe

Baze Malbus

Bodhi Rook

Pao

▼ Battle of Scarif

On sandy Scarif, the rogue rebels fight their way to the top-secret archive where the Death Star plans are kept. This set features locking doors on the archive's entrance, exploding floor panels, and two shoretroopers to keep Jyn and Cassian from their goal.

Set name	Battle on Scarif	
Number 75171		Pieces 419
Year 2017		Source R1

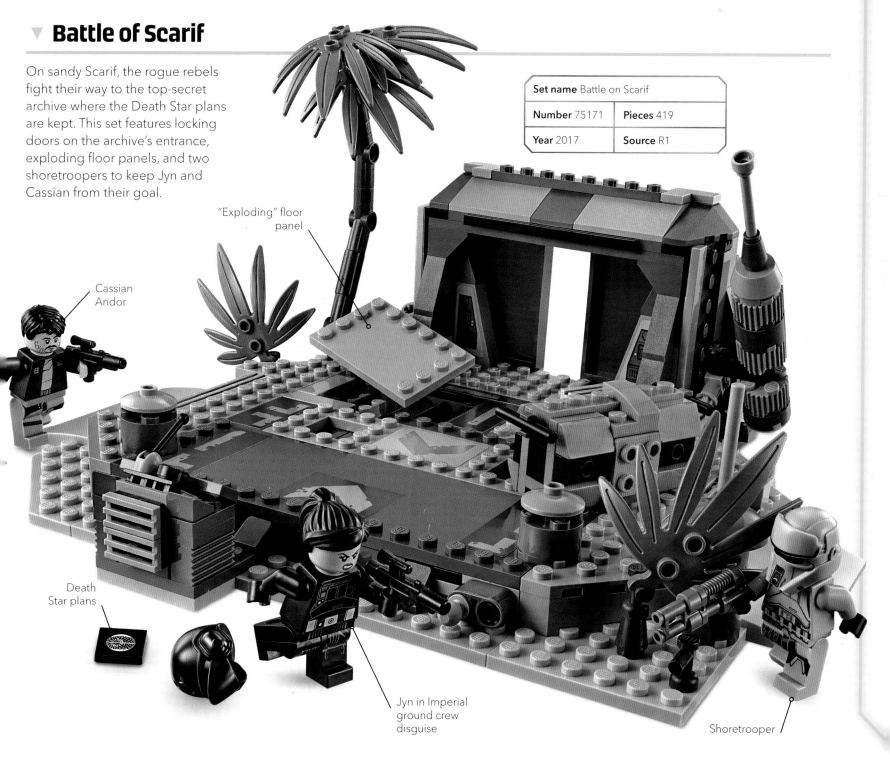

"Exploding" floor panel

Cassian Andor

Death Star plans

Jyn in Imperial ground crew disguise

Shoretrooper

Echo Base

On the ice planet Hoth, the Rebel Alliance establishes its secret Echo Base, protected by an immense energy shield. When the Empire discovers the location of the base, it deploys AT-ATs and AT-STs to destroy the shield generator. Even the combined strength of rebel artillery emplacements and snowspeeder squadrons cannot prevent one of the Alliance's worst battlefield defeats.

Protocol Droids

K-3PO is a white protocol droid who is given the rank of lieutenant in Hoth Rebel Base (set 7666). Exclusive to Hoth Echo Base (set 7879), R-3PO has special programming designed to ferret out Imperial spies.

C-3PO's head mold

Bright-red droid plating

K-3PO

R-3PO

Slide out pin to activate icicle trap

Rotating gun turrets with flick missiles

P-Tower laser cannon

Portable power unit

Catch secures base in "closed" play mode

▼ Wampa Cave

After a wampa captures Luke, the rebel hero must use the Force to escape from the beast. The wampa's hand can grip minifigures, but the ice monster also has an oversize turkey leg in case his prey should elude him.

Set name	Hoth Wampa Cave	
Number 8089	**Pieces** 297	
Year 2010	**Source** V	

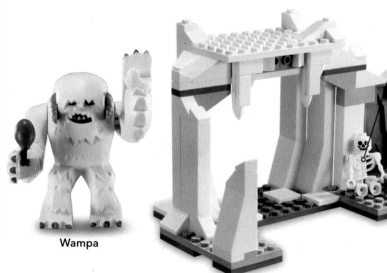

Wampa

Remnants of wampa's former meal

"Force" launcher for Luke's lightsaber

Head, torso, and tail is a single mold

Horn

Han Solo

Saddle for minifigures

Sharp claws on hands and feet for gripping ice

Tauntaun

Rebel troops on Hoth make patrols on domesticated snow lizards called tauntauns. Tauntauns can withstand freezing winds, but are not the sweetest-smelling animals!

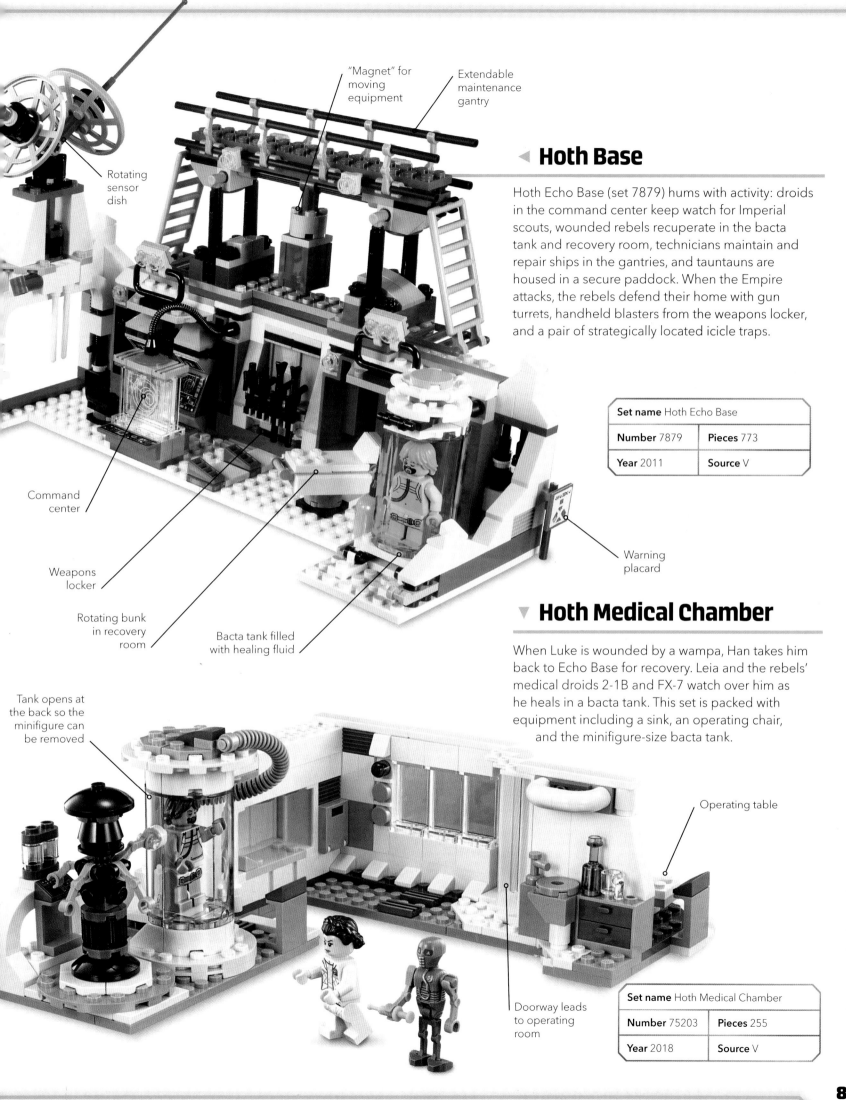

Rotating
sensor
dish

"Magnet" for
moving
equipment

Extendable
maintenance
gantry

◀ **Hoth Base**

Hoth Echo Base (set 7879) hums with activity: droids
in the command center keep watch for Imperial
scouts, wounded rebels recuperate in the bacta
tank and recovery room, technicians maintain and
repair ships in the gantries, and tauntauns are
housed in a secure paddock. When the Empire
attacks, the rebels defend their home with gun
turrets, handheld blasters from the weapons locker,
and a pair of strategically located icicle traps.

Set name Hoth Echo Base	
Number 7879	**Pieces** 773
Year 2011	**Source** V

Command
center

Weapons
locker

Rotating bunk
in recovery
room

Bacta tank filled
with healing fluid

Warning
placard

▼ **Hoth Medical Chamber**

When Luke is wounded by a wampa, Han takes him
back to Echo Base for recovery. Leia and the rebels'
medical droids 2-1B and FX-7 watch over him as
he heals in a bacta tank. This set is packed with
equipment including a sink, an operating chair,
and the minifigure-size bacta tank.

Tank opens at
the back so the
minifigure can
be removed

Operating table

Doorway leads
to operating
room

Set name Hoth Medical Chamber	
Number 75203	**Pieces** 255
Year 2018	**Source** V

Grenades
on torso

Goggles
attach to
helmet

Rebels on Hoth

After the rebels establish Echo Base in a secret location on Hoth, it is only a matter of time before Imperial probe droids track them down. Very soon the rebels have to use all their technology and firepower to counter an Imperial attack.

Hoth Rebel Soldier
The first Hoth soldiers, released in 1999, had yellow faces and brown visors. The latest minifigures have squared-off, movie-accurate ski goggles and detailed printing, which includes grenades on their torsos.

Set name Rebel Trooper Battle Pack	
Number 8083	Pieces 79
Year 2010	Source V

▼ Laser Ice Cutter

Turret rotates

Vehicles often break down in the bitter cold of Hoth, forcing the rebels to patrol on tauntauns or one-man laser ice cutters while technicians adapt their airspeeders to the frigid conditions. Laser ice cutters are combat speeders with swiveling gun turrets and skirts designed to push through accumulated ice and snow.

Snow goggles

Hoth Rebel Officer

Flick-fire missile

Repulsorlift skirt

▼ Snowspeeder

Rebel snowspeeders are civilian T-47 airspeeders adapted for military use, with laser cannons bolted to the wings as well as souped-up engines and armor plating (but no shields). Although similar to previous models, the 2014 snowspeeder has redesigned wings and engines, with the back portion of the laser cannons being much larger. The harpoon can be triggered to launch a grappling hook, which is attached to a spool of rope.

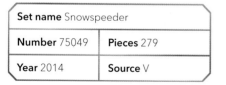

Hinged flap opens and closes

A clip on the grappling hook allows it to be fired

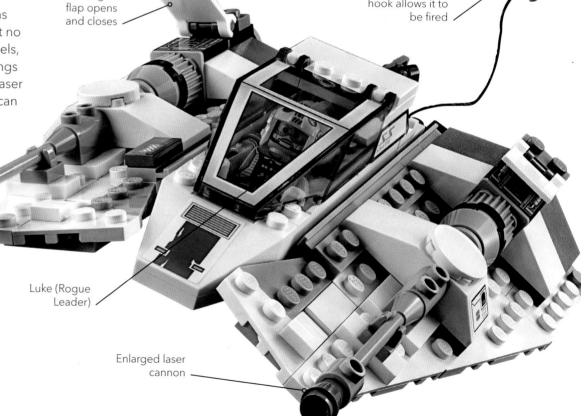

Set name Snowspeeder	
Number 75049	Pieces 279
Year 2014	Source V

Luke (Rogue Leader)

Enlarged laser cannon

▼ Imperial Battle Station

Flick-fire missile

Imperial officer

Hoth's rebels are under attack from Imperial invaders with giant AT-ATs and artillery squads. The squads' mobile equipment includes rotating gun turrets and sensor emplacements.

Weapons rack

Sensor dish

Set name Snowtrooper Battle Pack	
Number 8084	Pieces 74
Year 2010	Source V

Happy Days
Zev Senesca looks happy—probably because he is the one who finds Luke and Han after they are lost for a night on Hoth. Zev's minifigure is one of many to wear the bright-orange rebel flight suit, but his latest variant has a unique gunmetal helmet with silver printing to show scratches.

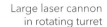

Zev Senesca

▶ Turret Defense

In trenches and behind snow-packed ridges, rebel soldiers are the first line of defense against the Imperial troops. They are supported by tall, cylindrical anti-infantry batteries.

Large laser cannon in rotating turret

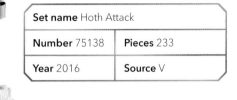

Knob turns rotating turret

Set name Hoth Attack	
Number 75138	Pieces 233
Year 2016	Source V

Power cable runs between tower and control panel

Snowy terrain is hinged so it can be rearranged

Imperial Probe Droid
Probe droids (or probots) are programmed to seek out the rebels and report back to Imperial officers. A probot detects telltale signs of habitation on Hoth, prompting Vader to initiate a full-scale Imperial assault.

▼ Tower Cannon and Trench

Echo Base is protected by an energy shield and a ring of trenches and artillery emplacements manned by brave rebel troopers. These soldiers defend their base against AT-ATs, snowtrooper scouts on speeder bikes, and Imperial artillery squads.

General Rieekan
Rieekan is Echo Base's grim commander. His gray hair piece can be switched for a cap.

Flick-fire missile

Pickax for digging trenches

Rebel gunner

P-Tower laser cannon

Command center station

Trench sections are hinged

Hidden dugout shelters troopers

Set name Battle of Hoth	
Number 75014	Pieces 426
Year 2013	Source V

Swiveling Mark II repeating blaster

Jedi in Hiding

After swearing allegiance to the Sith, Anakin Skywalker helps Darth Sidious hunt down the Jedi and turn the Republic into the Galactic Empire. The few Jedi who survive become refugees, hoping to avoid detection by Darth Vader and his Emperor. Obi-Wan Kenobi gives the infant Luke Skywalker to the Lars family on Tatooine and then lives in the desert, while Yoda hides on a little-known planet in the Outer Rim.

Lightsabers attract suspicion under the Empire

Young Ben Kenobi
Obi-Wan Kenobi still has youthful looks and auburn hair when he is forced into exile as "Ben." After rescuing a young Princess Leia, he hides his lightsaber away and goes into hiding for years.

Ben Kenobi

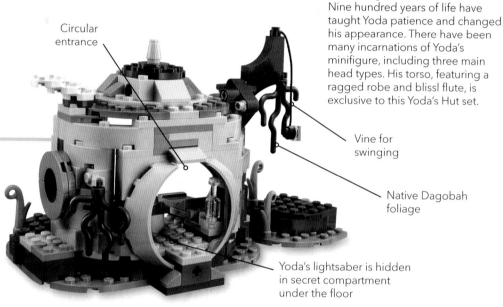

Circular entrance

Yoda (Dagobah)
Nine hundred years of life have taught Yoda patience and changed his appearance. There have been many incarnations of Yoda's minifigure, including three main head types. His torso, featuring a ragged robe and blissl flute, is exclusive to this Yoda's Hut set.

Vine for swinging

Native Dagobah foliage

Yoda's lightsaber is hidden in secret compartment under the floor

► Yoda's Hut

Yoda survives the Jedi Purge at the end of the Clone Wars to live in exile on the planet Dagobah. He lands on the planet in an escape pod, which he makes into a hut. Yoda's lifestyle on the swamp planet is frugal: his dwelling is furnished with a simple bed, table, cooking pot, and barrels.

Set name Yoda's Hut	
Number 75208	**Pieces** 229
Year 2018	**Source** V

▼ Obi-Wan's Hut

Obi-Wan settles in an abandoned hovel on the edge of Tatooine's Dune Sea. From here, he keeps a quiet watch over Luke, Anakin's son, waiting for the day he can teach him about the Force. Finally Luke turns up with a familiar-looking droid and a distress call from Princess Leia.

Ben Kenobi (Tatooine)
In exile on Tatooine, Obi-Wan keeps away from people as much as possible. He leads a solitary life under the new identity of "Ben Kenobi."

Ben Kenobi (Jedi Master)
Obi-Wan's exile comes to an end when he receives a distress call from Princess Leia. He puts on his Jedi cloak and hood to lead Luke on a rescue mission.

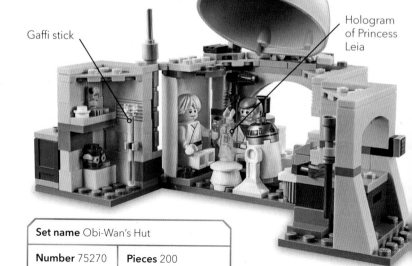

Traditional Tatooine pourstone dome

Hologram of Princess Leia

Gaffi stick

Set name Obi-Wan's Hut	
Number 75270	**Pieces** 200
Year 2020	**Source** IV

Boba Fett

Son of the bounty hunter Jango Fett, Boba Fett follows in his father's footsteps to become the most feared bounty hunter in the galaxy. He brings in many "impossible" bounties, thanks to his talent and an arsenal of exotic weapons. Working for Darth Vader, Fett captures Han Solo and loads Solo's carbon-frozen body into his starship.

▶ Boba Fett's Starship

Boba Fett inherited his *Firespray*-class patrol and attack ship from his father, Jango. He has added modifications of his own, including several upgraded weapons systems. The 2021 version features an opening cargo bay, a cockpit, and wings that automatically rotate into flight mode. It is armed with spring-loaded cannons and swiveling short-range twin blasters on the tail, and the hold carries an unlucky Gamorrean who has been frozen in carbonite.

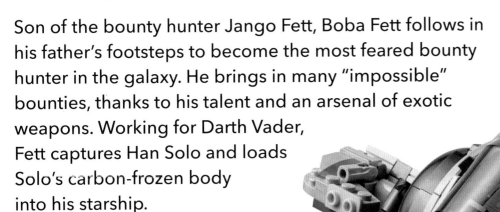

Boba Fett in pilot's seat

Armor plating

Blaster cannon

Access to hold

Wing extension strut

Set name Boba Fett's Starship	
Number 75312	**Pieces** 593
Year 2021	**Source** M, BBF

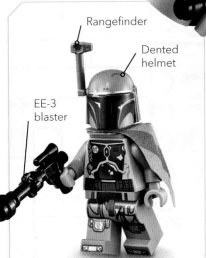

Rangefinder

Dented helmet

EE-3 blaster

Boba Fett
Boba Fett's minifigure features repainted Mandalorian armor, a helmet, jetpack, swiveling rangefinder, and cape.

Galactic Rogues
After the Battle of Hoth, Darth Vader hires bounty hunters to pursue the *Millennium Falcon*. Among those answering his call are Boba Fett, the Trandoshan Bossk, the scarred human named Dengar, the insectoid Zuckuss, assassin droid IG-88, and renegade protocol droid 4-LOM.

Blaster rifle

Flight suit

Turban

IG-88

Bossk

Dengar

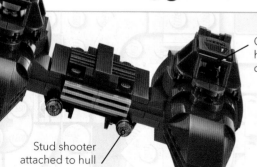

Cloud City

Custom-made shirt

Dashing cape

Lando Calrissian
The 2018 Lando minifigure features a beautifully textured cape.

After the Battle of Hoth, Han Solo and Chewbacca escape with Leia and C-3PO to Cloud City, a floating resort and mining colony, located near the gas planet Bespin. Its administrator, Lando Calrissian, is Han's longtime friend and sometime rival. Their arrival, however, is preceded by that of Boba Fett and Darth Vader, who spring a trap and lure Luke Skywalker to Cloud City for a confrontation with Vader himself!

Interrogation chamber

Cloud car pilot

▼ Duel with Vader

When Luke arrives at Cloud City to rescue his friends, Vader is waiting for him in the carbon freezing chamber. They ignite their lightsabers and duel through the chamber into a control room that overlooks a huge reactor shaft. Luke is sucked through a smashed window and a final clash takes place on a treacherous gantry.

Luke and Vader engaged in an epic duel

LEGO foil piece used for top of atmosphere sensor

Turning lever encases Solo in carbonite

Han Solo is about to be frozen!

Opulent dining room for entertaining guests

Cloud car has two cockpits

Cloud City Car
The Cloud City pilots use these fast vehicles to patrol the area surrounding Cloud City. The LEGO version of the craft has space for one pilot in each cockpit. The top and the outer side of each pod open up to let them in.

Stud shooter attached to hull

BRICK FACTS

Released in 2018, the Betrayal at Cloud City set is the first set of the Master Builder Series (MBS). These large playsets are complicated builds with exciting dioramas, many play functions, and a large assortment of minifigures.

Boba Fett's Starship

Boba Fett's ship is a powerful vehicle. Its wings change position depending on whether the ship is in flight or landing mode. The Han Solo in carbonite piece can fit under the ship's hull.

Cloud City guard

Lando Calrissian

◀ **Landing Platform**

Starships dock on a landing platform outside the main wall of Cloud City. When Han and the others arrive in the *Millennium Falcon*, Lando Calrissian meets them there.

Sith Surprise

Lando escorts Han and his friends to a dining room—but it's a trap. The Dark Lord Darth Vader and his stormtroopers are waiting there to capture them.

C-3PO has discovered a stormtrooper

This beam can lock the door in an open position

Conical hat piece used for micro Cloud City build

Set name Betrayal at Cloud City	
Number 75222	**Pieces** 2,812
Year 2018	**Source** V
Dimensions Length more than 56 cm (22 in); width more than 56 cm (22 in); height more than 16 cm (6 in)	
Minifigures 19—Luke Skywalker, Han Solo (Hoth outfit and Bespin outfit), Princess Leia (Hoth outfit and Bespin outfit), Chewbacca, C-3PO, Lando Calrissian, Lobot, 2 Cloud City Guards, 2 Cloud Car Pilots, Ugnaught, Darth Vader, 2 Stormtroopers, Boba Fett, and IG-88, plus R2-D2	

Jabba the Hutt

A gigantic, sluglike Hutt with slimy skin, an unfathomable appetite, and a large, hungry mouth, Jabba lives to strike shady deals with other members of the galactic underworld. He is protected by thugs and hirelings on whose loyalty he keeps a careful eye. Luke Skywalker and his friends seek to rescue Han Solo from Jabba's clutches, but they run the risk of becoming the gangster's latest victims.

Shrewd expression

Jabba the Hutt
Jabba's single-mold figure shows him with wrinkles of flesh, catlike eyes, and a tattoo on his arm.

Thick, leathery skin

Muscular tail

Belly filled with gorg snacks

Rotta the Huttlet
Jabba's son Rotta can be clipped onto a minifigure's hand through a circle at his base. He comes with AT-TE Walker (set 7675) and The Twilight (set 7680), which re-creates his kidnap and rescue at the beginning of Star Wars: The Clone Wars.

Rotta

▶ Jabba's Palace

Jabba's palace once belonged to a mysterious order of B'omarr monks, who continue to go about their business on the lower levels to this day. The palace is armed against external attacks with gun emplacements and missiles, and further dangers await those foolish enough to enter. The fortress is riddled with secret compartments, trapdoors, and other unwelcome surprises—not to mention the depraved thugs and criminals who call its dank passages home.

Set name Jabba's Palace		
Number 9516		Pieces 717
Year 2012		Source VI

Lookout post

Gamorrean guard

Trapdoor

Guard tower

Weapons cache

Binoculars

Salacious B. Crumb

Water pipe

Flick-fire missile defends palace

Domed temple roof

Jabba the Hutt seated on dais

Chewbacca

Han Solo frozen in carbonite

Lever opens trapdoor to rancor pit

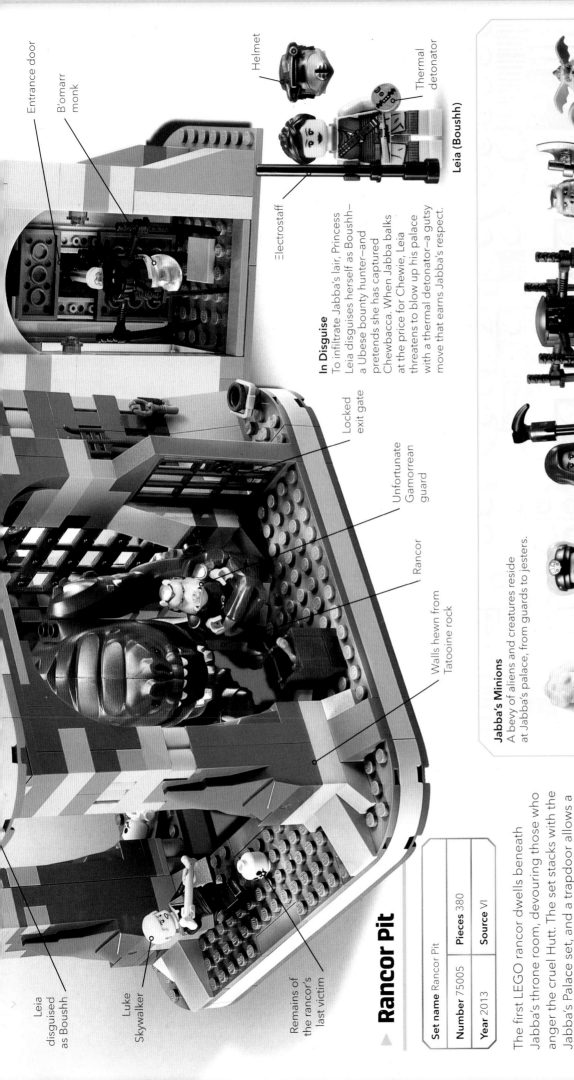

Entrance door

B'omarr monk

Helmet

Thermal detonator

Electrostaff

Leia (Boushh)

In Disguise

To infiltrate Jabba's lair, Princess Leia disguises herself as Boushh—a Ubese bounty hunter—and pretends she has captured Chewbacca. When Jabba balks at the price for Chewie, Leia threatens to blow up his palace with a thermal detonator—a gutsy move that earns Jabba's respect.

Locked exit gate

Unfortunate Gamorrean guard

Rancor

Walls hewn from Tatooine rock

Leia disguised as Boushh

Luke Skywalker

Remains of the rancor's last victim

▲ Rancor Pit

Set name	Rancor Pit	
Number 75005	**Pieces** 380	
Year 2013	**Source** VI	

The first LEGO rancor dwells beneath Jabba's throne room, devouring those who anger the cruel Hutt. The set stacks with the Jabba's Palace set, and a trapdoor allows a minifigure to fall between the two while Jabba's minions watch from above. A portcullis keeps the rancor in its dreary pen. Accessories include a key, pitchfork, and bucket.

Rancor is 10 cm (3 in) tall

Movable arms and jointed fingers

Rancor

Jabba's Minions

A bevy of aliens and creatures reside at Jabba's palace, from guards to jesters.

Bib Fortuna
Twi'lek Bib Fortuna is Jabba's chief lieutenant. His updated minifigure has a fierce expression with bared teeth (set 9516).

Oola
A green-skinned Twi'lek with printed details and a unique head piece, Oola falls through the trapdoor and is eaten by the hungry rancor.

Malakili
Malakili cares for the rancor. Turning his head after the rancor's defeat reveals a tearful alternative face—Malakili was fond of the beast.

B'omarr Monk
These strange monks house their brains in jars that are ferried around by spiderlike droid bodies. The legs are repurposed samurai swords.

Gamorrean Guard
These piglike guards serve Jabba as dim-witted muscle. This third incarnation has printed legs and a torso rich in detail.

Salacious B. Crumb
This Kowakian monkey-lizard, made from a single LEGO piece, serves as court jester. He loves to cackle at guests' misfortunes.

Jabba's Sail Barge

Jabba's sail barge is a giant repulsorlift pleasure craft that carries the crime lord and his undesirable entourage from his palace to podraces, gladiatorial contests, and other, shadier activities. It also transports Jabba to the Great Pit of Carkoon where he hopes to watch Luke Skywalker being fed to the hungry beast that inhabits this basin in the desert.

Fabric sails

Rear View

▶ The *Khetanna*

No respectable—or unrespectable—Hutt is complete without an opulent sail barge. Originally just a traveling pleasure craft, the *Khetanna* has been upgraded with prison cells, guards, armor plating, and a custom-mounted deck gun, testament to Jabba's need for protection from rival gangs. Jabba's 2013 LEGO sail barge also has the addition of a large cannon that slides out of the heavily armored hull. Three sides of the model fold down so Jabba has an unobstructed view of Luke's planned execution without the inconvenience of having to leave his throne.

Rear-mounted crossbow

Sides and back fold down on hinge with LEGO Technic connection

▼ Sand Skiff

Sand skiffs are repulsorlift platforms used to ferry passengers or prisoners to and from Jabba's palace. Han battles with a skiff guard before Luke is forced to walk the plank over the Sarlacc pit.

Set name	Desert Skiff Escape	
Number 75174	**Pieces** 277	
Year 2017	**Source** VI	

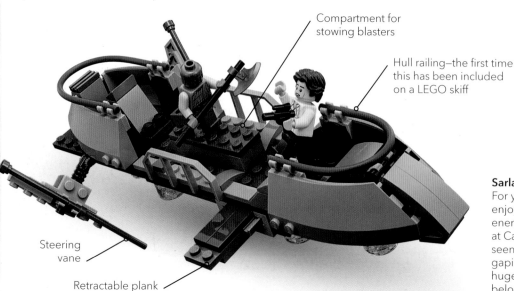

Compartment for stowing blasters

Hull railing—the first time this has been included on a LEGO skiff

Steering vane

Retractable plank

Exploratory tentacle

Opening mouth large enough to hold minifigure

Teeth prevent victims escaping

Sarlacc Pit
For years, Jabba has enjoyed feeding his enemies to the Sarlacc at Carkoon. All that can be seen of the Sarlacc is its gaping mouth. The rest of its huge, tentacled body is hidden below the desert sand.

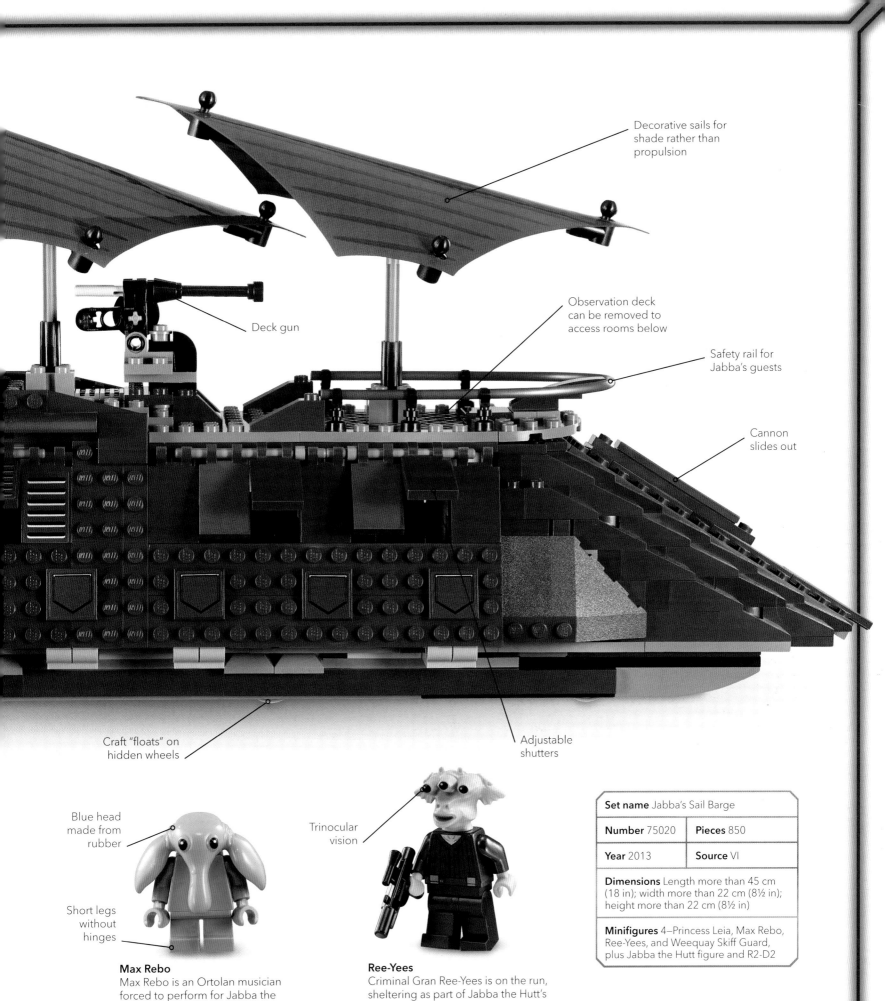

Decorative sails for shade rather than propulsion

Deck gun

Observation deck can be removed to access rooms below

Safety rail for Jabba's guests

Cannon slides out

Craft "floats" on hidden wheels

Adjustable shutters

Blue head made from rubber

Short legs without hinges

Max Rebo
Max Rebo is an Ortolan musician forced to perform for Jabba the Hutt. His hands play his red ball jet organ, but also absorb food, which is his only payment.

Trinocular vision

Ree-Yees
Criminal Gran Ree-Yees is on the run, sheltering as part of Jabba the Hutt's court. This hiding place does not do him much good, though, when the sail barge is blown up—with him on board.

Set name Jabba's Sail Barge	
Number 75020	**Pieces** 850
Year 2013	**Source** VI
Dimensions Length more than 45 cm (18 in); width more than 22 cm (8½ in); height more than 22 cm (8½ in)	
Minifigures 4—Princess Leia, Max Rebo, Ree-Yees, and Weequay Skiff Guard, plus Jabba the Hutt figure and R2-D2	

▼ A-Wing

The rebels constructed this lightning-fast starfighter in secret before the Battle of Endor to use as an escort craft. A trio of A-wings plays a crucial role in the battle, destroying Darth Vader's gigantic ship, the *Executor*.

Set name A-Wing Starfighter	
Number 75175	**Pieces** 358
Year 2017	**Source** VI

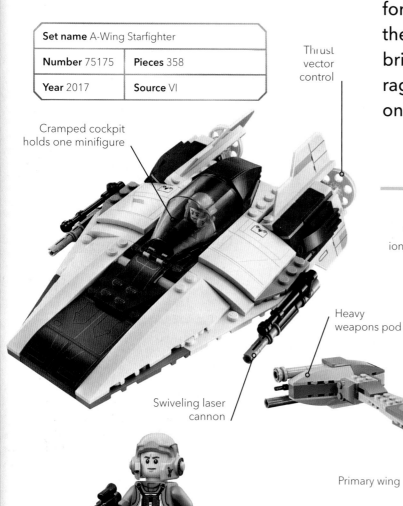

Thrust vector control

Cramped cockpit holds one minifigure

Swiveling laser cannon

A-Wing Pilot

Battle of Endor

The Empire's second Death Star is protected by a defensive shield, projected from a generator on the forest moon of Endor. The rebels must concentrate all their resources on a concerted strike that will ultimately bring down the hated Empire. The Battle of Endor rages in space around the Death Star and below, on the surface of the forest moon.

▼ B-Wing

The B-wing is the most powerful starfighter in the rebel fleet. Its S-foil wings can be deployed for flight and attack modes, and folded for landing. Its vast array of weapons is operated by spring-loaded mechanisms.

Set name B-Wing	
Number 75050	**Pieces** 448
Year 2014	**Source** VI

Wingtip ion cannon

Heavy weapons pod

Navigation sensor array

Primary wing

Rotating cockpit

Cooling system intake

Ion cannon

▼ Rebel Control Center

The rebels direct their forces at Endor from a mobile command center on board a massive Mon Calamari star cruiser. A-wings, B-wings, and Y-wings are launched from hangars in the ship as well.

Repulsorlift crane

Tool sled

Set name B-Wing at Rebel Control Center	
Number 7180	**Pieces** 338
Year 2000	**Source** VI

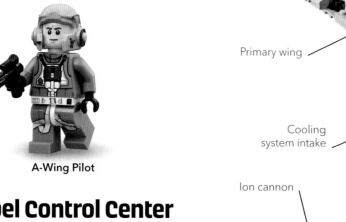

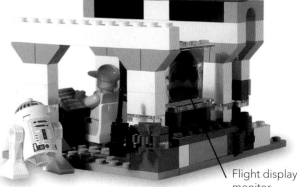

Flight display monitor

Ewok Weapons

Endor's forest moon is inhabited by Ewoks, who help the rebels defeat the Imperial forces guarding the shield generator bunker (including, in this set, a stormtrooper and a scout trooper on a speeder bike). The Ewoks use weapons that are crude—simple wooden catapults and gliders—but these furry creatures are tough and resourceful.

Ewok spear

Plants for camouflage

LEGO fishing rod pieces

Animal-pelt wing

Spare rocks for ammunition

Catapult

Wicket

Glider

Set name	The Battle of Endor	
Number 8038		**Pieces** 890
Year 2009		**Source** VI

Walls collapse when round dish piece is pressed

Shield Generator Bunker

The Imperial shield generator is housed in a bunker on Endor's moon. A rebel commando team, led by Han Solo, Princess Leia, Chewbacca and two commandos, must evade two Imperial scout troopers to gain entry to the secret back entrance and overpower the Death Star trooper inside.

Front View

Set name	The Battle of Endor	
Number 8038		**Pieces** 890
Year 2009		**Source** VI

Sliding blast doors can be "blown off"

Forest vegetation

Power generator array

Control monitor

Blaster rack

Death Star trooper

Interior View

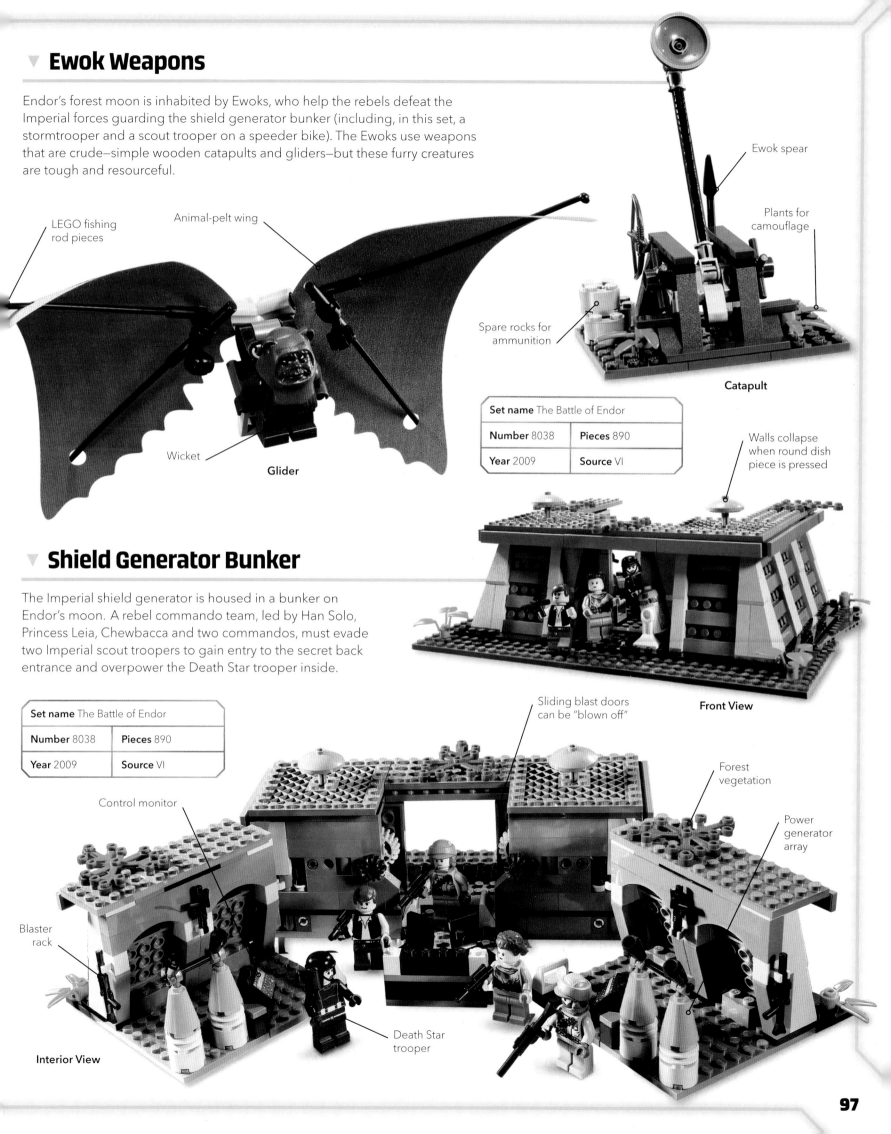

Bright Tree Village

Deep in the primeval woodland of Endor's forest moon is Bright Tree Village, the home of the Ewoks. Although the wooden building materials are primitive, the resourceful Ewoks have created a complex network of treetop dwellings, protected by hidden fortifications. When the rebels stumble into Ewok territory, they get a mixed reception, but soon win over the furry creatures—who prove to be invaluable allies.

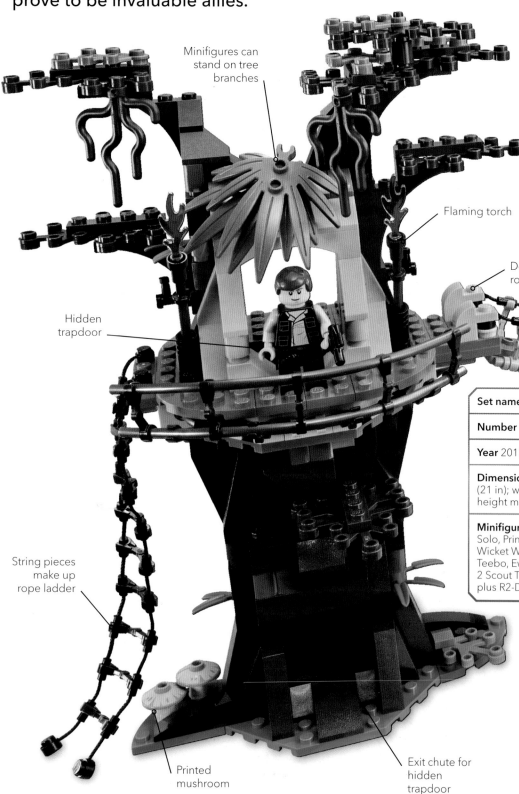

Minifigures can stand on tree branches

Vine lever controls crashing logs

Bendable tubes make guardrails

Princess Leia

Luke with artificial hand

Flaming torch

Detachable rope bridge

Hidden trapdoor

String pieces make up rope ladder

Printed mushroom

Exit chute for hidden trapdoor

Set name Ewok Village	
Number 10236	**Pieces** 1,990
Year 2013	**Source** VI

Dimensions Length more than 55 cm (21 in); width more than 35 cm (13 in); height more than 35 cm (13 in)

Minifigures 16—Luke Skywalker, Han Solo, Princess Leia, Chewbacca, C-3PO, Wicket W. Warrick, Chief Chirpa, Logray, Teebo, Ewok Warrior, 2 Rebel Soldiers, 2 Scout Troopers, and 2 Stormtroopers, plus R2-D2

Ewoks
The five Ewoks in this set have more detailed printing than previous Ewok minifigures—for example, more elaborate bones and feathers with which the Ewoks adorn themselves as hunting trophies.

Stitching detail

Wicket W. Warrick

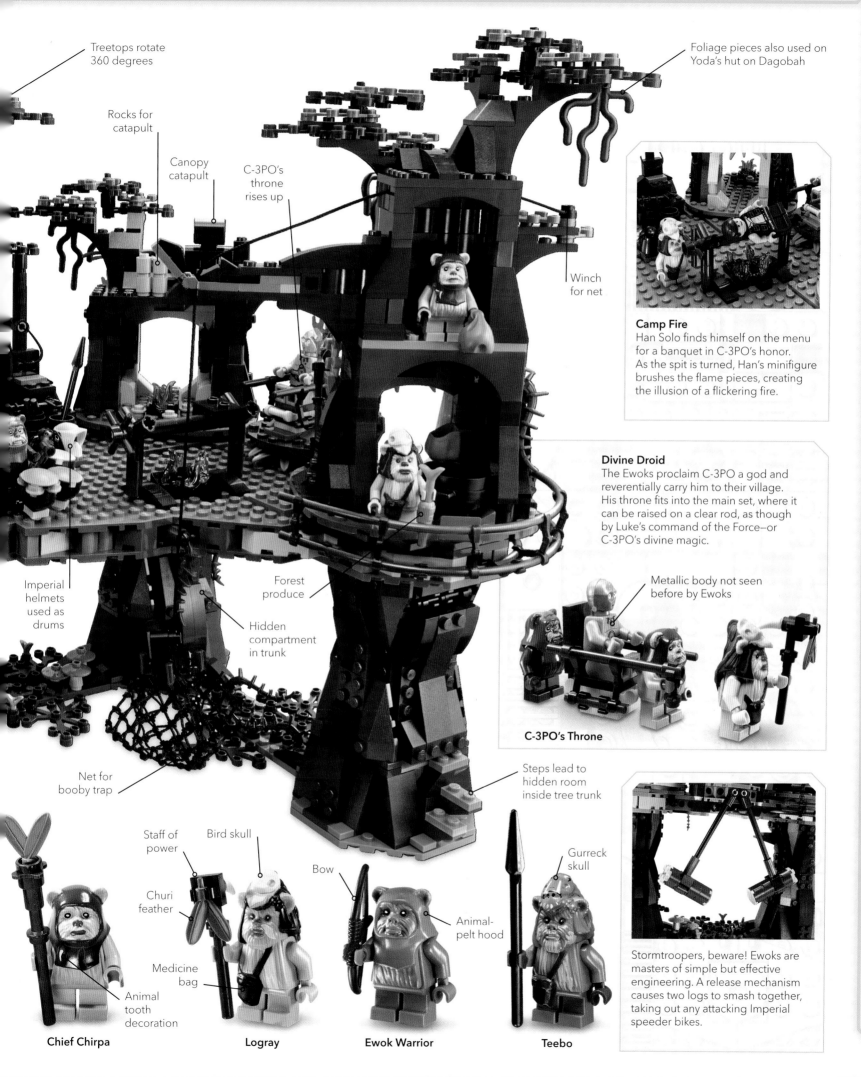

Treetops rotate
360 degrees

Rocks for
catapult

Canopy
catapult

C-3PO's
throne
rises up

Foliage pieces also used on
Yoda's hut on Dagobah

Winch
for net

Camp Fire
Han Solo finds himself on the menu
for a banquet in C-3PO's honor.
As the spit is turned, Han's minifigure
brushes the flame pieces, creating
the illusion of a flickering fire.

Divine Droid
The Ewoks proclaim C-3PO a god and
reverentially carry him to their village.
His throne fits into the main set, where it
can be raised on a clear rod, as though
by Luke's command of the Force—or
C-3PO's divine magic.

Metallic body not seen
before by Ewoks

Imperial
helmets
used as
drums

Forest
produce

Hidden
compartment
in trunk

C-3PO's Throne

Net for
booby trap

Steps lead to
hidden room
inside tree trunk

Staff of
power

Bird skull

Bow

Gurreck
skull

Churi
feather

Animal-
pelt hood

Medicine
bag

Stormtroopers, beware! Ewoks are
masters of simple but effective
engineering. A release mechanism
causes two logs to smash together,
taking out any attacking Imperial
speeder bikes.

Animal
tooth
decoration

Chief Chirpa

Logray

Ewok Warrior

Teebo

Din Djarin

Known to many as "the Mandalorian" or "Mando," Din Djarin is a lone bounty hunter with a fearsome reputation. As a child, he was raised as a Mandalorian foundling in keeping with the Way—a set of ancient beliefs and rules followed by the Mandalorian group called the Children of the Watch.

Helmet is never removed by the Children of the Watch

Old and New Armor
Two of Djarin's minifigures wear brown durasteel armor plates, while five boast his new silver beskar armor. It's made from melting down the Imperial-stamped beskar he earns from a client.

Amban phase-pulse blaster

New Beskar Armor

▼ Secret Forge

Deep in the Outer Rim, a hidden Mandalorian forge lies below the sewers of Nevarro City. The LEGO forge set includes everything the skilled Armorer needs to craft armor from beskar—one of the strongest metals in the galaxy. The Armorer follows the path of her Mandalorian ancestors, doing everything according to the Way. Knowledgeable and wise, she provides Djarin and other Mandalorians with advice and guidance along with her metalwork.

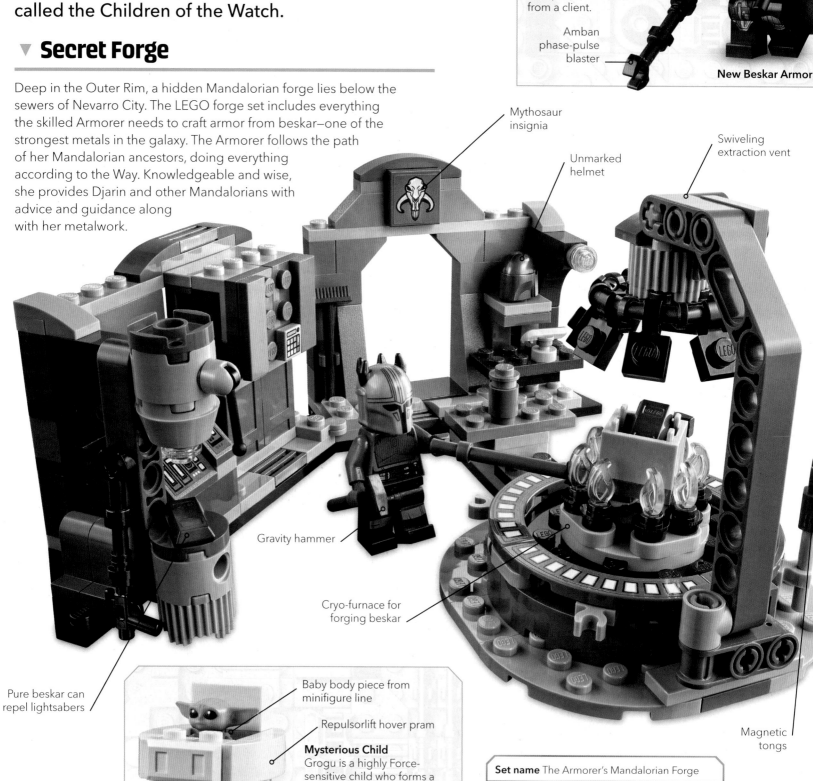

Mythosaur insignia

Unmarked helmet

Swiveling extraction vent

Gravity hammer

Cryo-furnace for forging beskar

Magnetic tongs

Pure beskar can repel lightsabers

Baby body piece from minifigure line

Repulsorlift hover pram

Mysterious Child
Grogu is a highly Force-sensitive child who forms a deep bond with Djarin. They become a clan of two with a mudhorn as their signet.

Set name	The Armorer's Mandalorian Forge	
Number 75319	Pieces 258	
Year 2021	Source M	

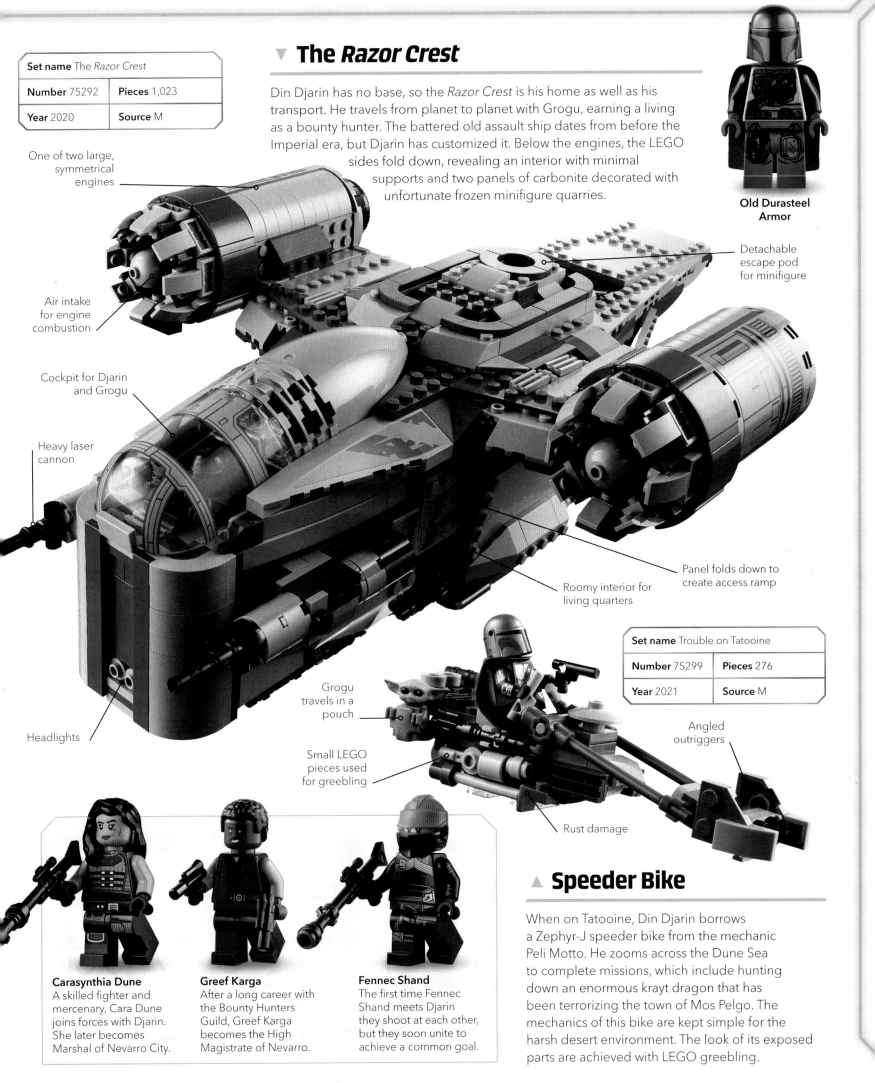

The *Razor Crest*

Set name	The *Razor Crest*	
Number	75292	Pieces 1,023
Year	2020	Source M

Din Djarin has no base, so the *Razor Crest* is his home as well as his transport. He travels from planet to planet with Grogu, earning a living as a bounty hunter. The battered old assault ship dates from before the Imperial era, but Djarin has customized it. Below the engines, the LEGO sides fold down, revealing an interior with minimal supports and two panels of carbonite decorated with unfortunate frozen minifigure quarries.

Old Durasteel Armor

One of two large, symmetrical engines

Air intake for engine combustion

Detachable escape pod for minifigure

Cockpit for Djarin and Grogu

Heavy laser cannon

Panel folds down to create access ramp

Roomy interior for living quarters

Headlights

Grogu travels in a pouch

Small LEGO pieces used for greebling

Set name	Trouble on Tatooine	
Number	75299	Pieces 276
Year	2021	Source M

Angled outriggers

Rust damage

▲ Speeder Bike

When on Tatooine, Din Djarin borrows a Zephyr-J speeder bike from the mechanic Peli Motto. He zooms across the Dune Sea to complete missions, which include hunting down an enormous krayt dragon that has been terrorizing the town of Mos Pelgo. The mechanics of this bike are kept simple for the harsh desert environment. The look of its exposed parts are achieved with LEGO greebling.

Carasynthia Dune
A skilled fighter and mercenary, Cara Dune joins forces with Djarin. She later becomes Marshal of Nevarro City.

Greef Karga
After a long career with the Bounty Hunters Guild, Greef Karga becomes the High Magistrate of Nevarro.

Fennec Shand
The first time Fennec Shand meets Djarin they shoot at each other, but they soon unite to achieve a common goal.

Troubled Times

In an era of turmoil, Din Djarin takes on the Imperial Remnant, criminal syndicates, and pirate gangs. He discovers that Mandalore, the homeworld of his people, is not as damaged as legend says, though it holds other dangers. Most troubling of all, he finds himself without a ship.

Powerful Darksaber

▶ Din Djarin

Djarin's minifigure wields the ancient Mandalorian Darksaber. The first LEGO version of this precious relic has the same mold as a lightsaber, but the second has a unique blade. Printed on the Mandalorian's right arm is a whipcord launcher and his and Grogu's mudhorn signet. The left arm has a gauntlet for firing whistling bird explosives.

Set name	The Mandalorian's Starfighter	
Number 75325		Pieces 412
Year 2022		Source M, BBF

Engine attaches on LEGO® Technic pins

Customized domed viewport for Grogu

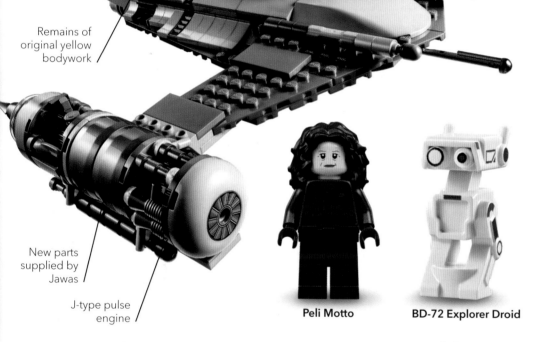

Remains of original yellow bodywork

New parts supplied by Jawas

J-type pulse engine

◀ The Mandalorian's N-1 Starfighter

The destruction of the *Razor Crest* leaves Din Djarin without a ship. Friendly mechanic Peli Motto finds a battered old N-1 starfighter (once the pride of the Naboo Royal Guard) and upcycles it into a speedster with extra thrust and weapons. She removes the astromech socket—Djarin doesn't like droids—and creates a special spot for Grogu. The mostly gray model is a little larger than the yellow LEGO N-1 starfighters flown by Anakin Skywalker.

Peli Motto

BD-72 Explorer Droid

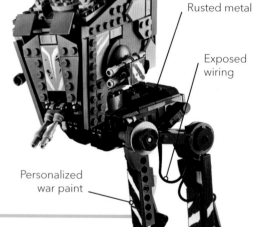

Rusted metal

Exposed wiring

Personalized war paint

Two-piece helmet

Klatooinian Raiders

▶ AT-ST Raider

The AT-ST raider has a similar construction to previous LEGO AT-STs, but this one shows signs of a lot of wear and tear. Criminals have made the most of abandoned Imperial machinery, and the AT-ST raider—with different color legs—is a hodgepodge of scavenged parts. Despite creaks, rust, and exposed wiring, the walker is good enough for Klatooinians to terrorize villages on the planet Sorgan—until Din Djarin and Cara Dune put a stop to their raids.

Set name	AT-ST Raider	
Number 75254		Pieces 540
Year 2019		Source M

Spider Tank

Deep in the gloom of the polluted mines of Mandalore there lurks a mysterious cyborg. The small creature controls a large, menacing droid tank and uses traps to capture its victims—including Din Djarin. The set uses different types of joint as well as LEGO Technic pieces to capture the movements of the machine's articulated legs and pincers.

Set name Spider Tank	
Number 75361	Pieces 526
Year 2023	Source M

New arm prints

Bo-Katan Kryze

Lethal serrated pincers

Opening hatch for cockpit

Legs pierce ground

Pirate Snub Fighter

Pirate king Gorian Shard leads his gang's assault on Nevarro, many of them flying nimble, ferocious snub fighters. These compact craft bristle with weapons—four laser cannons plus two LEGO stud shooters—but they are no match for Mandalorians. All but one of the snub fighters are destroyed, and the Nikto pirate Vane flees in it.

Set name Pirate Snub Fighter	
Number 75346	Pieces 285
Year 2023	Source M

LEGO roller skate adds mechanical detail

One of four laser cannons

Nikto Pirates
The snub fighter pilot wears a unique yellow flight suit, and Vane has a specially molded bandanna piece.

TIE Interceptor

Four daggerlike wings differentiate the TIE interceptor from other TIE starfighters. It is part of a fleet commanded by Imperial officer-turned-warlord Moff Gideon, who has his sights set on destroying the Mandalorians. The set includes a Fang fighter and two Mandalorian warriors who are ready to battle it out with the TIE Interceptor's pilot and R2 droid.

Set name Mandalorian Fang Fighter vs. TIE Interceptor	
Number 75348	Pieces 957
Year 2023	Source M

R2-E6

Mandalorian fleet commander

Triple ion engines

Set name Mandalorian Fang Fighter vs. TIE Interceptor	
Number 75348	Pieces 957
Year 2023	Source M

Mandalorian Fang Fighter

Beaten but not out, the Mandalorians are rebuilding their naval power. Key to the fleet is the nimble, powerful *Fang*-class Mandalorian starfighter with hyperdrive capability. Swift and maneuverable, the craft can dodge incoming fire while launching its own attacks from both its wing-mounted laser cannons and a concealed proton torpedo launcher.

Fleet Commander
The Mandalorian captain's minifigure is equipped with a jetpack and thermal detonator.

Printed canopy piece

Daimyo on Tatooine

Everyone thought they had seen the last of Boba Fett when he fell into the deadly Sarlacc. But instead of being digested, the bounty hunter escaped. After being restored to health, he eventually seizes control of Mos Espa's criminal empire, becoming the new Daimyo in town.

Boba Fett in cockpit

▶ Boba Fett's Starship

Emerging from the carnivorous Sarlacc, Boba is still alive—barely—but without his starship and customized Mandalorian armor he's no longer the legendary bounty hunter he used to be. With the help of Fennec Shand, Boba steals his ship back from a well-guarded hangar. Luckily, it still flies. There are many LEGO versions of his starship, and this is the Microfighters one. Unusually for a Microfighter, the set fully encloses the minifigure, who can sit in the craft in two different positions depending on whether the ship is in flight or landing mode.

Green macaroni tile

Wings swivel on LEGO Technic joints

Starship coloring matches Boba's armor

Flick-fire missile

Set name	Boba Fett's Starship Microfighter	
Number 75344		Pieces 85
Year 2023		Source BBF

Barrel contains thermal detonators

A Fresh Start
Finally reunited with his cherished Mandalorian beskar armor, Boba gives the shabby pieces a bright coat of paint, highlighting the yellow plates.

Landing Mode

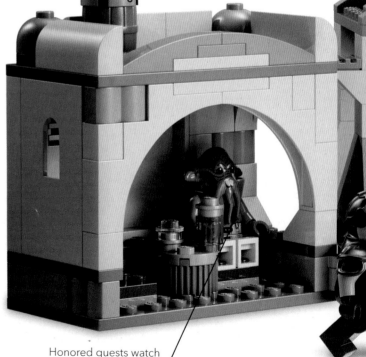

Honored guests watch the entertainment

Fennec Shand   Gamorrean Guard   Bib Fortuna   Theelin Dancer   Quarren   Weequay Guard

▼ Daimyo's Throne Room

The first LEGO models of the palace on Tatooine's Dune Sea are ruled by Jabba the Hutt. After Jabba's demise, his majordomo servant, Bib Fortuna, grabs the opportunity to take his place as crime lord in this 2022 set. Unfortunately for him, Boba Fett comes along and defeats him, claiming the throne and the title of Daimyo for himself. The six other minifigures included with the palace set must now swear loyalty to him and pay tribute—or face the consequences.

Set name	Boba Fett's Throne Room	
Number 75326	Pieces 732	
Year 2022	Source BBF	

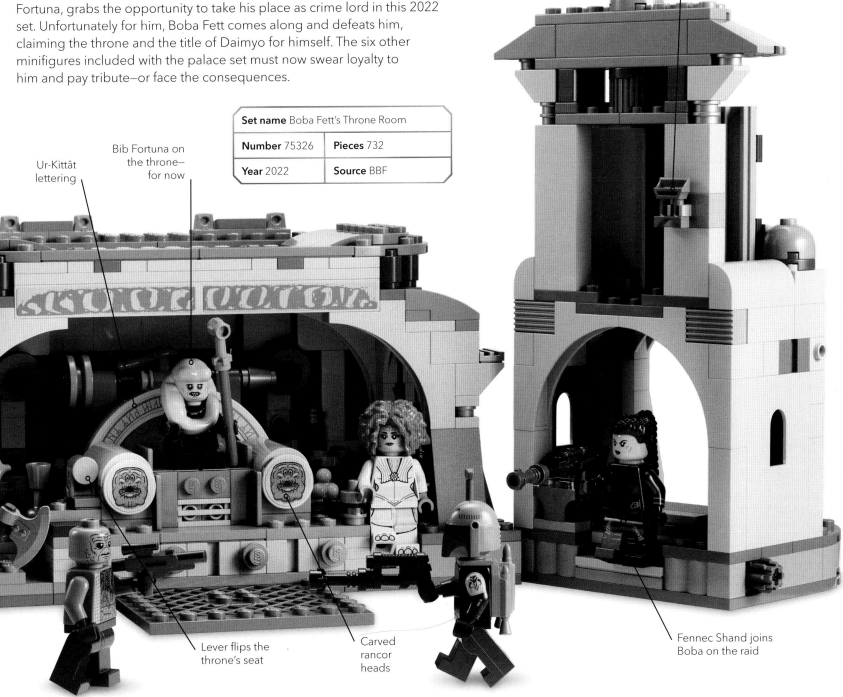

Macrobinoculars for sentry duty on the tower

Ur-Kittât lettering

Bib Fortuna on the throne— for now

Lever flips the throne's seat

Carved rancor heads

Fennec Shand joins Boba on the raid

Remnants of the Empire

Just because the Empire has collapsed, that doesn't mean local Imperial leaders will give up their positions. In fact, they continue to use Imperial craft, weapons, and soldiers to increase their power and pursue their own interests, away from the control of the New Republic.

Moff rank indicator

Moff Gideon
With a striking red-and-black double-sided cape, Moff Gideon uses all his Imperial might as he attempts to destroy every remaining Mandalorian.

▼ Imperial Light Cruiser

Not many Imperial light cruisers remain, but one is under the command of the ruthless Moff Gideon in the Outer Rim. Its whole front section opens up to reveal a large cabin, containing a hologram comms table and space for the minifigure passengers to stow their thermal detonators, electrobinoculars, and blasters. A mechanism launches mini LEGO TIE fighters from the front of the craft.

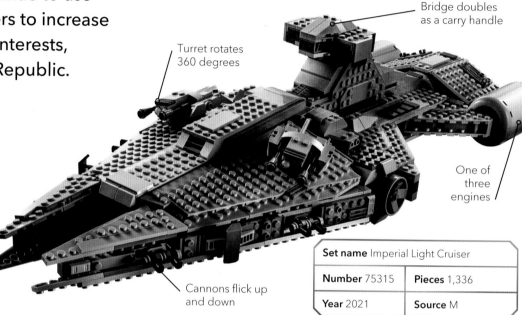

Bridge doubles as a carry handle

Turret rotates 360 degrees

One of three engines

Cannons flick up and down

Set name Imperial Light Cruiser	
Number 75315	**Pieces** 1,336
Year 2021	**Source** M

▶ Imperial Armored Marauder

Once an Imperial troop transport, this repulsorlift Trexler Armored Marauder is under Moff Gideon's command on Nevarro. The set comes with two stormtroopers and a brand-new artillery trooper with a yellow pauldron and backpack, but will they be enough to stop the craft from being stolen by Greef Karga? With many opening panels, the model can seat four minifigures.

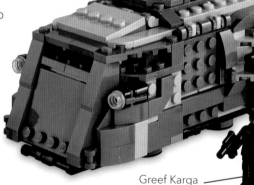

Rotating rear laser turret

Greef Karga

Set name Imperial Armored Marauder	
Number 75311	**Pieces** 478
Year 2021	**Source** M

Imperial-style lights in elevator

◀ Dark Trooper Attack

Aboard Moff Gideon's Imperial light cruiser, a hooded and cloaked Luke Skywalker arrives to rescue Grogu. The elevator spins around to reveal a closed door, and Dark Trooper minifigures can be rotated or flung backward by Luke's Force attacks.

Function pulls back floor

Set name Dark Trooper Attack	
Number 75324	**Pieces** 166
Year 2022	**Source** M

Dark Trooper
Moff Gideon commands advanced battle droids with armor-plated exoskeletons and red photoreceptors.

Ahsoka Tano

With the defeat of the Empire and the start of the New Republic, life in the galaxy looks bright. But only a few years in, Ahsoka Tano senses a threat from new dark forces: those who believe that the heir of the Empire can rise and restore Imperial glory.

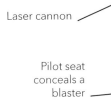

Protective gauntlet

Independent Togruta
Ahsoka trained as a Jedi during the Clone Wars, but she became disillusioned with the Jedi Order. She left to walk her own path, helping those fighting for peace and justice.

Laser cannon

Pilot seat conceals a blaster

Astromech droid fits sideways

LEGO core creates hexagonal structure

Hinge plates allow nose to taper slightly

▲ New Republic E-Wing

Known for its distinctive curved wings, the E-wing has been used by several different factions, including the New Republic, piloted by Captain Porter. A modified version, Jek-14's Stealth Starfighter (set 75018), is also flown in LEGO *Star Wars: The Yoda Chronicles*.

▼ Shin Hati's Starfighter

In an electrifying dogfight, dark-side apprentice Shin Hati tangles with New Republic pilot Captain Porter. Hati's nonsymmetrical fighter is built using a rare mix of dark-red and dark-yellow bricks. Hati, who opposes both Ahsoka Tano and the New Republic, is joined in this set by minifigures of her master—Baylan Skoll—and Morgan Elsbeth, the coldhearted Magistrate of Calodan.

Stickers show wear and tear

Set name	New Republic E-Wing vs. Shin Hati's Starfighter	
Number 75364		**Pieces** 1,056
Year 2023		**Source** AH

Hidden hatch for lightsaber

Angled wing shape created with LEGO Technic pieces

Landing Mode

New Republic Astromech Droid

Captain Porter

Shin Hati

Morgan Elsbeth

Baylan Skoll

Chapter 3
The Rise of the
First Order

Rey

Abandoned by her parents, Rey has grown up on her own on the desert world of Jakku. A lonely scavenger, she teaches herself to fly and repair ships and to defend herself against attack. A chance meeting with Resistance droid BB-8 sees her calling on all those skills to escape the First Order—and discovering new ones as a gifted Force user.

Rey
Rey wears tightly bound robes to keep the sun and sand at bay on the harsh desert plains of Jakku.

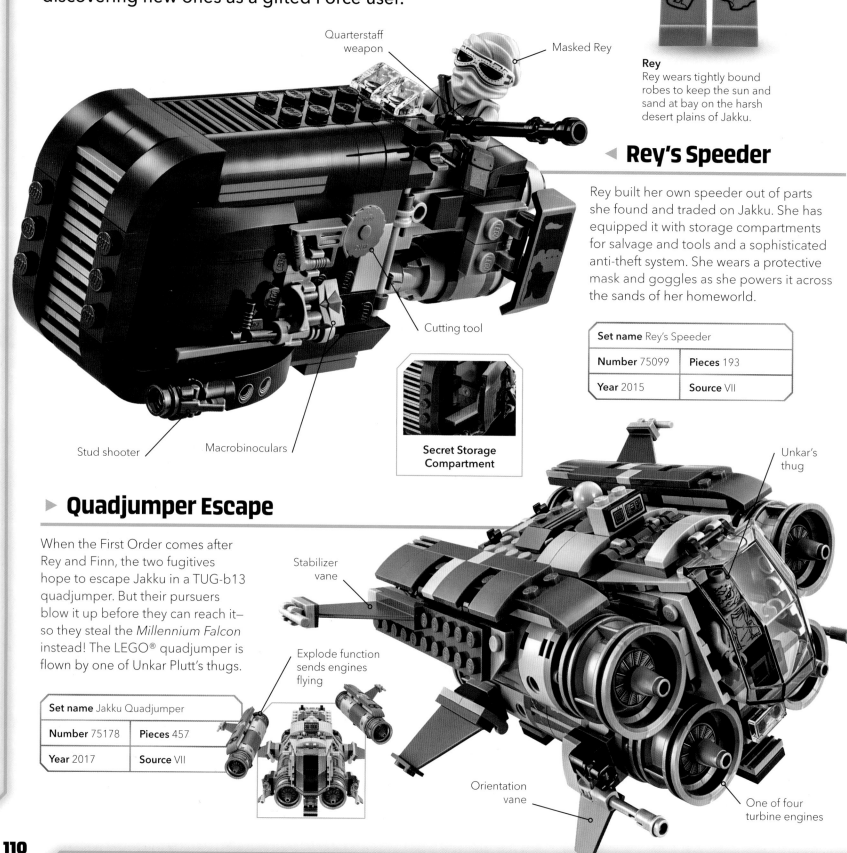

Quarterstaff weapon

Masked Rey

Cutting tool

Stud shooter

Macrobinoculars

Secret Storage Compartment

◄ Rey's Speeder

Rey built her own speeder out of parts she found and traded on Jakku. She has equipped it with storage compartments for salvage and tools and a sophisticated anti-theft system. She wears a protective mask and goggles as she powers it across the sands of her homeworld.

Set name Rey's Speeder	
Number 75099	**Pieces** 193
Year 2015	**Source** VII

► Quadjumper Escape

When the First Order comes after Rey and Finn, the two fugitives hope to escape Jakku in a TUG-b13 quadjumper. But their pursuers blow it up before they can reach it—so they steal the *Millennium Falcon* instead! The LEGO® quadjumper is flown by one of Unkar Plutt's thugs.

Set name Jakku Quadjumper	
Number 75178	**Pieces** 457
Year 2017	**Source** VII

Stabilizer vane

Explode function sends engines flying

Unkar's thug

Orientation vane

One of four turbine engines

▶ Niima Outpost

Before she leaves Jakku, Rey survives by trading salvage for food at Niima Outpost. Ruthless Unkar Plutt calls the shots at this makeshift marketplace, and Rey has no choice but to accept whatever rations he offers.

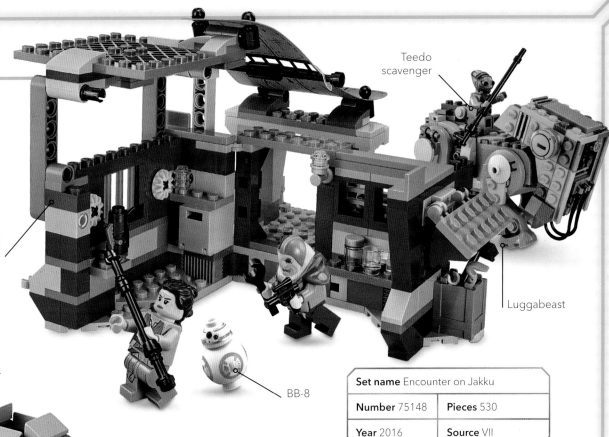

Teedo scavenger

Unkar Plutt's concession stand

Luggabeast

Unkar Plutt
Cruel Plutt uses hired thugs to enforce his stranglehold on barter. His minifigure has a sculpted, detailed head.

BB-8

Set name Encounter on Jakku	
Number 75148	Pieces 530
Year 2016	Source VII

Luke's hut has a lift-off roof

Ragged cloth curtain

◀ Jedi Training

When Rey meets Jedi Master Luke Skywalker, she hopes he will leave the planet Ahch-To to fight the First Order. He refuses, but agrees to teach her how to use her Force powers instead.

Rey uses Luke's old lightsaber

Set name Ahch-To Island Training	
Number 75200	Pieces 241
Year 2018	Source VIII

Porg
Porgs are sea-dwelling birds native to Ahch-To Island where Luke Skywalker is in exile.

Luke's fire pit

Luke's staff

Revolving platform

Jedi Missions
After leaving Ahch-To, Rey dons gray and then white robes. Until she builds her own yellow-bladed lightsaber, she uses Luke's blue one.

Rey
Rey's 2018 minifigure shows her in her training attire and comes with two facial expressions.

Luke Skywalker
Master Luke Skywalker dons a majestic robe with gold detail and a large, textured cape.

Finn and Friends

When stormtrooper FN-2187 is ordered to destroy a village on the planet Jakku, he sees the true horror of the First Order and disobeys. He flees in a TIE fighter with help from the Resistance pilot Poe Dameron, who gives him the new name Finn and sets him on the path to becoming a Resistance fighter.

FN-2187
This minifigure of Finn in a weathered First Order stormtrooper uniform comes in a LEGO polybag (set 30605).

That's So Poe
When Finn and Poe crash on Jakku, all Finn can find of his new friend is his jacket, which he puts on in place of his stormtrooper armor.

Guavian security soldier

Chewbacca

◀ Rebels and Rathtars

Aided by Rey, Finn gets away from Jakku, and the pair soon run into the famous rebels Han Solo and Chewbacca. Han and his copilot aren't sure about Finn at first, but they become friendlier after they all survive a rathtar attack inside Han's sprawling freighter, the *Eravana*.

Set name Rathtar Escape	
Number 75180	**Pieces** 836
Year 2017	**Source** VII

Rathtar

Han Solo

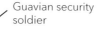

Exploding wall function

Kylo Ren

▶ Maz Kanata

Finn and Rey go with Han to Takodana, where they meet the mysterious "pirate queen" Maz Kanata. Finn thinks about leaving his new friends here, but when the First Order attacks Maz entrusts Finn with Luke Skywalker's old lightsaber, and he chooses to fight and, later, get the weapon to Rey.

Maz Kanata

Set name Battle on Takodana	
Number 75139	**Pieces** 409
Year 2016	**Source** VII

Fallen tree

Finn with lightsaber

Bacta Fashion
For DK's LEGO® *Star Wars™: Visual Dictionary: New Edition*, the LEGO Group produced a brand-new, exclusive Finn minifigure. The wounded hero has been recovering in a flexypoly bacta suit.

Rose and the Resistance

At first, Finn insists that his loyalty is to Rey only and not to the Resistance. But when he and Resistance technician Rose Tico set out on a dangerous mission in a tiny transport pod, he begins to realize the importance of taking a side in the battle between good and evil.

Finn

Rose Tico

Two-seater transport pod

Stud shooter

Set name Resistance Transport Pod	
Number 75176	Pieces 294
Year 2017	Source VIII

AT-ST Pilot

Throughout Finn's adventures, BB-8 is never far from his side. The tiny, ball-shaped droid even saves Finn's life when he and Rose are taken prisoner by Captain Phasma—by piloting an AT-ST walker to save them.

Set name First Order AT-ST	
Number 75201	Pieces 370
Year 2018	Source VIII

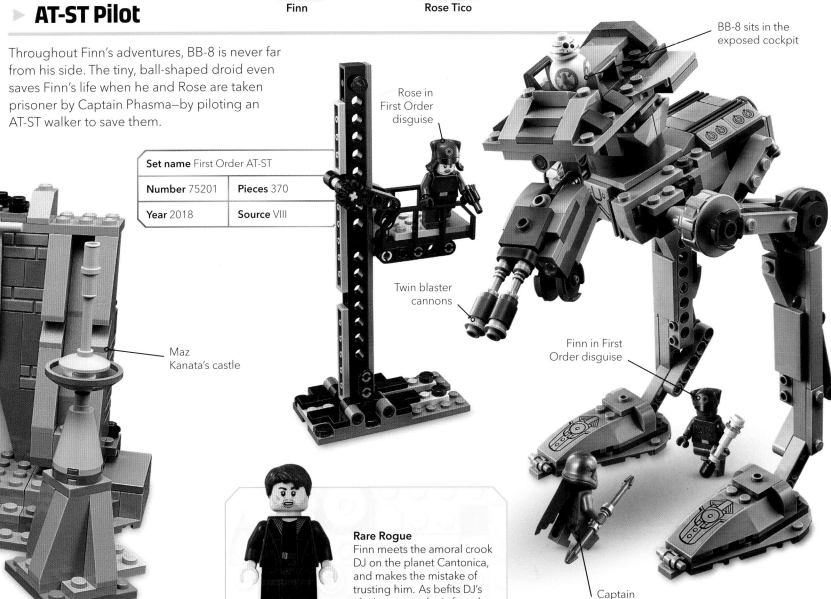

Maz Kanata's castle

Rose in First Order disguise

Twin blaster cannons

BB-8 sits in the exposed cockpit

Finn in First Order disguise

Captain Phasma

Rare Rogue
Finn meets the amoral crook DJ on the planet Cantonica, and makes the mistake of trusting him. As befits DJ's elusive nature, he is found in just one limited edition LEGO polybag (set 40298).

The Resistance

When the Galactic Empire falls, a New Republic grows up to replace it. Its leaders believe in a peaceful future, and most turn their backs on military matters. But Leia Organa still senses threats to the galaxy, so she forms the Resistance to fight the evil First Order.

Lifelong friend
Protocol droid C-3PO has served General Leia for almost as long as she can remember. He has been damaged and repaired many times over the years and, during the early days of the Resistance, sports a red replacement arm.

C-3PO

Hinged canopy folds down

◄ Black Ace

Black Ace is a TIE interceptor racer flown by racing pilot Griff Halloran. Once a pilot in the Imperial Navy, he defects and goes on to serve in Ace Squadron, defending the *Colossus* mobile aircraft refueling station near the planet Castilon, and helping the Resistance cause. He heavily customizes the former Imperial craft to to make it more formidable in racing competitions.

Kaz Xiono
Kazuda Xiono trained as a pilot with the New Republic Navy, but later becomes a spy for the Resistance.

Long strut design evokes podracers

Set name	Black Ace TIE Interceptor	
Number 75242	**Pieces** 396	
Year 2019	**Source** RES	

Racing modification

Cockpit

► Resistance Bomber

The MG-100 StarFortress SF-17—otherwise known as a Resistance bomber—is designed to drop proton bombs from its long lower hull, while a pair of gunners in rotating ball turrets defend the ship. The LEGO incarnation includes all these features, plus lift-off sections that reveal the cockpit, flight deck, and targeting station.

Targeting station

Set name	Resistance Bomber	
Number 75188	**Pieces** 780	
Year 2017	**Source** VIII	

Rear ball turret

Ventral ball turret

Resistance Gunner Paige Tico
Gunner Paige is Rose Tico's sister. Her helmet has a distinctive, colorful print. She comes with two face paintings— including one wearing breathing gear.

Vice Admiral Holdo
Vice Admiral Holdo's minifigure features a pale-purple hair piece true to the movie character.

Proton bomb

The Battle of Crait

When the Resistance is all but wiped out by the First Order, its remaining members make their stand on the planet Crait. Using the defenses and ski speeders from an old rebel base, they narrowly survive to fight another day.

Twin medium laser cannon

V-4X-D ski speeder

Rebel command tower

Open-air cockpit

Mono-ski

Set name Defense of Crait	
Number 75202	Pieces 746
Year 2018	Source VIII

General Leia
After her experience leading the rebels, Leia now has the formal title of General—along with her first minifigure dressed in green Resistance gear.

Boolio
Boolio works undercover as a secret ally to help the Resistance with intelligence and resources. The Ovissian has two sets of horns on his head.

General Ematt
Caluan Ematt earned his stripes with the Rebel Alliance, and his first minifigure is ready to face the First Order with a promotion to general.

Lando Calrissian
Lando, now with a few gray hairs, assembles a ragtag Citizen's Fleet to help the Resistance turn the tide of the battle at Exegol against the First Order.

D-O
Once owned by a Sith assassin, this data storage and retrieval droid holds information that proves very useful to the Resistance.

▶ A-Wing Starfighter

The RZ-2 A-wing starfighter is a speedier, more powerful version of the A-wing used by the Rebel Alliance. Some Resistance pilots are old-timers, including Snap Wexley, and they're supported by younger operators including Kaydel Ko Connix.

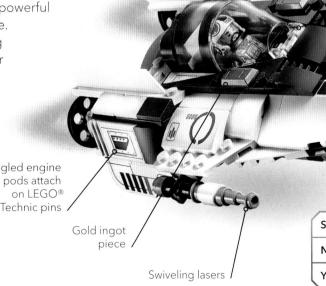

Cockpit opens with front hinge

Control for spring-loaded shooters on underside of craft

Angled engine pods attach on LEGO® Technic pins

Gold ingot piece

Swiveling lasers

Temmin "Snap" Wexley

Lieutenant Connix

Set name Resistance A-Wing Starfighter	
Number 75248	Pieces 269
Year 2020	Source IX

115

Poe Dameron

One of the greatest pilots in the galaxy, Poe Dameron has been flying since he was a child, when his mom taught him to pilot her A-wing starfighter. Poe is a Resistance hero with lots of potential, though he often annoys his superiors by being hotheaded and only following the orders he wants to. General Leia mentors him, helping him grow into a responsible leader.

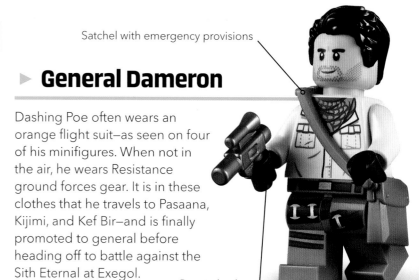

Satchel with emergency provisions

▶ General Dameron

Dashing Poe often wears an orange flight suit—as seen on four of his minifigures. When not in the air, he wears Resistance ground forces gear. It is in these clothes that he travels to Pasaana, Kijimi, and Kef Bir—and is finally promoted to general before heading off to battle against the Sith Eternal at Exegol.

Runyip-leather flying gloves

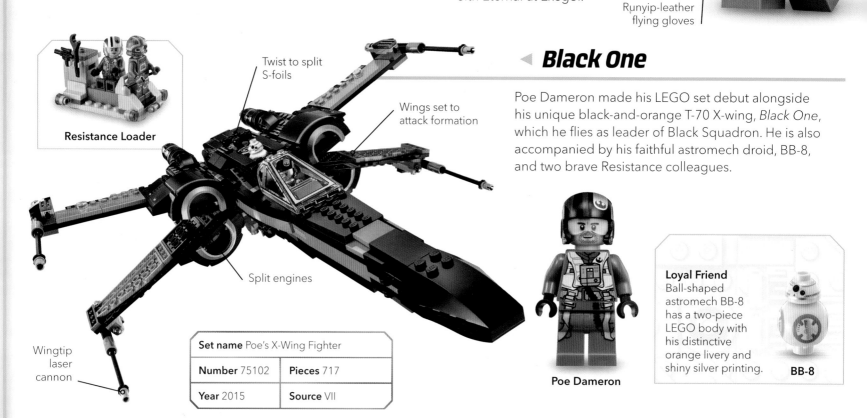

Resistance Loader

Twist to split S-foils

Wings set to attack formation

Split engines

Wingtip laser cannon

Set name Poe's X-Wing Fighter	
Number 75102	Pieces 717
Year 2015	Source VII

◀ Black One

Poe Dameron made his LEGO set debut alongside his unique black-and-orange T-70 X-wing, *Black One*, which he flies as leader of Black Squadron. He is also accompanied by his faithful astromech droid, BB-8, and two brave Resistance colleagues.

Loyal Friend
Ball-shaped astromech BB-8 has a two-piece LEGO body with his distinctive orange livery and shiny silver printing.

BB-8

Poe Dameron

▶ Blue Squadron X-Wing Starfighter

For younger fans, Poe flies with Blue Squadron in this LEGO T-70 X-wing set. This model is an easier build for beginners, but the craft still has moving S-foil wings, Poe in his cockpit, and BB-8 navigating from the back. A larger and more detailed 740-piece version of this blue-and-gray craft was released with Poe in Resistance X-Wing Fighter (set 75149) in 2016.

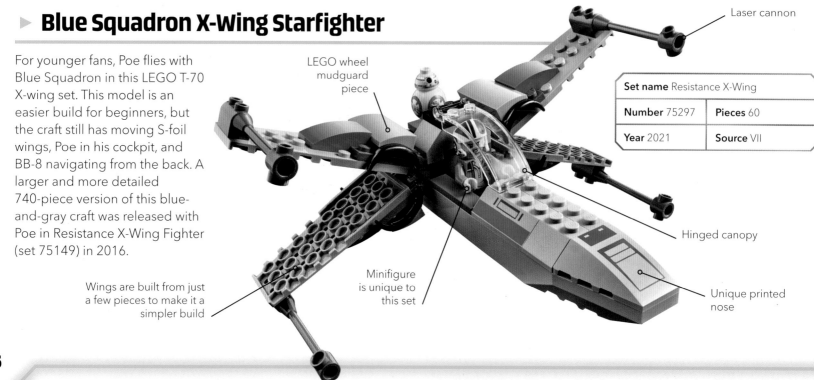

LEGO wheel mudguard piece

Laser cannon

Set name Resistance X-Wing	
Number 75297	Pieces 60
Year 2021	Source VII

Hinged canopy

Unique printed nose

Minifigure is unique to this set

Wings are built from just a few pieces to make it a simpler build

Poe's T-70 X-Wing Starfighter

The Resistance fleet uses T-70 X-wings, which are upgrades of previous Rebel Alliance models. Poe's signature *Black One* doesn't survive the evacuation from D'Qar, and his replacement X-wing is orange and white with splashes of blue. Unlike previous LEGO Resistance X-wings, which have a twisting mechanism to open and close the S-foil wings, this build has a lever and push function.

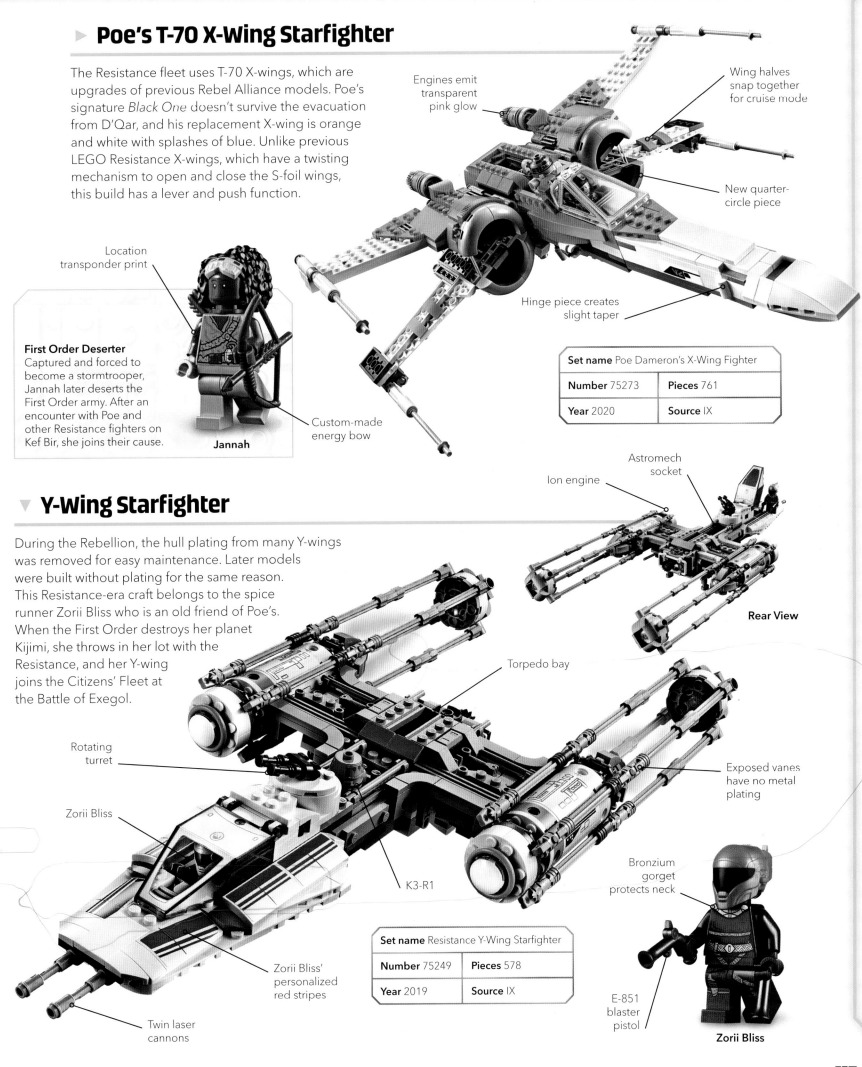

Engines emit transparent pink glow

Wing halves snap together for cruise mode

New quarter-circle piece

Hinge piece creates slight taper

Location transponder print

First Order Deserter
Captured and forced to become a stormtrooper, Jannah later deserts the First Order army. After an encounter with Poe and other Resistance fighters on Kef Bir, she joins their cause.

Jannah

Custom-made energy bow

Set name	Poe Dameron's X-Wing Fighter	
Number 75273		**Pieces** 761
Year 2020		**Source** IX

Y-Wing Starfighter

During the Rebellion, the hull plating from many Y-wings was removed for easy maintenance. Later models were built without plating for the same reason. This Resistance-era craft belongs to the spice runner Zorii Bliss who is an old friend of Poe's. When the First Order destroys her planet Kijimi, she throws in her lot with the Resistance, and her Y-wing joins the Citizens' Fleet at the Battle of Exegol.

Ion engine

Astromech socket

Rear View

Torpedo bay

Rotating turret

Zorii Bliss

K3-R1

Exposed vanes have no metal plating

Bronzium gorget protects neck

Zorii Bliss' personalized red stripes

Twin laser cannons

E-851 blaster pistol

Zorii Bliss

Set name	Resistance Y-Wing Starfighter	
Number 75249		**Pieces** 578
Year 2019		**Source** IX

Kylo Ren

The Force-sensitive son of Han Solo and Leia Organa, Kylo Ren was lured to the dark side by Supreme Leader Snoke. He longs to be as powerful and confident as his grandfather, Darth Vader, and has risen to become Supreme Leader of the First Order by destroying his former master, Snoke.

Wings go vertical for landing

Kylo Ren
This Kylo Ren minifigure (set 75179) has a facial scar. Its alternative face printing shows an even angrier expression.

Top half of wing folds down and locks in place

▶ Command Shuttle

The *Upsilon*-class command shuttle is a high-tech transport reserved for only the most senior First Order officials—and Kylo Ren has his own. The wings' flight and landing positions can be switched by lifting the craft or placing it down.

Crossguard lightsaber

Knights of Ren mask

Behind the Mask
Three Kylo Ren minifigures wear a Vaderlike mask that can swapped for a hair piece, and a fourth has the mask printed on the head piece, so it can be worn with a hood. Seven Kylo Ren minifigures carry a red cruciform lightsaber.

Twin heavy laser cannon

Command bridge

Sith Trooper
Stormtrooper minifigures with bright-red armor spark terror. They have no Force powers but are loyal to the Sith Eternal— a secret group plotting the return of the Sith.

Sith Jet Trooper
Identical to jet trooper minifigures except for their color, Sith jet troopers provide air cover while being too small and nimble to be threatened by aircraft.

Sith Fleet Officer
Followers of the Sith Eternal can train to become military officers. They wear black trimmed with red and display the Sith Eternal crest on their hats and belts.

Set name Kylo Ren's Shuttle	
Number 75256	Pieces 1,005
Year 2019	Source IX

In Control
Kylo Ren takes the driver's seat of the command shuttle. There is space in the cockpit behind him for two of his followers or subordinates.

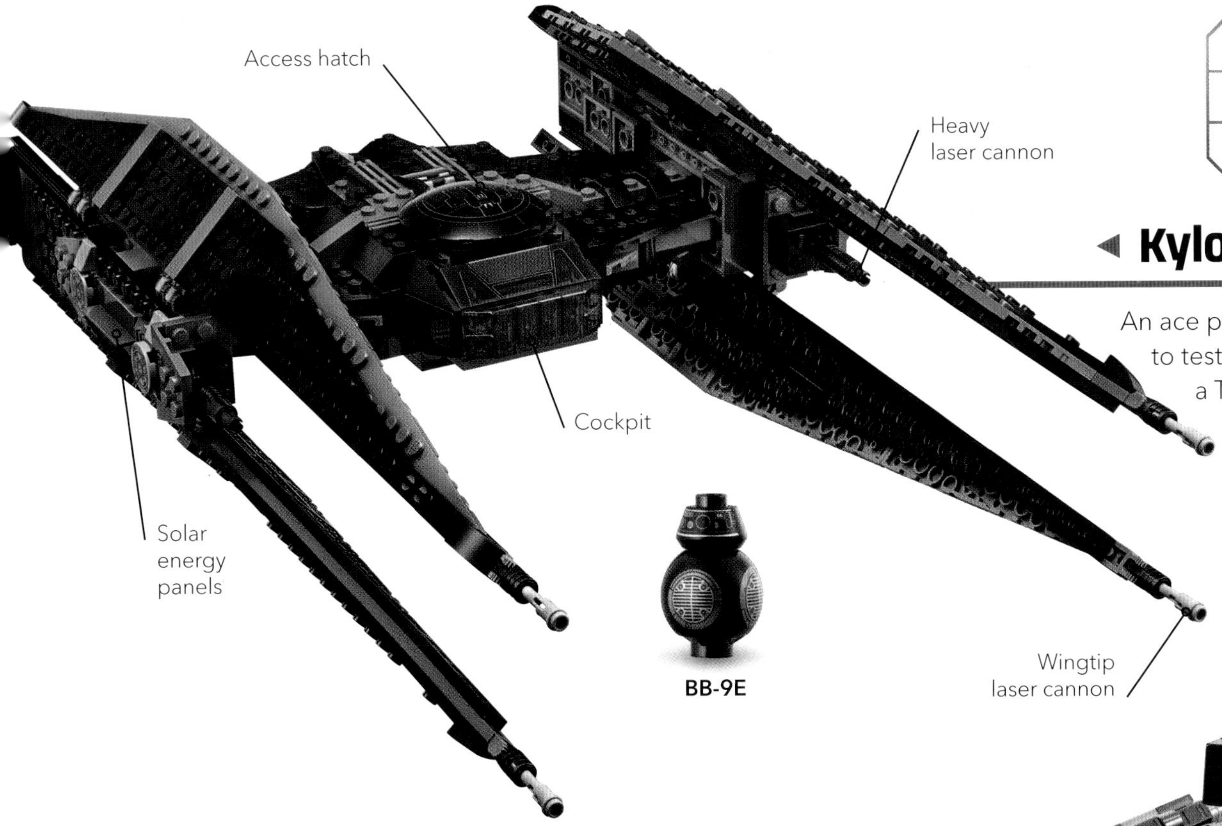

Access hatch

Heavy
laser cannon

Set name	Kylo Ren's TIE Fighter	
Number 75179		Pieces 630
Year 2017		Source VIII

◀ Kylo Ren's TIE Fighter

An ace pilot, Kylo Ren is the perfect choice
to test this prototype TIE craft, known as
a TIE silencer. Faster and more
powerful than a standard First
Order TIE fighter, it is also
equipped with stealth technology
to baffle enemy sensors.

Cockpit

Solar
energy
panels

BB-9E

Wingtip
laser cannon

Radar dish

▼ Knights of Ren Transport Ship

Once a prison ship, this *Oubliette*-class transport was
commandeered by the Knights of Ren, who modified
it and renamed it the *Night Buzzard*. It is now heavily
armed with tough plating and more
powerful thrusters. The craft comes
with Knight of Ren Kuruk
as pilot, Knight of Ren
Cardo, and Rey.

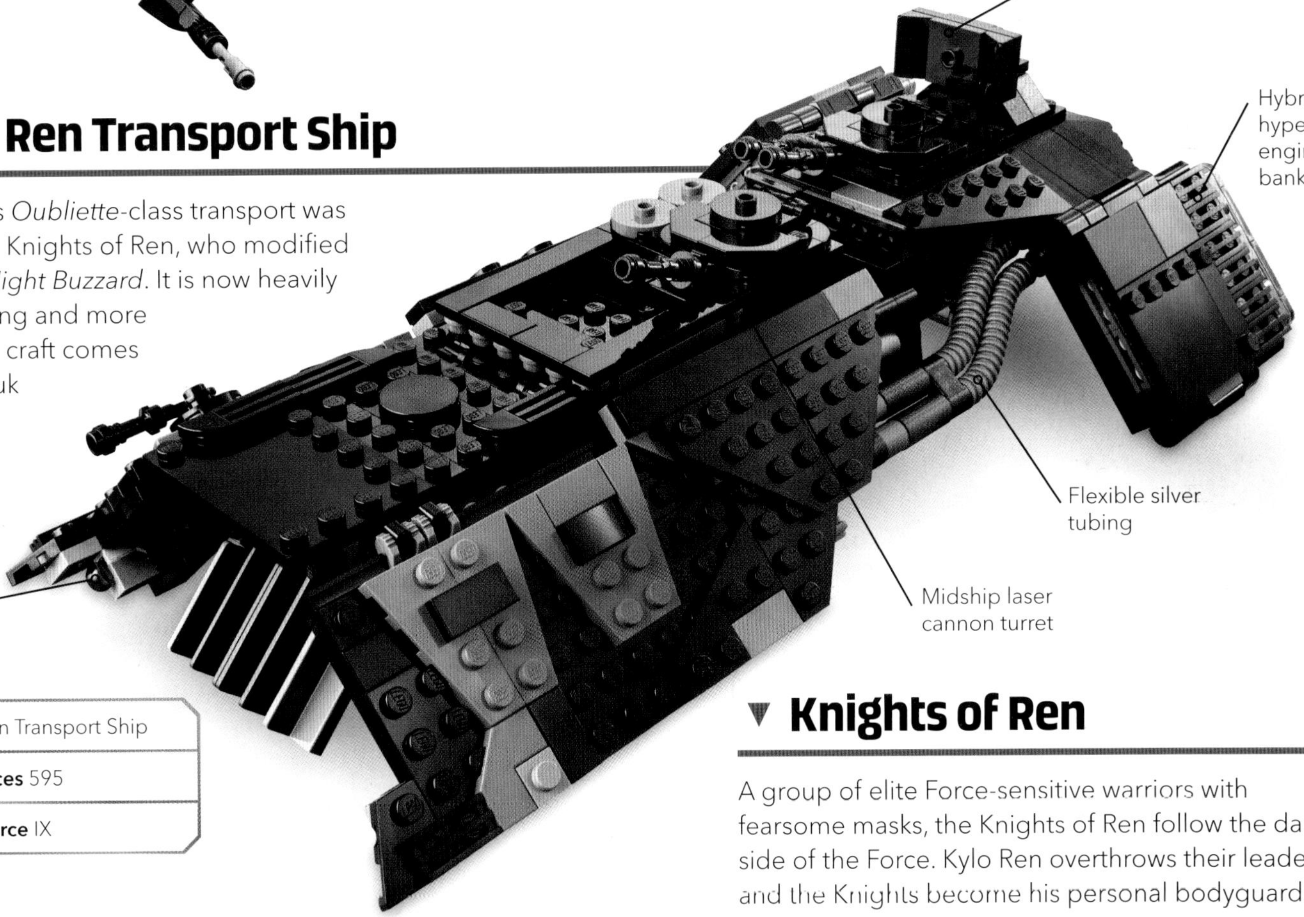

Hybrid
hyperdrive
engine
bank

Flexible silver
tubing

Spring-loaded
missile

Midship laser
cannon turret

▼ Knights of Ren

Set name	Knights of Ren Transport Ship	
Number 75284		Pieces 595
Year 2020		Source IX

A group of elite Force-sensitive warriors with
fearsome masks, the Knights of Ren follow the dark
side of the Force. Kylo Ren overthrows their leader,
and the Knights become his personal bodyguards.

Ap'lek    Ushar    Trudgen    Vicrul    Kuruk    Cardo

The First Order

The First Order is amassing a great military force. Its navy has drawn on Imperial-era designs for its craft, but they are more powerful than ever. Some models are built in secret by a hidden Sith cult. Little is known about Snoke, the Force user who leads the First Order—he prefers to operate in the shadows.

Loaded stud shooter

Command bridge

Interior View

◀ First Order Star Destroyer

A master manipulator, Snoke likes to remain out of sight. However, if you open up the *Resurgent*-class Star Destroyer using its LEGO Technic hinges, you'll find his first ever minifigure, along with various First Order officials and the devious droid BB-9E.

Ship opens along center line

LEGO Technic hinge

Snoke

Set name First Order Star Destroyer	
Number 75190	**Pieces** 1,416
Year 2017	**Source** VIII

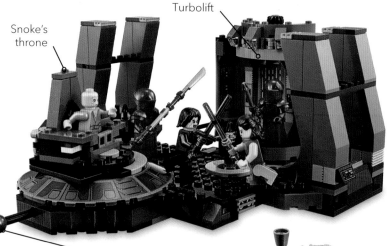

Snoke's throne

Turbolift

Operate lever to rotate throne

▲ Snoke's Throne Room

Snoke rules the First Order from a throne room on board the *Mega*-class Star Dreadnought *Supremacy*. Kylo brings Rey to see Snoke here, and a battle ensues between the Force users and the Praetorian Guard.

Set name Snoke's Throne Room	
Number 75216	**Pieces** 492
Year 2018	**Source** VIII

▼ Praetorian Guard Battle Pack

Similar in appearance to the Imperial Guard that protected Emperor Palpatine, Snoke is flanked by fearsome, mysterious minifigures in blood-red armor. Called the Praetorian Guard, they train with each other and with droids to hone their skills.

Set name Elite Praetorian Guard Battle Pack	
Number 75225	**Pieces** 109
Year 2019	**Source** VIII

Bilari electro-chain whip

Twin vibro-arbir blade

Vibro-voulge

Electro-bisento

Praetorian Guard

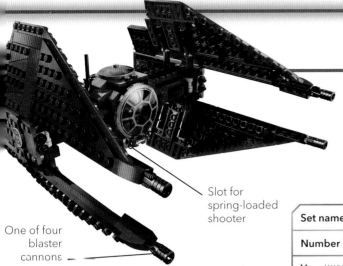

◀ # Major Vonreg's TIE Fighter

In the early days of the First Order, when it was still operating in secret, this TIE fighter was flown by crimson-uniformed Major Elrik Vonreg. He led a First Order squadron and reported to Captain Phasma. This craft is his personal TIE baron space superiority interceptor, which he flew during a dogfight with Poe Dameron.

Slot for spring-loaded shooter

One of four blaster cannons

Solar panel powers flight indefinitely

Set name	Major Vonreg's TIE Fighter	
Number	75240	Pieces 496
Year	2019	Source RES

▼ Sith TIE Fighter

Twin triangular wings are trimmed with red to declare this starfighter's allegiance to the Sith Eternal. Also known as the TIE dagger, this Sith craft is flown by a regular TIE pilot minifigure in a cockpit that is accessible from both the front and the top. The two-layered wings have spring-loaded shooters between them.

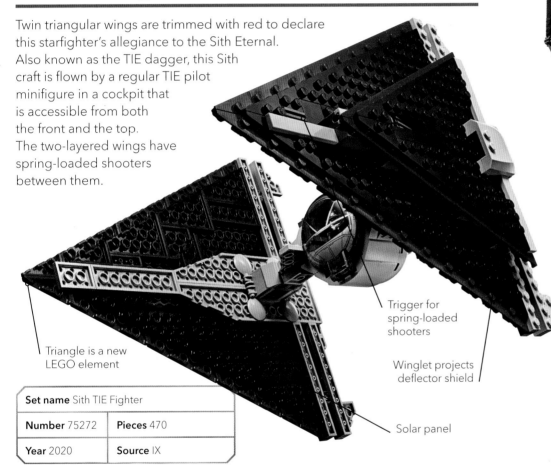

Triangle is a new LEGO element

Trigger for spring-loaded shooters

Winglet projects deflector shield

Solar panel

Heavy weapons turret

▲ Special Forces TIE Fighter

While most TIE fighters have only one seat, the Special Forces TIE has room for two minifigures. This allows the pilot to focus on flying while a dedicated gunner controls the mission-specific heavy weapons.

Set name	First Order Special Forces TIE Fighter	
Number	75101	Pieces 517
Year	2015	Source VII

Set name	Sith TIE Fighter	
Number	75272	Pieces 470
Year	2020	Source IX

▼ First Order Navy and Special Forces

The pilots and crew of the First Order navy are essentially the stormtroopers of the skies—though they operate ground vehicles such as walkers, too. Special Forces are a separate, elite part of the navy. Its members combine the skills of both pilots and troopers.

TIE Pilot

Special Forces TIE Pilot

Shuttle Pilot

First Order Fleet Engineer

Walker Pilot

First Order Forces

Under the command of General Armitage Hux, the First Order military is an ever-growing threat to peace in the galaxy. Inspired by the might of the old Imperial Navy, its firepower now outstrips that of the Empire at its peak.

▷ Snowspeeder

Properly known as the Light Infantry Utility Vehicle or LIUV, the First Order snowspeeder is a rugged repulsorlift craft well suited to the icy conditions on Starkiller Base. It is designed for patrol duty and supply runs rather than assault missions.

Snowtrooper officer

Stud shooter

Transparent wheels for hovering effect

Set name	First Order Snowspeeder	
Number	75100	Pieces 444
Year	2015	Source VII

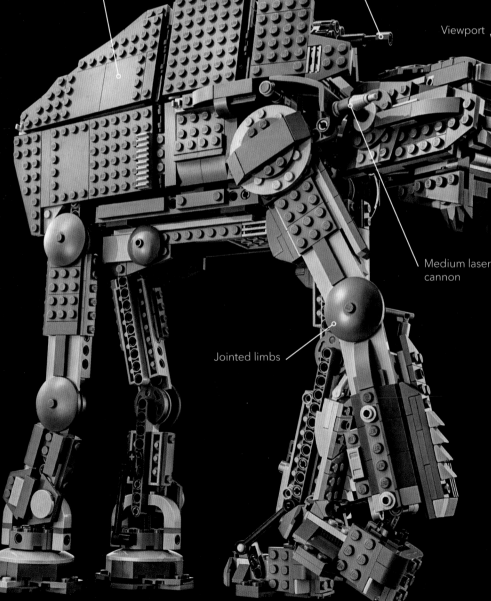

Armor plating opens for access to storage bay

MegaCaliber Six turbolaser cannon

Viewport

◁ Heavy Assault Walker

The biggest walker in the First Order fleet is the All Terrain MegaCaliber Six (AT-M6), named for the huge MegaCaliber cannon on its back. It has tough armor-plate detailing and a posable head with a cockpit that opens.

Set name	First Order Heavy Assault Walker	
Number	75189	Pieces 1,376
Year	2017	Source VIII

Medium laser cannon

Jointed limbs

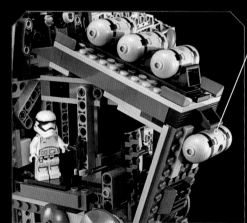

Fuel canisters can be ejected at rear

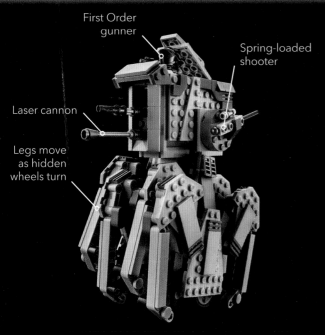

First Order gunner

Spring-loaded shooter

Laser cannon

Legs move as hidden wheels turn

▲ Scout Walker

The All Terrain Heavy Scout, or AT-HS, crawls along on eight spiderlike legs. Unlike other small walkers—which can topple if just one limb is attacked—it can withstand the destruction of several legs and still keep scuttling on.

Set name First Order Heavy Scout Walker	
Number 75177	Pieces 554
Year 2017	Source VIII

▼ Treadspeeder Bike

First Order troopers on hostile planets have more advanced tech and brute force built into their speeder bikes than their Imperial predecessors did. The treadspeeder bike can drive over rugged terrain, or hover when needed thanks to repulsorlift engines. Chunky and robust, the bike is armed for offense and shielded for defense. On Pasaana, however, Finn reveals a weakness when he feeds rope into the speeder's tread mechanism, and the bike winds itself to destruction.

Set name Pasaana Speeder Chase	
Number 75250	Pieces 373
Year 2019	Source IX

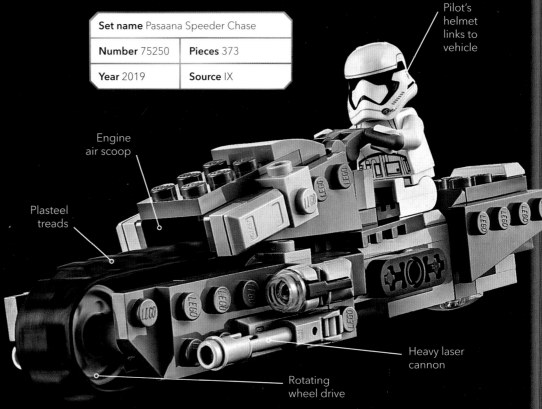

Pilot's helmet links to vehicle

Engine air scoop

Plasteel treads

Heavy laser cannon

Rotating wheel drive

▼ Transporter

Designed to deliver troops from bigger ships into ground battles, First Order transporters are little more than heavily armored flying boxes. Even seats are considered a luxury, so stormtroopers have to stand inside as they wait for the deployment ramp to drop.

Set name First Order Transporter	
Number 75103	Pieces 792
Year 2015	Source VII

Emergency escape hatch

Pilot's cabin

Flametrooper

Captain Phasma

Deployment ramp

Dial raises and lowers ramp

First Order Troops

The fighting men and women of the First Order are trained to be emotionless. The majority of the troops are stormtroopers and pilots, who are conditioned for combat from childhood and given ID numbers instead of names. Others are allowed to retain a small amount of their individuality as officers—though their loyalty to the organization must still be absolute.

First Order Stormtrooper
With updated armor and streamlined helmets, standard First Order stormtroopers are easy to tell apart from their Imperial predecessors. Though they are not clones, their minifigures all have the same fierce face beneath their headgear.

Snowtrooper
Specially trained to serve in cold conditions, First Order snowtroopers wear insulated belt-capes, glare-resistant helmets, and armor with built-in heating.

Treadspeeder Driver
125-Z treadspeeder bikes are driven by specialist troopers. They wear shin guards and extra padding on the legs instead of the standard leg armor.

Heavy Assault Trooper
Armed with oversize blasters, heavy assault troopers can be identified by the extra equipment strapped to their chests and sometimes worn on their backs, too.

First Order Jet Trooper
Agile jet troopers have specialized insulated armor with built-in jetpacks. On Pasaana, jet troopers launch off the rear of treadspeeders for aerial assaults.

Flametrooper
With fuel tanks on their backs and incinerator guns in their grasp, the fearsome flametroopers are outfitted in fireproof armor and glare-resistant helmets.

Walker Driver
A gray helmet flash and gray jumpsuit are unique to the stormtroopers who drive the heavy assault walkers, such as the one that tramps across the salt crust of Crait.

▼ First Order Army

Riot Trooper
Wearing standard-issue First Order stormtrooper armor, riot control units carry betaplast shields and electroshock batons to subdue unrest among civilian populations.

Executioner
Bold black markings and black arm pieces denote executioner troopers, who serve to strike fear into their fellow stormtroopers—reminding them of the need for total obedience!

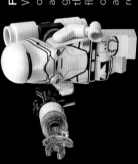

Betaplast Ballistic Riot Shield

First Ordnance
Most First Order weapons are made by the Sonn-Blas Corporation—a company set up especially to do business beyond the reach of New Republic law. They can supply arms for every occasion!

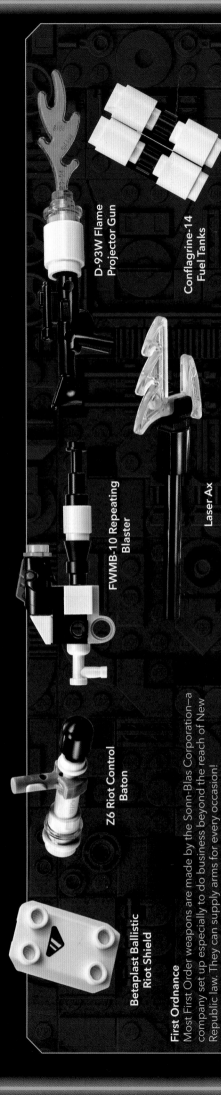

D-93W Flame Projector Gun

Conflagrine-14 Fuel Tanks

FWMB-10 Repeating Blaster

Laser Ax

Z6 Riot Control Baton

Stormtrooper Leaders

A few stormtroopers who show particular aptitude can rise a little way through the ranks. The stormtrooper squad leader shows his status with a white cloth pauldron with black edging, while a red pauldron with black marks out a stormtrooper or snowtrooper officer.

Snowtrooper Officer

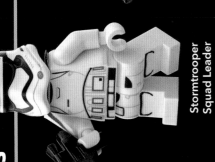

Stormtrooper Officer

Stormtrooper Squad Leader

Chromium Captain
Clad in unique chromium-plated armor, Captain Phasma is the First Order's most senior stormtrooper. She loathes the Resistance fighter Finn, who once served under her command, and longs to make him pay for his desertion.

Armorweave cape

First Order Hierarchy

The First Order military is run using a hierarchical system of rank. Every member must obey orders from ranks higher than them. Generals outrank officers, who outrank stormtrooper officers. While white-clad stormtroopers are sent into battle, the soldiers in dark uniforms and matching command caps mostly serve on bases and aboard capital ships.

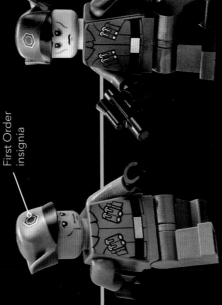

First Order insignia

First Order Lieutenant or Captain

First Order Lieutenant or Captain

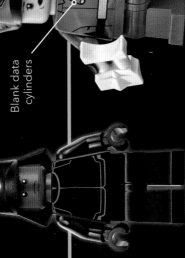

Blank data cylinders

First Order Officer

First Order Crew Member

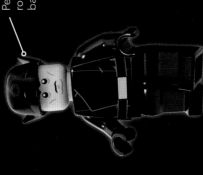

Peak wraps round the back of cap

First Order General

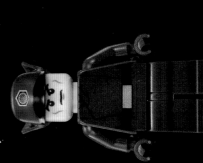

First Order Major or Colonel

General Enric Pryde

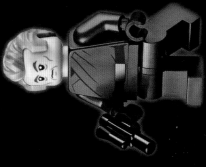

General Armitage Hux

BB-9E
First Order warships rely on dark, shiny BB astromech units to make sure procedures are followed. BB-9E keeps a sharp photoreceptor out for infiltrators, saboteurs, and other threats to Supreme Leader Snoke's flagship. BB-9E has a run-in with his counterpart Resistance droid, BB-8, in *Star Wars: The Last Jedi*.

BB-9E

Chapter 4
Specialist Sets

LEGO® Legends

In 2014 Lucasfilm reclassified the *Star Wars* canon, with many stories now considered Legends. These tales come from many different eras of *Star Wars* history and a range of media. The LEGO Group has produced many sets based on these Legends.

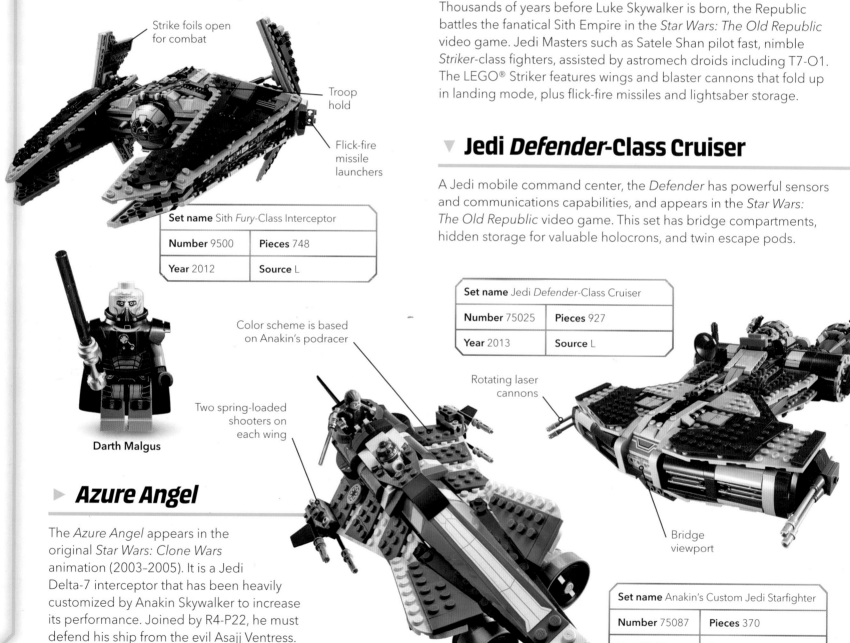

Sublight engines

Cockpit

Wings unfolded in attack mode

Sensor package

Blaster cannon swivels forward for combat

▼ Sith *Fury*-Class Interceptor

Based on the *Star Wars: The Old Republic* video game, this set depicts the Fury interceptor. The heavily shielded and armed starship's development is personally overseen by the ruthless Sith Lord Darth Malgus. Packed with weapons and filled with Sith troopers, these vicious craft are serious threats to the Republic and the Jedi.

Strike foils open for combat

Troop hold

Flick-fire missile launchers

Set name Sith *Fury*-Class Interceptor	
Number 9500	**Pieces** 748
Year 2012	**Source** L

Darth Malgus

▶ *Azure Angel*

The *Azure Angel* appears in the original *Star Wars: Clone Wars* animation (2003–2005). It is a Jedi Delta-7 interceptor that has been heavily customized by Anakin Skywalker to increase its performance. Joined by R4-P22, he must defend his ship from the evil Asajj Ventress.

Color scheme is based on Anakin's podracer

Two spring-loaded shooters on each wing

Set name Republic *Striker*-Class Starfighter	
Number 9497	**Pieces** 376
Year 2012	**Source** L

▲ Republic *Striker*-Class Starfighter

Thousands of years before Luke Skywalker is born, the Republic battles the fanatical Sith Empire in the *Star Wars: The Old Republic* video game. Jedi Masters such as Satele Shan pilot fast, nimble *Striker*-class fighters, assisted by astromech droids including T7-O1. The LEGO® Striker features wings and blaster cannons that fold up in landing mode, plus flick-fire missiles and lightsaber storage.

▼ Jedi *Defender*-Class Cruiser

A Jedi mobile command center, the *Defender* has powerful sensors and communications capabilities, and appears in the *Star Wars: The Old Republic* video game. This set has bridge compartments, hidden storage for valuable holocrons, and twin escape pods.

Set name Jedi *Defender*-Class Cruiser	
Number 75025	**Pieces** 927
Year 2013	**Source** L

Rotating laser cannons

Bridge viewport

Set name Anakin's Custom Jedi Starfighter	
Number 75087	**Pieces** 370
Year 2015	**Source** L

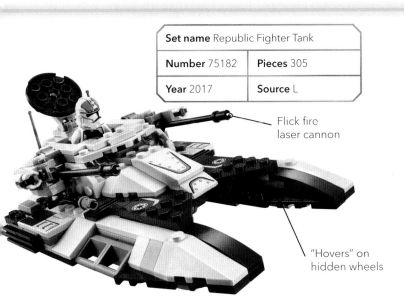

Set name	Republic Fighter Tank	
Number 75182		Pieces 305
Year 2017		Source L

Flick fire
laser cannon

"Hovers" on
hidden wheels

▲ Republic Fighter Tank

The TX-130 *Saber*-class vehicle first appeared in the *Star Wars: The Clone Wars* video game. It is a fast-attack tank equipped with laser cannons and concussion missiles. Clone troopers normally pilot this tank, though Jedi have been known to take control, too.

▼ TIE/D

In the *Star Wars: Dark Empire* comic series, the Empire develops prototype pilotless fighters with programmable droid brains. The droid brain figure can be removed from the pod casing.

Droid Brain

Droid
brain pod

High-
performance
solar panels

Blaster
cannon

Firing rocket

▶ Rogue Shadow

The *Rogue Shadow* is a unique starship found in the *Star Wars: The Force Unleashed* video games. It has an experimental cloaking device, sophisticated sensor arrays, and high-performance sublight engines. Darth Vader's secret apprentice, Galen Marek, and female Imperial pilot Juno Eclipse (with whom Marek falls in love) pilot the ship.

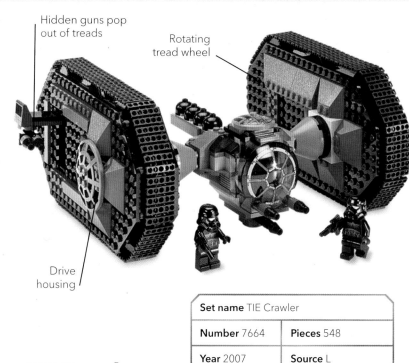

Hidden guns pop
out of treads

Rotating
tread wheel

Drive
housing

Set name	TIE Crawler	
Number 7664		Pieces 548
Year 2007		Source L

▲ TIE Crawler

First appearing in the *Star Wars: Dark Empire* comic series, the unusual TIE crawler marries the familiar cockpit of a TIE fighter with tread wheels borrowed from a ground-assault vehicle to make a cheap, effective option for ground combat. The treads rotate, elevating the cockpit to avoid obstacles or shoot the principal flick-fire missiles. The set comes with two shadow stormtroopers, feared servants of the Emperor.

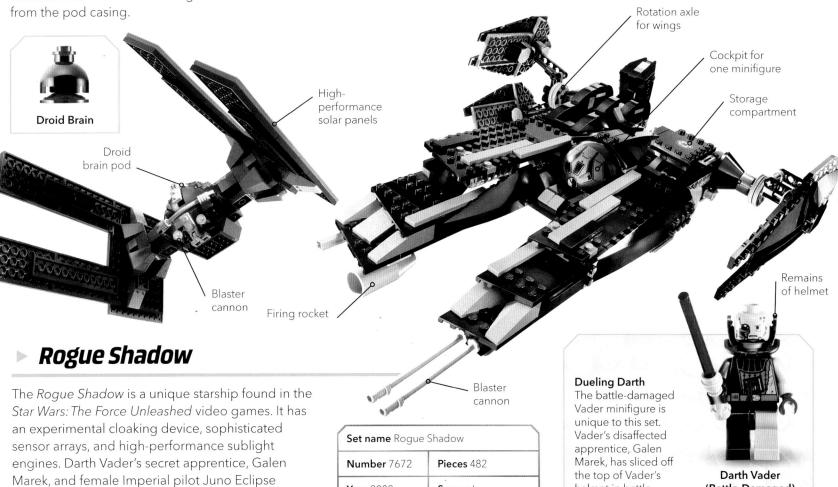

Rotation axle
for wings

Cockpit for
one minifigure

Storage
compartment

Remains
of helmet

Blaster
cannon

Set name	Rogue Shadow	
Number 7672		Pieces 482
Year 2008		Source L

Dueling Darth
The battle-damaged Vader minifigure is unique to this set. Vader's disaffected apprentice, Galen Marek, has sliced off the top of Vader's helmet in battle.

**Darth Vader
(Battle-Damaged)**

LEGO® Creations

As well as featuring hundreds of sets based on existing locations and spacecraft, the LEGO® *Star Wars*™ theme has occasionally introduced its own inventions to the *Star Wars* universe. Designed for animated TV shows that take place in a brick-built version of the galaxy far, far away, they naturally lend themselves to being LEGO® sets as well!

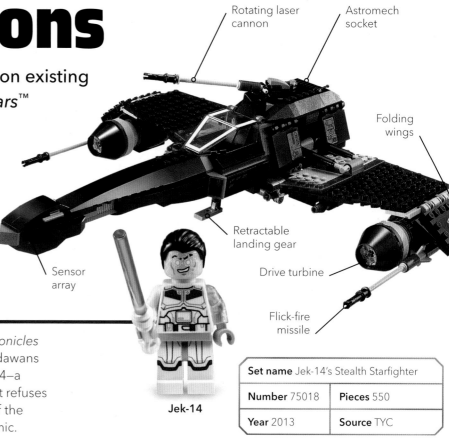

Rotating laser cannon

Astromech socket

Folding wings

Retractable landing gear

Drive turbine

Flick-fire missile

Sensor array

► Jek-14's Stealth Starfighter

In 2013, the animated TV series LEGO *Star Wars: The Yoda Chronicles* charted the adventures of Jedi Master Yoda and a group of Padawans during the Clone Wars. The characters they meet include Jek-14—a powerful Force-sensitive clone who was created by the Sith, but refuses to fight for either the Separatists or the Republic. The design of the starfighter was first visualized in the *Star Wars: Dark Empire* comic.

Jek-14

Set name	Jek-14's Stealth Starfighter	
Number 75018	Pieces 550
Year 2013	Source TYC

◄ Jedi Scout Fighter

Rotating dual laser cannon

Noga-ta in gunner's seat

Detachable cockpit

Jek-14 in pilot's seat

Astromech droid

Jek-14 returned in new episodes of *The Yoda Chronicles* in 2014. Now a friend of the remaining Jedi in the early days of the Empire, he agrees to help the Ithorian Jedi Knight Noga-ta retrieve vital holocrons from the abandoned Jedi Temple on Coruscant. For this mission, he is equipped with a two-seater Jedi fighter.

Set name	Jedi Scout Fighter	
Number 75051	Pieces 490
Year 2014	Source TYC

▼ StarScavenger

Launched in 2016, LEGO *Star Wars: The Freemaker Adventures* is an action-packed animated TV series following the exploits of Force-sensitive Rowan Freemaker and his family of scrap merchants. When we first meet them, all they want is to make a living on board their modular salvage ship, the *StarScavenger*.

Spring-loaded missile launcher

Fold-out engines

Breakaway cockpit

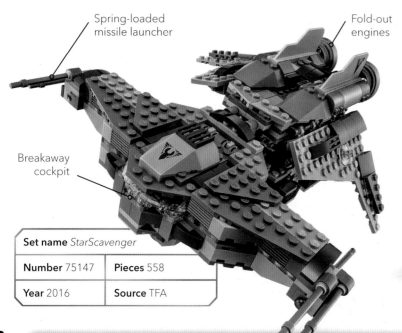

Set name	*StarScavenger*	
Number 75147	Pieces 558
Year 2016	Source TFA

Kordi Freemaker

Zander Freemaker

Rowan Freemaker

R0-GR

▶ Eclipse Fighter

When Rowan Freemaker starts to flex his untrained Force powers he attracts some unwanted attention, including from the Sith agent Naare and the bounty hunter Dengar. Naare pretends to be a Jedi and helps the Freemakers at first, but is soon pursuing them in her powerful ship, the *Eclipse Fighter*!

Naare in cockpit

Wings folded back for combat mode

Set name *Eclipse Fighter*	
Number 75145	**Pieces** 363
Year 2016	**Source** TFA

Wingtip blaster cannons

Zander at the controls

Kyber crystal power source

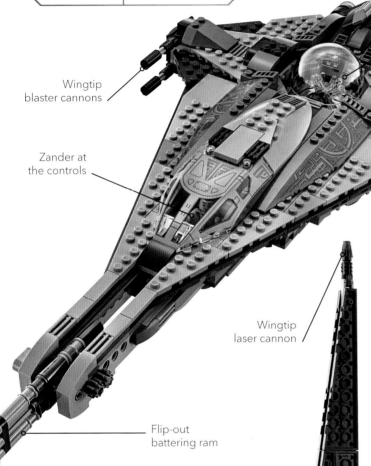

Dengar on speeder bike

◀ The *Arrowhead*

As Rowan Freemaker's Force powers grow, he experiences a vision of a powerful new ship. With the help of the seasoned Mon Calamari shipbuilder Quarrie, he succeeds in building the *Arrowhead*—a new kind of fighter, powered by a giant kyber crystal. The Freemakers hope it can bring down the Empire!

Set name The *Arrowhead*	
Number 75186	**Pieces** 775
Year 2017	**Source** TFA

Wingtip laser cannon

Flip-out battering ram

M-OC

Initially Funny
Droid M-OC comes with the *Tracker I* (set 75185). The Emperor created the hunter droid M-OC with his own hands. His name is an in-joke inspired by initials used by many LEGO fan builders—which stands for "My Own Creation."

▶ Tracker I

When Emperor Palpatine realizes the threat posed by the Freemakers, he dispatches the Imperial hunter droid M-OC to find and capture Rowan. The multitalented M-OC pilots the sleek and stealthy *Tracker I*—a fast-moving ship with a built-in prison cell that even a Force user can't escape from!

Set name *Tracker I*	
Number 75185	**Pieces** 557
Year 2017	**Source** TFA

Spring-loaded shooter

Open prison cell

Planet Sets

In 2012 and 2013 the LEGO Group released a dozen mini-ships, each accompanied by a minifigure, a planet (or other celestial phenomenon) introduced in the first six *Star Wars* movies, and a plaque. The planets can be hung from a wire for display, and several of the minifigures are unique or reworked from their previous LEGO set appearances.

Set name Naboo Starfighter & Naboo	
Number 9674	Pieces 56
Year 2012	Source I

Naboo

Droid is silver stud

Flight goggles

Naboo Pilot

▼ Death Star

Built in secret on the Emperor's orders, the first Death Star destroys the planet Alderaan and threatens to extinguish freedom in the galaxy. The Death Star has a great deal of detail, from the indented superlaser "dish" to the trenches on its surface.

Death Star

▲ Naboo

The planet Naboo is a lush world co-inhabited by human settlers known as the Naboo and the aquatic Gungan species. Naboo's starfighter pilots defend their home against the droid fighters of the Trade Federation.

Set name TIE Interceptor & Death Star	
Number 9676	Pieces 65
Year 2012	Source IV

TIE Pilot

Cockpit window shared with TIE bomber

Binoculars used as cannon

Set name X-Wing Starfighter & Yavin 4	
Number 9677	Pieces 77
Year 2012	Source IV

Yavin 4

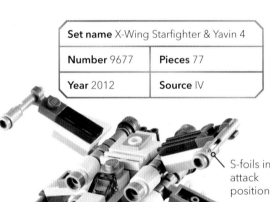

S-foils in attack position

Nose commonly used as roof tile

X-Wing Pilot

◄ Bespin

Bespin is a gas giant in the galaxy's Outer Rim, notable for the floating habitation known as Cloud City. Lobot's minifigure is reworked from his 2002 incarnation, now with a realistic skin tone and holding a blaster.

"Radiator grille" is common part

Set name Twin-Pod Cloud Car & Bespin	
Number 9678	Pieces 78
Year 2012	Source V

Bespin

Lobot

▲ Yavin 4

Yavin 4 is the jungle moon in the Outer Rim that provides a home for the main rebel base. The X-wing pilot shares a helmet with Dak Ralter, whose minifigure first appeared in the Snowspeeder set in 1999 and was updated in 2004 and 2007.

► Tatooine

A forlorn desert world in the Outer Rim, Tatooine is controlled by the Hutts and populated by hard-working moisture farmers, Jawas, and Sand People. Sebulba comes with a wrench for fixing (or perhaps building) his podracer.

Transparent pink lightsaber blades

Control pod "floats" on clear rod

Tatooine

Sebulba

Set name Sebulba's Podracer & Tatooine	
Number 9675	Pieces 80
Year 2012	Source I

Forest Moon of Endor

The Empire builds its second Death Star above Endor's forest moon, home to the Ewoks. AT-STs guard a shield generator and bunker constructed among the trees.

Forest Moon

Head swivels

Unique printed panel

Set name	AT-ST & Endor	
Number 9679		Pieces 65
Year 2012		Source VI

AT-ST Driver

Bridge made from saber hilt and stud

Coruscant

Coruscant is the capital of the Republic (and later the Empire) and is an immensely crowded city-planet. This is one of only two LEGO versions of the Republic assault ship, which was first used in battle at Geonosis.

Set name	Republic Assault Ship & Coruscant	
Number 75007		Pieces 74
Year 2013		Source II

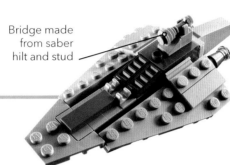

Clone Trooper

Coruscant

Hoth

The remote ice planet Hoth is the hiding place of the rebels after the destruction of the first Death Star. They fly snowspeeders to defend their base against the Empire.

Hoth

Cockpit is clear roof tile

Cockpit is unique printed piece

Snowspeeder Pilot

Unique printing

Set name	Snowspeeder & Hoth	
Number 75009		Pieces 69
Year 2013		Source V

Endor

Above the giant gas planet of Endor, rebels battle in B-wings against the Empire. The B-wing pilot has been updated with a detailed body, legs, and visor.

Folding wings

B-Wing Pilot

Endor

Set name	B-Wing Starfighter & Endor	
Number 75010		Pieces 83
Year 2013		Source VI

Set name	Jedi Starfighter & Kamino	
Number 75006		Pieces 61
Year 2013		Source II

Kamino

Republic symbol is unique

R4-P17

Kamino

The stormy water world of Kamino is home to a cloning facility that builds the massive clone army. This set includes the first full-body version of astromech droid R4-P17.

Set name	TIE Bomber & Asteroid Field	
Number 75008		Pieces 60
Year 2013		Source V

Bent solar-paneled wings

Asteroid Field

Cockpit window shared with TIE fighter

Second pod holds munitions

TIE Bomber Pilot

Asteroid Field

After the *Millennium Falcon* flees Hoth, TIE bombers search for the freighter amid the tumbling rocks of a nearby asteroid field.

Antenna used as gun turret

Set name	*Tantive IV* & Alderaan	
Number 75011		Pieces 102
Year 2013		Source IV

Alderaan

Element known as a "palisade brick"

Alderaan

Long a center for culture and learning, the Core World of Alderaan is Princess Leia's homeworld and the base of operations for her Blockade Runner, known as the *Tantive IV*.

Rebel Trooper

Microfighters

The galaxy got a little smaller in 2014 with the launch of LEGO® Star Wars™ Microfighters. Designed with exaggerated details for a fun, stylized look, each set depicts a classic vehicle or creature in miniature, with room for a minifigure on top. Built for battle, every Microfighters set comes with flick-fire missiles or stud shooters, and dual sets contain two builds and two minifigures.

▼ Sith Infiltrator

Two transparent slope pieces for the cockpit

Radiator fins can open and close

In 2012, the first iteration of the Sith Infiltrator at this scale was an exclusive release for San Diego Comic-Con. The 2019 Microfighters version is smaller, but it has the addition of two stud shooters under its hull.

Set name Sith Infiltrator	
Number 75224	Pieces 92
Year 2019	Source I

▼ Naboo Starfighter

Flick-fire missile

Young Anakin and R2 bravely take part in the Battle of Naboo in this N-1 starfighter Microfighter. The ship's sleek design is achieved with a combination of angled and curved pieces.

Set name Naboo Starfighter	
Number 75223	Pieces 62
Year 2019	Source I

▶ Clone Turbo Tank

The first LEGO Clone Turbo Tank (set 7261) from 2005 had more than 800 pieces. The 2014 Microfighters version has just 96, but still boasts 10 turning wheels, two flick-fire missiles, and an exclusive clone trooper minifigure.

Flick-fire missile

Wheels are 2x2 round bricks

Set name Clone Turbo Tank	
Number 75028	Pieces 96
Year 2014	Source III

◀ Vulture Droid

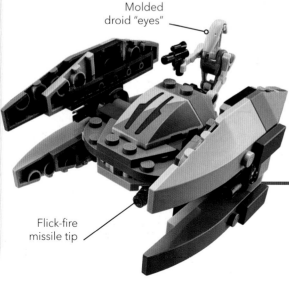

Molded droid "eyes"

Flick-fire missile tip

Standard Separatist vulture droids don't need an operator, but the Microfighters version comes with a pilot droid pal. The vulture droid's wings fold down to form four legs, so they can even go on walks together!

Set name Vulture Droid	
Number 75073	Pieces 77
Year 2015	Source III

The *Ghost*

In 2014, Microfighters-style versions of the *Ghost* piloted by Chopper and Kanan Jarrus were exclusively available at San Diego Comic-Con and Toronto FAN EXPO. Two years later, Hera Syndulla takes the controls in an even more compact edition.

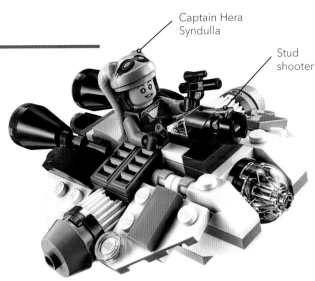

Captain Hera Syndulla

Stud shooter

Set name *The Ghost*	
Number 75127	Pieces 104
Year 2016	Source REB

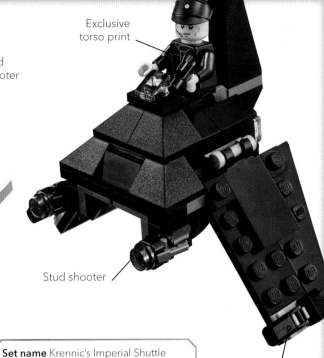

Exclusive torso print

Stud shooter

Wing in flight mode

▼ U-Wing

Just like the 659-piece version released the previous year, the Microfighters U-wing has two forward-facing S-foils that sweep backward in combat mode. It comes with an exclusive rebel pilot minifigure and a pair of stud shooters.

Set name U-Wing	
Number 75160	Pieces 109
Year 2017	Source R1

Stud shooter

S-foil

Unnamed rebel pilot

Set name Krennic's Imperial Shuttle	
Number 75163	Pieces 78
Year 2017	Source R1

▲ Krennic's Imperial Shuttle

Director Krennic himself is exclusive to the much larger version of Krennic's Imperial Shuttle (set 75156), so the Microfighters version is flown by an equally exclusive Imperial shuttle pilot. The craft's wings fold upward for landing.

▼ Escape Pod vs. Dewback

In the second wave of Microfighters dual packs, this set re-creates the Empire's hunt for the Death Star plans. Can C-3PO and R2-D2 evade the sandtrooper on a brick-built dewback?

Escape Pod

Set name Escape Pod vs. Dewback	
Number 75228	Pieces 177
Year 2019	Source IV

Ion engine

▲ Y-Wing

Based on the Y-wings in *Rogue One: A Star Wars Story*, this Microfighters set comes with a blue-clad rebel pilot from Blue Squadron. Like most minifigures in the range, his head can be turned to show happy or scared expressions.

LEGO roller skate piece

Head is connected by a ball joint to body

Dewback

Set name Y-Wing	
Number 75162	Pieces 90
Year 2017	Source R1

▼ Snowspeeder

Rebel snowspeeders have appeared in more than a dozen sets, but this one boasts an exclusive pilot's helmet! Two flick-fire missiles are hidden beneath the remarkably accurate angular hull, which fits together using click-hinge pieces.

Rebel Alliance symbol

Set name	Snowspeeder	
Number	75074	Pieces 97
Year	2015	Source V

Laser cannons made from LEGO® Technic pieces

▼ Tauntaun vs. AT-AT

A molded LEGO tauntaun appeared in Battle of Hoth sets in 2009 and 2011, but this is the first brick-built model of the snowy reptomammal. It carries Luke Skywalker, who faces off against an Imperial AT-AT on the icy plains of Hoth.

Horn shared with LEGO bantha

Set name	AT-AT vs. Tauntaun Microfighters	
Number	75298	Pieces 205
Year	2021	Source V

Handheld stud shooter

AT-AT

Tauntaun

▼ Bantha vs. T-16 Skyhopper

On Tatooine, a Tusken goes into battle on a bantha—a domesticated mammal with shaggy fur and curled horns. This is the first ever LEGO bantha, and it battles a T-16 Skyhopper pilot on the third LEGO version of this personal repulsorlift airspeeder.

Set name	T-16 Skyhopper vs Bantha Microfighters	
Number	75265	Pieces 198
Year	2020	Source IV

Minifigure unique to this set

Tusken's gaffi stick

▼ The *Razor Crest*

The first Microfighter to tie in with *The Mandalorian* live-action series, the *Razor Crest* is an ST-70-class Razor Crest M-111 assault ship flown by the Mandalorian, Din Djarin. It has two stud shooters, though Djarin isn't taking any chances—he carries a blaster as well.

Fusial thrust engine

New shooter introduced in 2022

Set name	The *Razor Crest* Microfighter	
Number	75321	Pieces 98
Year	2022	Source M

▼ N-1 Starfighter

After the *Razor Crest* is destroyed, Din Djarin acquires a new ship, a customized N-1 starfighter, and his minifigure gets a Microfighters version of the high-performing craft in 2023. This time, he's accompanied by a little passenger—the Force-sensitive child, Grogu.

Set name	The Mandalorian N-1 Starfighter Microfighter	
Number	75363	Pieces 88
Year	2023	Source M

Grogu

Castle turret-top piece

▼ Resistance X-Wing Fighter

Though the minifigure in this set is not named, his facial hair and helmet decals suggest he is Temmin "Snap" Wexley—a member of Poe Dameron's celebrated Black Squadron. The ship's four wingtip laser cannons are, in fact, flick-fire missiles.

Set name	Resistance X-Wing Fighter	
Number	75125	Pieces 87
Year	2016	Source VII

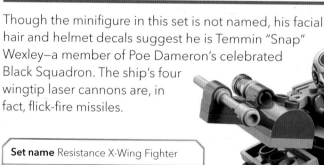

Adjustable wings

Sensor dish

Exclusive printed piece

▲ *Millennium Falcon*

In 2014, one of the first Microfighters sets released was the *Millennium Falcon* flown by Han Solo. This *Star Wars: The Last Jedi* 2018 update swaps flick-fire missiles for stud shooters, the round sensor dish for a rectangular one, and Han for his former copilot, Chewbacca.

Set name *Millennium Falcon*	
Number 75193	Pieces 92
Year 2018	Source VIII

Exclusive Resistance minifigure

Flick-fire missile

A-Wing

▶ First Order TIE Fighter

With its bold red flash, this ship resembles a First Order Special Forces TIE fighter, though its pilot does not wear a Special Forces helmet. It is the fourth TIE ship in the Microfighters range, after the TIE Interceptor (set 75031), TIE Advanced Prototype (set 75128), and TIE Striker (set 75161).

Set name First Order TIE Fighter	
Number 75194	Pieces 91
Year 2018	Source VII

First Order TIE pilot

Flick-fire missile port

Kylo Ren

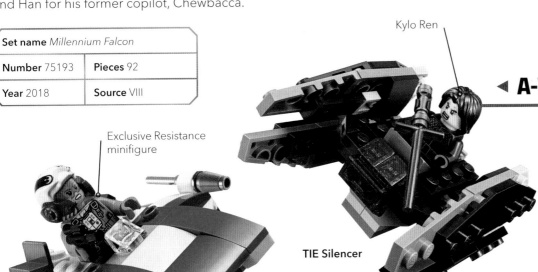

TIE Silencer

◀ A-Wing vs. TIE Silencer

In 2018, the first Microfighters dual packs hit the shelves. Each set included two vehicles and two minifigures, plus an extra bonus build. In A-Wing vs. TIE Silencer, the extra build is a small maintenance station that the Resistance pilot can use for repairs if her ship is damaged by Kylo Ren.

Set name A-Wing vs. TIE Silencer	
Number 75196	Pieces 188
Year 2018	Source VIII

▶ Ski Speeder vs. First Order Walker

The huge First Order heavy assault walker is brought down to size in this set that re-creates the Battle of Crait, along with a Resistance ski speeder. Both vehicles come with stud shooters and another is included as part of a defensive trench build that captures the distinctive red-and-white surface of Crait in just a few pieces.

Set name Ski Speeder vs. First Order Walker	
Number 75195	Pieces 216
Year 2018	Source VIII

Brand new hair-and-headphones piece

Head can turn in all directions

Each leg is jointed in two places

Ski Speeder

First Order Walker

Mini Sets

In 2002 the LEGO Group created the first mini sets. They are smaller than the normal sets, with fewer pieces. Though less detailed, mini sets are incredibly accurate. The LEGO Group has issued sets based on many vehicles from across the *Star Wars* saga.

Legs can be posed

30243 Umbaran MHC (2013)

▼ Separatist Forces

30058 STAP (2012)

Head pivots for walking mode

30055 Vulture Droid (2011)

30052 AAT (2011)

Pivoting wings

4493 Sith Infiltrator (2004)

30241 Mandalorian Gauntlet Fighter (2013)

▼ Republic Forces

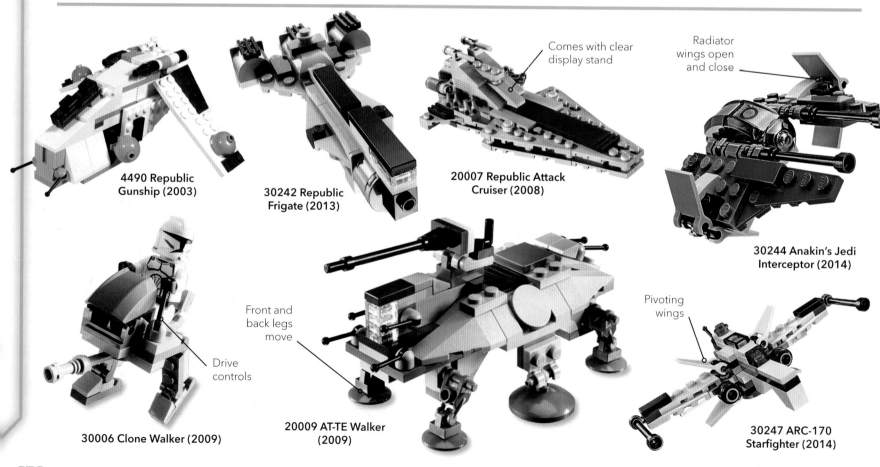

4490 Republic Gunship (2003)

30242 Republic Frigate (2013)

Comes with clear display stand

20007 Republic Attack Cruiser (2008)

Radiator wings open and close

30244 Anakin's Jedi Interceptor (2014)

Drive controls

30006 Clone Walker (2009)

Front and back legs move

20009 AT-TE Walker (2009)

Pivoting wings

30247 ARC-170 Starfighter (2014)

▼ Imperial Vehicles

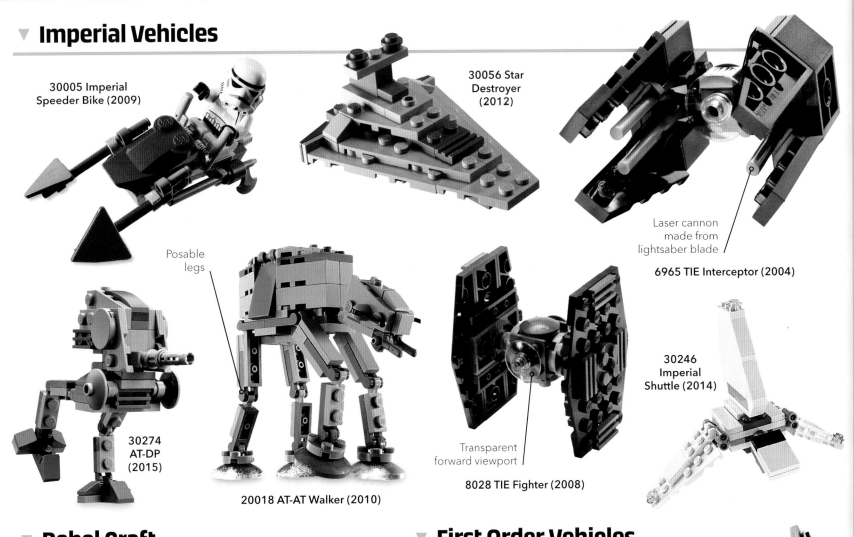

30005 Imperial Speeder Bike (2009)

30056 Star Destroyer (2012)

Laser cannon made from lightsaber blade

6965 TIE Interceptor (2004)

Posable legs

30274 AT-DP (2015)

20018 AT-AT Walker (2010)

Transparent forward viewport

8028 TIE Fighter (2008)

30246 Imperial Shuttle (2014)

▼ Rebel Craft

▼ First Order Vehicles

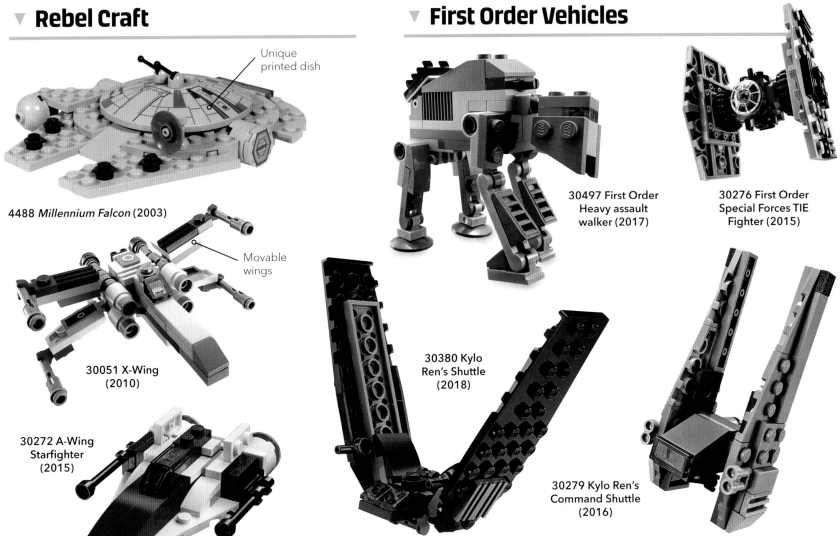

Unique printed dish

4488 Millennium Falcon (2003)

30497 First Order Heavy assault walker (2017)

30276 First Order Special Forces TIE Fighter (2015)

Movable wings

30051 X-Wing (2010)

30272 A-Wing Starfighter (2015)

30380 Kylo Ren's Shuttle (2018)

30279 Kylo Ren's Command Shuttle (2016)

Ultimate Collector Series

The LEGO Group has issued a number of highly detailed *Star Wars* models in the Ultimate Collector Series (or UCS). Intended for older builders and primarily for display, each set includes a collector's card and, in many cases, a display stand. Most are not scaled for minifigures, though some, such as the Imperial shuttle, are.

▼ Tantive IV

Princess Leia Organa's consular starship, *Tantive IV* (also known as a Blockade Runner), is one of the largest LEGO Ultimate Collector sets, at more than 60 cm (2 ft) long and almost 30 cm (1 ft) wide. The highly detailed model is made up of separate sections—front, mid, and rear engine blocks—built individually and then pegged together. The upper and lower turbolasers rotate, and the ship is supported on "landing gear" stands.

11 engines at the rear

Stickers add detail

Distinctive dark-red bricks (one of the first models to feature them)

Cockpit module slightly larger than the one on the ship in the movie

Set name	Rebel Blockade Runner	
Number	10019	Pieces 1,748
Year	2001	Source IV

▶ Darth Maul

Standing at 45 cm (18 in) tall, this remarkably detailed bust of Sith apprentice Darth Maul weighs almost 4 kg (9 lb). It has to be built from the bottom up and utilizes the same construction techniques used to create expert models at LEGOLAND® Parks.

Bust can be supported on a special stand

Set name	Darth Maul	
Number	10018	Pieces 1,868
Year	2001	Source I

▼ The *Razor Crest*

The most detailed portrayal of the *Razor Crest* yet, this set captures Din Djarin's signature ship and mobile home. It comes with an exclusive minifigure of the Mandalorian, Grogu in his hoverpram, a handcuffed captive Mythrol, and Kuiil riding a blurrg. Also included is a yellow "Baby on Board" sticker written in Aurebesh with a silhouette of Grogu's head.

Engine module lifts off easily

Laser cannon

Set name	The *Razor Crest*	
Number	75331	Pieces 6,187
Year	2022	Source M

▶

Brick Facts

The year 2000 saw the release of a UCS X-wing fighter (set 7191) with 1,304 pieces, a gearbox to operate the S-foils, moving controls in the cockpit, and an R2-D2 minifigure. The model is nearly 60 cm (2 ft) long, with a wingspan of 45 cm (18 in).

Imperial Star Destroyer

Bigger in every way than the 2002 UCS Imperial Star Destroyer (set 10030), the 2019 update is huge at 110 cm (43 in) long. It is staffed by two exclusive minifigures: an Imperial crew member and a junior lieutenant with dual-molded legs. Both UCSs include a scale model of the *Tantive IV* to re-create the opening scenes of *Star Wars: A New Hope*.

Two sections of bridge built separately from the main body

Navigation light

Reactor heat sink

Open Cockpit

Set name	Imperial Star Destroyer	
Number 75252	**Pieces** 4,784
Year 2019	**Source** IV–VI

Death Star II

The gigantic Death Star II is 63.5 cm (25 in) tall and 48 cm (19 in) wide. The partially constructed battle station features a superlaser (which Emperor Palpatine reveals to be operational) and an *Executor*-class Super Star Destroyer to scale. The model rests on a stand (constructed before the main model) with a plaque that gives detailed specifications.

Set name	Death Star II	
Number 10143	**Pieces** 3,449
Year 2005	**Source** VI

Rotating dual cannons

Wings fold landing

Cockpit holds four minifigures

Superlaser beams

Exposed "skeleton" construction

Set name	Imperial Shuttle	
Number 10212	**Pieces** 2,503
Year 2010	**Source** VI

Super Star Destroyer

▲ Imperial Shuttle

The *Lambda*-class shuttle that carries Luke Skywalker from Endor to the Death Star measures 57 cm (22½ in) wide with the wings unfolded and 71 cm (28 in) tall on its display stand. Keys at the rear raise and lower the wings, and the craft has landing gear that attaches to the bottom of the hull.

Areas under construction

Exterior armor plating

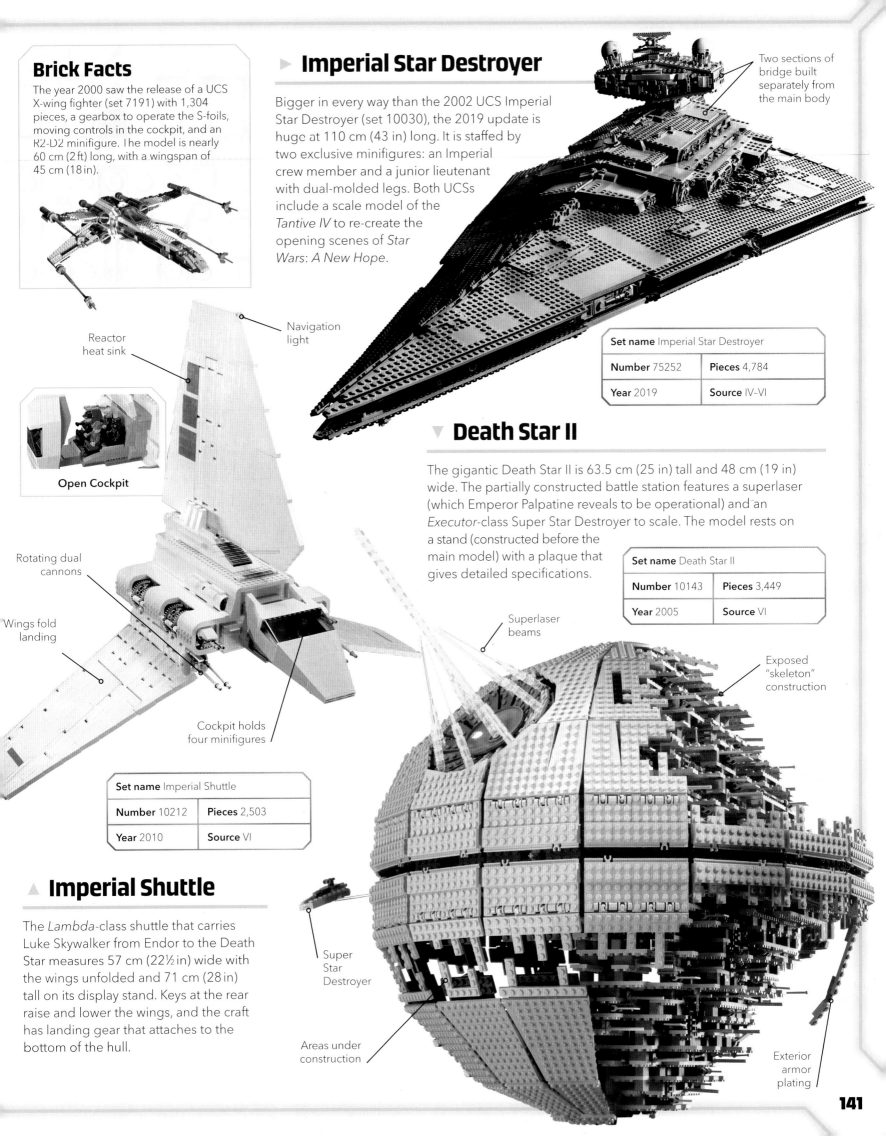

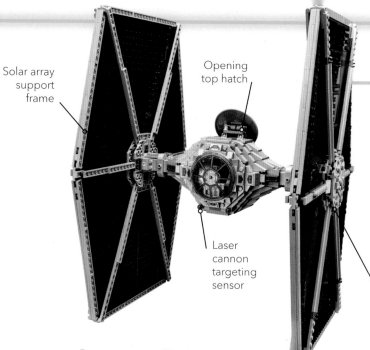

Solar array support frame

Opening top hatch

Laser cannon targeting sensor

◄ TIE Fighter

Standing 47 cm (18½ in) tall, the UCS TIE fighter rotates on its display stand so it can be admired from all angles without picking it up. It is also guarded by an exclusive TIE pilot minifigure.

Set name	TIE Fighter	
Number 75095	**Pieces** 1,685
Year 2015	**Source** IV

Exclusive TIE Pilot

Solar energy collector

► Y-Wing Starfighter

With 494 more pieces than the first UCS Y-wing, Dutch Vander's ship is based on the vessel seen in *Rogue One: A Star Wars Story*, complete with astromech navigator R2-BHD.

Set name	R2-D2
Number 10225	**Pieces** 2,127
Year 2012	**Source** IV-VI

Set name	Y-Wing Starfighter
Number 75181	**Pieces** 1,967
Year 2018	**Source** R1

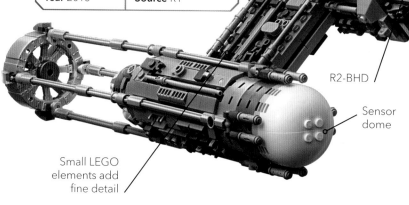

R2-BHD

Sensor dome

Small LEGO elements add fine detail

Head rotates 360 degrees

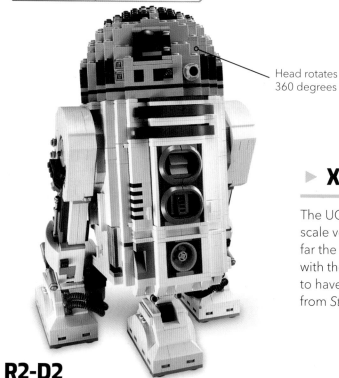

▼ R2-D2

Loyal astromech to both Anakin and Luke Skywalker, UCS R2-D2 stands 31 cm (12 in) high. A lever allows his retractable third leg to drop down, and lifting him locks the legs into "traveling" mode. Front panels hide a computer interface arm and a circular saw, while his spacecraft linkage arms unfold. An R2-D2 minifigure keeps his larger cousin company.

► X-34 Landspeeder

The UCS X-34 landspeeder is the fifth minifigure-scale version of Luke's classic transport, and is by far the largest at 49 cm (19¼ in) long. It comes with the first C-3PO minifigure to have a silver lower right leg from *Star Wars: A New Hope*.

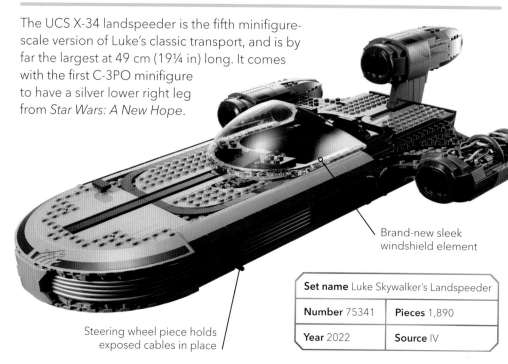

Brand-new sleek windshield element

Steering wheel piece holds exposed cables in place

Set name	Luke Skywalker's Landspeeder
Number 75341	**Pieces** 1,890
Year 2022	**Source** IV

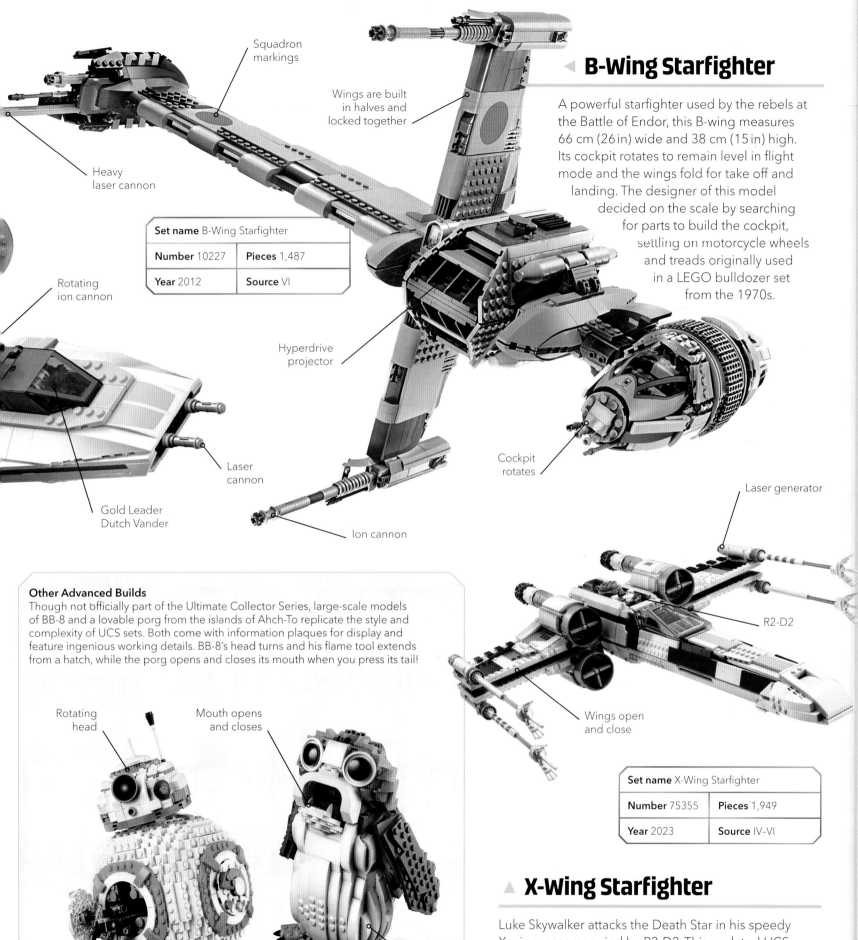

Squadron markings

Wings are built in halves and locked together

Heavy laser cannon

B-Wing Starfighter

A powerful starfighter used by the rebels at the Battle of Endor, this B-wing measures 66 cm (26 in) wide and 38 cm (15 in) high. Its cockpit rotates to remain level in flight mode and the wings fold for take off and landing. The designer of this model decided on the scale by searching for parts to build the cockpit, settling on motorcycle wheels and treads originally used in a LEGO bulldozer set from the 1970s.

Rotating ion cannon

Set name B-Wing Starfighter	
Number 10227	Pieces 1,487
Year 2012	Source VI

Hyperdrive projector

Laser cannon

Gold Leader Dutch Vander

Ion cannon

Cockpit rotates

Laser generator

R2-D2

Other Advanced Builds
Though not officially part of the Ultimate Collector Series, large-scale models of BB-8 and a lovable porg from the islands of Ahch-To replicate the style and complexity of UCS sets. Both come with information plaques for display and feature ingenious working details. BB-8's head turns and his flame tool extends from a hatch, while the porg opens and closes its mouth when you press its tail!

Wings open and close

Rotating head

Mouth opens and closes

Intricate feather detailing

Set name X-Wing Starfighter	
Number 75355	Pieces 1,949
Year 2023	Source IV-VI

Hatch opens to reveal welding torch

BB-8

Porg

▲ X-Wing Starfighter

Luke Skywalker attacks the Death Star in his speedy X-wing, accompanied by R2-D2. This updated UCS version of Luke's fighter is 55 cm (21½ in) long, 27 cm (11 in) high, and 44 cm (17½ in) wide, with new detailing on the thrusters, cockpit, and wings.

LEGO® Technic

LEGO® Technic is an advanced building range that utilizes gears and interconnecting rods to create complex models with moving parts. In 2000, the LEGO Group released the first LEGO Technic *Star Wars* models: a pit droid, a battle droid, and a destroyer droid (or droideka). Since then, new LEGO Technic sets have appeared for each Prequel Trilogy movie as well as the Classic Trilogy movies.

▼ Pit Droid

Elastic bands help the pit droid fold up into its compressed form (for storage). Like in the movies, a tap on the nose makes the model stand up again.

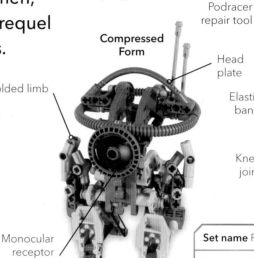

Podracer repair tool

Compressed Form

Folded limb

Head plate

Elastic band

Knee joint

Monocular receptor

Set name Pit Droid	
Number 8000	**Pieces** 217
Year 2000	**Source** I

▼ Battle Droid

The battle droid measures more than 33 cm (13 in) tall when standing and can fold for transportation. A dial on its back turns to make one arm reach to the side of its backpack to grab a blaster. The model comes with spare parts to convert it into a security droid or a battle droid commander.

Battle droid blaster

Set name Battle Droid	
Number 8001	**Pieces** 328
Year 2000	**Source** I

▶ Destroyer Droid

The LEGO Technic destroyer droid can fold into a ball and roll, then it will stop after a few turns and unfold into attack position with its blasters raised—just like it does in the movie. To achieve this, elastic bands are part of the model's construction.

Sensor antenna

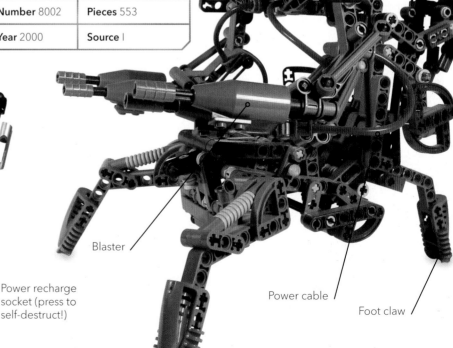

Set name Destroyer Droid	
Number 8002	**Pieces** 553
Year 2000	**Source** I

Vocoder plate

▶ C-3PO

C-3PO stands 33 cm (13 in) tall when upright. Just like the scene in *The Empire Strikes Back* when a stormtrooper blasts C-3PO, the model's head and arms can blow off when the "belly button" socket is pressed.

Power recharge socket (press to self-destruct!)

Blaster

Power cable

Foot claw

Set name C-3PO	
Number 8007	**Pieces** 339
Year 2001	**Source** I

► Stormtrooper

Standing 33 cm (13 in) tall, the stormtrooper carries a firing BlasTech E-11 rifle blaster. A wheel on the model's back allows the arms to move, so the trooper can aim the blaster—it could even hit C-3PO's socket to blow him up!

Set name Stormtrooper	
Number 8008	Pieces 361
Year 2001	Source IV–VI

► R2-D2

R2-D2 has a rotating dome and, when the front is pressed, a third leg extends for stability (the other two treads also roll). A lever mechanism at the back of the model operates one of R2-D2's utility/repair arms.

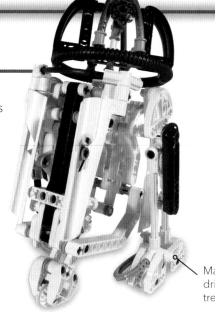

Set name R2-D2	
Number 8009	Pieces 242
Year 2002	Source I–VI

Main drive tread

▼ Darth Vader

The LEGO Technic model of Darth Vader is armed with his lightsaber, which the figure's hands can grasp and hold. The lightsaber can be raised and lowered using a lever on the back of the model. The cape is made from real cloth.

Set name Darth Vader	
Number 8010	Pieces 400
Year 2002	Source IV–VI

Sith red eyes

Real fabric cape

▼ Jango Fett

All Jango Fett's limbs and digits (and antenna) are movable, and a missile can be launched from his jetpack when the model is leaned forward.

Set name Jango Fett	
Number 8011	Pieces 429
Year 2002	Source II

Blaster

Brick Facts

In 2008, a LEGO Technic model of General Grievous was issued as an Ultimate Collector set (set 10186). Unusually, it consisted of a mix of regular LEGO bricks alongside LEGO Technic pieces.

▼ Super Battle Droid

The super battle droid's wrist blasters can be raised and lowered using a lever on the back of the model. BIONICLE® parts allow extra movement.

Set name Super Battle Droid	
Number 8012	Pieces 381
Year 2002	Source II

Eye stalks

All limbs are posable

Wrist blaster

▼ Hailfire Droid

This sturdy model of the hailfire droid rolls on its giant hoop wheels. The central blaster gun snaps into place and flick-fires missiles. The model, which is not packaged as a LEGO Technic set, is in proportion to LEGO *Star Wars* minifigures.

Set name Hailfire Droid	
Number 4481	Pieces 681
Year 2003	Source II

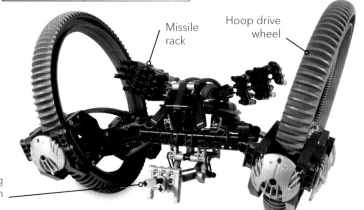

Missile rack

Hoop drive wheel

Flick-firing blaster gun

Buildable Figures

Designed to stand up to rough-and-ready action play, these large-scale posable figures hit the shelves in 2015, featuring unique head and helmet pieces. Using ball-and-socket connections rather than traditional LEGO bricks, each figure is posable for play and display, and many have mechanical arm functions and firing weapons for full-on battle movement.

Flexible lightsaber blade piece

Printed battle-damage detail

Exclusive fabric cape

◄ Obi-Wan Kenobi

With a stylized beard and modified clone armor, this buildable figure is based on General Kenobi's appearance in *Star Wars: The Clone Wars*. He stands ready to battle with General Grievous (set 75112), whose four-armed figure was released at the same time.

Set name Obi-Wan Kenobi	
Number 75109	**Pieces** 83
Year 2015	**Source** CW

Antenna is a minifigure fencing sword

Thin arms are buildable figure lightsaber hilt pieces

► Darth Vader

Standing more than 28 cm (11 in) tall, the Dark Lord of the Sith towers above most other buildable figures—and is seven times taller than his minifigure equivalent! This updated Vader figure from 2018 has a creepy white face beneath his mask.

Without Mask

Unique helmet piece

▲ K-2SO

One of six buildable figures released to tie in with *Rogue One: A Star Wars Story*, the distinctive rebel droid K-2SO features an adjustable arm-swinging battle function, operated by a wheel built into its back.

Limbs can angle in any direction

Set name Darth Vader	
Number 75534	**Pieces** 168
Year 2018	**Source** VI

Set name K-2SO	
Number 75120	**Pieces** 169
Year 2016	**Source** R1

Brick-Built Figures

In addition to the buildable figures for action play, some characters and droids can be made into large-scale models using regular LEGO bricks. They are designed for different ages, but are all for display, and each has a plaque, similar to those in the Ultimate Collector Series sets.

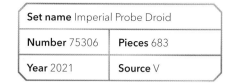

Set name Imperial Probe Droid	
Number 75306	Pieces 683
Year 2021	Source V

Sensor for tracking rebels on Hoth

◄ Imperial Probe Droid

Presented in a sleek black box and labeled 18+ like the Helmet line, this Imperial probe droid seeks out the rebels on Hoth. The model stands 27 cm (10½ in) tall, and each of its posable robotic arms is unique, combining LEGO elements such as an ice skate, a candle, and a unicorn horn.

Set name The Child	
Number 75318	Pieces 1,073
Year 2020	Source M

Expressive ears can be repositioned

Storage for three LEGO stim canisters

► BD-1

Before *The Mandalorian*'s BD-72, fans of the video game *Star Wars Jedi: Fallen Order* were familiar with BD-1, a BD explorer droid who assists Jedi Eno Cordova. His 31-cm (12-in) tall build has intricate mechanical details, including LEGO whip pieces for exposed cables.

Set name BD-1	
Number 75335	Pieces 1,062
Year 2022	Source JFO

Favorite toy—a shifter knob from the *Razor Crest*

Studs-out building technique re-creates rough texture of cloak

Mechanism for moving head

◄ D-O

Standing 27 cm (10½ in) tall, D-O's build has a small gearbox for turning and nodding its head to express the skittish nature of this data storage and retrieval droid. Its large unitread wheel has 1x4 curves around two pneumatic hoses. Like BD-1 and the Child, the set comes with a minifigure of the character.

Circular panel covers multicolor core

▲ The Child

When this set was released in 2020, the character was still known only as "the Child" (or "Baby Yoda" by fans). His name, Grogu, was soon revealed in Season 2 of the *Mandalorian*. Cute character Grogu is too young to speak yet, but both he and his LEGO counterpart can express a wide range of emotions: his ears move on LEGO ball joints, and his head is on a large LEGO ball joint.

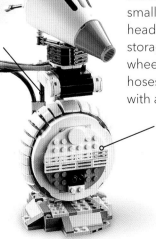

Set name D-O	
Number 75278	Pieces 519
Year 2020	Source IX

Helmets

A new initiative aimed at adult collectors began in 2020, with the first three Helmet sets tying in to the 40th anniversary of *Star Wars: The Empire Strikes Back*. The stylish models have creative building techniques and are designed for display rather than play.

▶ TIE Fighter Pilot

Like all Helmet sets, this pilot's model has a cuboid core with side studs (and window frame pieces). Sub-assemblies are then added onto the sides and top of the build to create curved surfaces.

Set name	TIE Fighter Pilot Helmet	
Number 75274	**Pieces** 724
Year 2020	**Source** IV

Train wheels threaded onto flexible hose piece

◀ The Mandalorian

LEGO plates layer up to create the curved structure of the helmet. Din Djarin's concave cheek panels are achieved with layers of curved and angled plates. Like all Helmet sets, it comes with a brick-built stand and a display name plaque.

Drum-lacquered metallic finish

Set name	The Mandalorian Helmet	
Number 75328	**Pieces** 584
Year 2022	**Source** M

◀ Luke Skywalker (Red Five)

Luke's helmet at the Battle of Yavin, with the call sign Red Five, posed a new challenge for LEGO designers as it has an open face and visible interior. They gave the model the same core as other helmets, but it is smaller and sits in the top section.

Set name	Luke Skywalker (Red Five) Helmet	
Number 75327	**Pieces** 675
Year 2022	**Source** IV

◀ Stormtrooper

A feared sight throughout the galaxy, this stormtrooper helmet is only for display. White bricks conceal the multicolor core, and black details complete the iconic look. The striped LEGO tile used for the air vent is shared only with the TIE pilot's helmet.

Rangefinder swivels down

▶ Boba Fett

A curved structure of layered plates forms the top of Boba Fett's helmet, unlike the Mandalorian's, which has a central ridge. The sand-green surface is disrupted by a gray dent because of battle damage.

Set name	Stormtrooper Helmet	
Number 75276	**Pieces** 647
Year 2020	**Source** IV-VI

Rounded breathing filters are 1x4 curved slopes

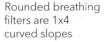

Set name	Boba Fett Helmet	
Number 75277	**Pieces** 625
Year 2020	**Source** V

Mechs

Star Wars minifigures went super-powered in 2023. Drawing on the successful LEGO® Marvel Mech range, sturdy, brick-built humanoid mechs made their appearance in the galaxy far, far away. Each is armored, armed, and posable for endless play value.

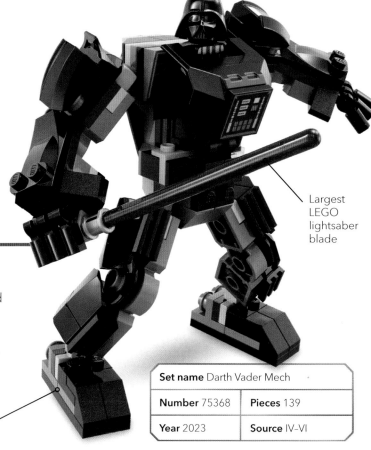

Largest LEGO lightsaber blade

▶ Darth Vader Mech

Missile on top of jetpack

Darth Vader depends on a mechanized suit to keep his damaged body alive, but that's taken a step further with this huge mechanical body to stomp around in. Encased at the top, he controls the machine, which is tougher, taller, and stronger than him. It also carries a supersize lightsaber with a LEGO Technic hilt and large red blade.

Armored feet crush enemies

Set name	Darth Vader Mech	
Number	75368	Pieces 139
Year	2023	Source IV–VI

Hinged, posable joints

▼ Stormtrooper Mech

The plastoid armor of Imperial stormtrooper gear keeps them safe, but that's like Andorian jelly compared to the protection offered by this large, plated stormtrooper mech. The mech's right hand is armed with a large brick-built stud shooter, and clips on the hips can store extra blasters for the minifigure.

Every mech's chestplate has a unique print

Imperial symbol

Set name	Stormtrooper Mech	
Number	75370	Pieces 138
Year	2023	Source IV–VI

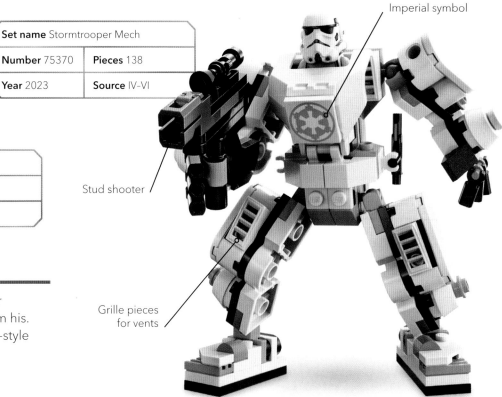

Stud shooter

Set name	Boba Fett Mech	
Number	75369	Pieces 155
Year	2023	Source V

▲ Boba Fett Mech

All mechs raise up their minifigure to give them a higher vantage point, but Boba Fett gets even more height from his. Like Boba himself, the mech is fitted with a Mandalorian-style jetpack so the whole thing can take off and carry Boba's minifigure through the skies. The mech features a large, built-in stud-shooter blaster on one arm.

Grille pieces for vents

Dioramas

Following the Helmets range, the LEGO Group launched another line for adults in 2022 with a series of dioramas. Built on a black stage for display, these scenes capture 3D snapshots of iconic moments from the Original Trilogy and also include a famous quote.

Luke's X-wing

Death Star Trench Run
Small LEGO elements create the detailed backdrop to this high-speed Death Star chase. The tiny vehicles, reminiscent of Advent Calendar builds, fly on clear antenna pieces and fire lightsaber-blade lasers.

R2-D2 as a 1x1 tile

Vader's TIE Advanced

Movable wall

Set name	Death Star Trench Run Diorama	
Number	75329	Pieces 665
Year	2022	Source IV

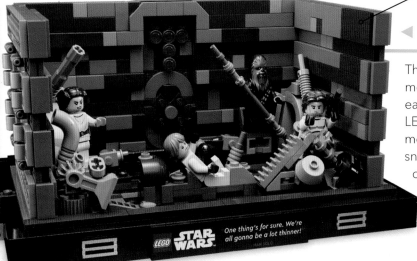

◄ Death Star Trash Compactor

This cluttered scene is about to get a lot more compact: both side walls slide toward each other, like in the movie. The room's LEGO contents slot together as the walls move in, including the red-eyed dianoga, snuggled up to Luke. Hidden from the front of the set, R2-D2 and C-3PO stand behind the door, at the back of the model, trying to help their friends.

Walls Closing Together

Set name	Death Star Trash Compactor Diorama	
Number	75339	Pieces 802
Year	2022	Source IV

Set name	Dagobah Jedi Training Diorama	
Number	75330	Pieces 1,000
Year	2022	Source V

► Emperor's Throne Room

The stage is set for the ultimate showdown between the Emperor, Darth Vader, and Luke aboard the Death Star, with a dramatic frame around a uniquely printed large radar dish. Flexible hoses hold a series of LEGO window frames in place to create the curved backdrop.

Set name	Emperor's Throne Room Diorama	
Number	75352	Pieces 807
Year	2023	Source VI

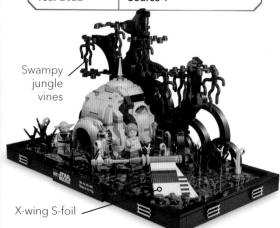

Swampy jungle vines

X-wing S-foil

Compartment hides Force lightning pieces

Set name	Endor Speeder Chase Diorama	
Number	75353	Pieces 608
Year	2023	Source VI

▲ Dagobah Jedi Training

Welcome to Dagobah, where Yoda's humble home is built on a swamp. Its rippling surface is created with 107 transparent green tiles. Luke closes his eyes to focus on raising his X-wing from the swamp, while a mud-splattered R2-D2 looks on. Inside the hut is a cooking pot and a hidden lightsaber, and a white feather piece at the back looks like smoke from the chimney.

Endor Speeder Chase
Here, Leia and Luke chase a scout trooper, but their bikes, which "float" on clear lightsaber blades and angled stands, can be swapped or reangled—or even crashed into a tree.

40th anniversary brick for *Star Wars: Return of the Jedi*

Seasonal Sets

Since 2011, the LEGO Group has released an annual seasonal set offering minifigures and parts for building micro *Star Wars* sets. Children (or adults) open a window on each day of Advent for the countdown to Christmas, revealing a toy. Each seasonal set has surprises, such as a Christmas object or a unique minifigure or two dressed in garb appropriate for the holiday season.

Brick Facts

Attendees of the 2011 San Diego Comic-Con could take home that year's advent calendar in special packaging telling them to open it by December 1. Only 1,000 were made.

▼ 2011 Advent Calendar

The countdown to Christmas 2011 began for LEGO fans with a miniature Republic Cruiser and ended with Yoda resplendent in a Santa costume. Other highlights included a Republic gunship with movable wings, tools, and weapons racks, and a Christmas tree from a galaxy far, far away. The calendar art shows Yoda and a rebel pilot watching the Battle of Endor unfold.

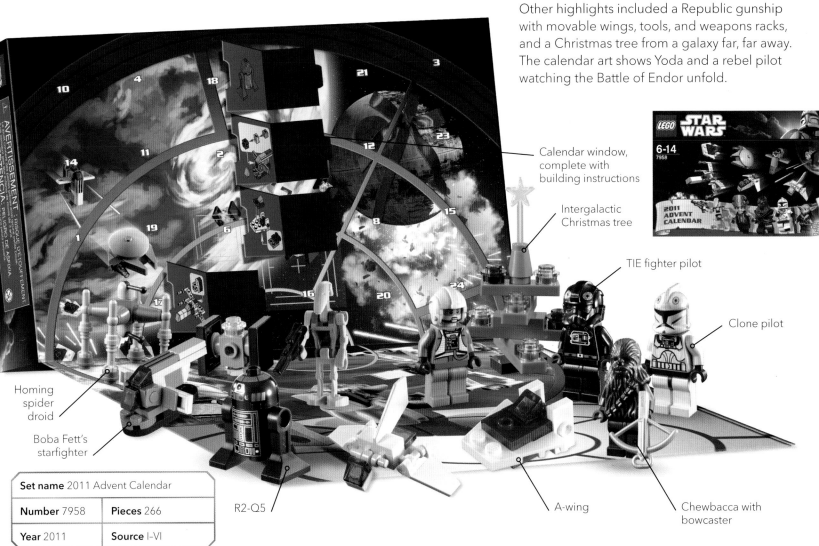

Calendar window, complete with building instructions

Intergalactic Christmas tree

TIE fighter pilot

Clone pilot

Homing spider droid

Boba Fett's starfighter

R2-Q5

A-wing

Chewbacca with bowcaster

Set name	2011 Advent Calendar	
Number 7958		**Pieces** 266
Year 2011		**Source** I–VI

Festive Figures
LEGO fans delight in seeing their favorite minifigures in Christmas gear. Many of these merry minifigures were seen on screen in the LEGO *Star Wars: Holiday Special* (2020) and LEGO *Star Wars: Summer Vacation* (2022).

Sack full of goodies

Bowcaster shoots snowballs

Festive sweater

Yoda (2011)   Darth Vader (2014)   Chewbacca (2016)   Grogu (2021)   R2-D2 (2022)   C-3PO (2022)   Palpatine (2023)

Chapter 5
Beyond the Brick

Meet the Team

Everything LEGO® *Star Wars*™ is designed in Billund, Denmark, home of the LEGO Group, though the team is drawn from places as far flung as Portugal, the US, and Australia. To mark the exciting 25th anniversary of LEGO *Star Wars*, DK spoke to the designers about their passion for the theme and how they love to share it with fans. One designer is such a big fan that he made his own Mandalorian outfit, described by some as the best costume at *Star Wars* Celebration! Here is what the team had to say.

Back row *(left to right)*: Jens Kronvold Frederiksen (Creative Lead, Design Director), Lucy Bilgin, Niels Bundesen, Christian Minick Vonsild, Jason Zapantis, Gus McLaren, Madison Andrew O'Neil
Front row *(left to right)*: Jme Wheeler, Jan Neergaard Olesen, Henrik Andersen, César Carvalhosa Soares, Martin Fink, Jackson Hughes, Michael Lee Stockwell

LEGO® *Star Wars*™ has reached the incredible milestone of being a LEGO theme for 25 years. Why do you think it's so popular?

Part of the ongoing popularity of LEGO® *Star Wars*™ is that Lucasfilm's world lends itself so well to the sets—all the vehicles and locations work perfectly with the LEGO building system.

At first, we linked the sets to the Prequel Trilogy movies, which were being released at the time. But then LEGO *Star Wars* became popular in its own right, and we were able to create our own universe and add our LEGO humor into it. We've kept it going by innovating with new ideas and new lines, such as the LEGO *Star Wars* computer games, while all the time reinforcing the existing universe.

"The *Star Wars* galaxy lends itself so well to the LEGO building system."

Compared to 25 years ago, the creation of LEGO *Star Wars* sets relies a lot more on digital processes. Like all minifigures, Bo Katan from Spider Tank (set 75361) has a digital Minifigure Design Sheet, showing all her sides, as well as her accessories, alternative head pieces, and color references.

How has the process of making LEGO *Star Wars* changed since the beginning, back in 1999?

All those years ago, the design process was much more manual than today. We had to take a physical model apart in order to count how many pieces it had; now we can just press a button. In the early days, one designer was responsible for all aspects of the product design—the building and the graphics, etc. These days we are a company of highly specialized designers.

"Many things have changed since 1999."

Using technology that wasn't around 25 years ago, the design process for new elements now involves 3D printing prototypes. These four samples of Huyang's head grow more detailed as you go from left to right.

What has been a highlight of the last 25 years?

One moment that really stands out is our launch of the Ultimate Collector Series (UCS) in 2000. It was the first time we targeted children aged 14+. We discussed whether older children would buy LEGO sets. But they did! And because the *Star Wars* universe has an adult fanbase, lots of adults love LEGO *Star Wars*, too. It all started with sets for kids, but now we have dedicated adult lines, such as the Helmet and Diorama collections. For these, we focus on the display aspect of sets so adult fans can embrace their passion for LEGO *Star Wars*. These sets also give adult fans the opportunity to enjoy more advanced building techniques—and designers can get creative with their engineering skills! For example, the round window in the Emperor's Throne Room Diorama (set 75352) was a really fun design challenge.

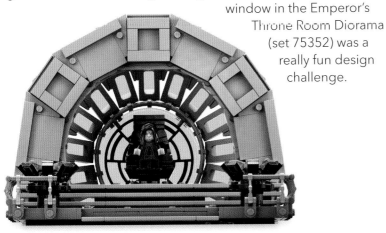

The Emperor's Throne Room Diorama (set 75352) has a circular window with panels around it at various angles. A lot of design time was spent working with the quality department to ensure that the bricks in the model were not under any strain.

Building at a variety of scales enables designers to create the same vehicle for different people, whether as part of kids' play sets, enormous display models, or smaller display models like Executive Star Destroyer (set 75356), which has condensed details inspired by its huge USC counterpart.

"It all started with sets for kids, but now adults are a big part of LEGO *Star Wars*, too."

What else have you learned about the people who like LEGO *Star Wars* sets?

LEGO *Star Wars* appeals to people of different generations and it brings families together. It can be a family event to build a model and then, after that, there are hours of play. *Star Wars* lends itself well to LEGO models because many parents rediscover their love for it through their kids. Perhaps they haven't played with LEGO models for a long time and then they're reminded, "this is really fun." It becomes something parents and kids do together, which is really cool. There are people out there who tell us that they can't wait to pass on their sets to their kids. We support this idea of LEGO play being a family experience with new products, such as the Yavin 4 Rebel Base (set 75365).

"LEGO *Star Wars* brings families together."

The Mos Eisley Cantina (set 75290) is an 18+ set. Working on it was a bonanza for the graphic designers. The printed and stickered decorations include lots of tiny details, which are hugely appreciated by fans.

When revisiting subjects for sets, designers review what has gone before as well as trying out new building techniques. The rubber-band mechanism used to open S-foils was revised between the 2013 Red Five X-Wing Starfighter (set 10240) and the 2023 X-Wing Starfighter (set 75355).

What can you tell us about the elements (LEGO pieces) that are used in LEGO *Star Wars* sets?

We are always trying to come up with new elements to make our models and minifigures better and better. Some elements are, of course, character driven. Hair pieces or headphones for a minifigure can be very specific. However, whenever possible, we try to design new LEGO elements in such a way that they offer the most potential for building. That's partly so we can use them in our future models, but it's also so that when they end up in a box of bricks in a kid's room, they can use them in lots of different ways. We don't want it to be too specialized or odd-looking. LEGO *Star Wars* has led to the creation of many new pieces, for example, the lightsaber hilt piece has found its way into many other sets and models, and it has many uses.

LEGO *Star Wars* has always been full of innovation. The first ever minifigure with a special head sculpt was Jar Jar Binks in 1999. Then the first short minifigure leg pieces were for Yoda, young Boba Fett, and two Ewoks in 2002. In 2018 we made a curved skirt piece for Barriss Offee. We spent a lot of time working out the perfect design and the right connection, and now it has become the standard element for skirts—and wizard robes—across all themes.

"LEGO *Star Wars* has led to the creation of many new pieces."

Grogu is too young to speak so his expressive face is key to his communication. We experimented with many elements and building styles to find the best way to capture his expressions for The Child (set 75318).

How do you involve kids in developing your sets?

We hold test sessions when children come to our office and we watch them interact with the models—they have smaller hands and different motor skills than adults. There's always something new for us to discover. Once, we designed a model with big wings. Adults intuitively avoided picking it up by the wings, but we saw that kids didn't. It's our job as model designers to ensure that the wing design is strong enough for them to pick it up like that so we redesigned the model.

Kids are very insightful. They always come up with things we've not thought about. We once asked if a child thought a minifigure needed a coffee mug. They replied, "No, I don't drink coffee. Just something for water." Kids have also pointed out that a cockpit with gaps around it won't work because you can't fly into space like that!

"There's always something new for us to discover from kids."

It's enjoyable trying to think like a kid about building and play experiences. Death Star Final Duel (set 75093) has loads of play functions that kids love, including these collapsing stairs, swing-out side sections, a rotating throne, and a hidden lightsaber pop-up function.

How do you engage with the LEGO *Star Wars* fan community?

We're very interested in hearing what fans have to say. The design team pays attention to online product reviews and listens to what YouTubers have to say about our sets. We go to events like *Star Wars* Celebration, attend product releases, and do box signings in stores. Those are fun ways to meet fans, hear what they think, and receive some of their energy, which is really rewarding. We also ask fans for input on the development of sets as well. The UCS Republic Gunship (set 75309) was decided on by a poll of fans.

"We're very interested in hearing what fans have to say."

For the Clone Commander Cody (set 75350) and the other Helmet sets, we went back to our roots, with more studs and more stacking. After many, many testing rounds, we concluded that this more traditional LEGO approach with visible studs and bricks was the best. Fans wanted a LEGO model to look like a LEGO model, rather than relying only on specially shaped elements.

As well as focus testing, what other kinds of tests do you do?

We put a lot of effort into making sure the quality of our models is up to scratch. All new elements have to pass a lot of different tests, too. We have many quality-control processes for things such as core stability and heat tolerance. Heat can change plastic—even on a sunny windowsill—so models are put in ovens. Or, if they're too big, like the USC *Millennium Falcon* (set 75192), we place them in a sauna! Oils in skin can also react with plastics and damage them. Our test known as "the butter test" simulates the possible effect that oils from human hands can have on LEGO bricks.

The USC AT-AT (set 75313) had 20 kg (44 lb) placed on top of its legs for months to ensure their strength before we could move forward with the project. We use special weights that look like 2x6 LEGO bricks but weigh nearly 50 g (2 oz) each.

The rubber suspension of the Spider Tank (set 75361) was tested by a robot arm. The arm pushed down on the model about 500 times to ensure the model's strength and stability.

> ## "We put a lot of effort into making sure the quality of our models is up to scratch."

Do you have a final message for fans in this special anniversary year?

We want to reach out to all fans, young and old, with our new range of products for this celebratory year. Our team hopes to share our excitement and we invite fans to engage with us and share the love we all have for LEGO *Star Wars*!

AN EXCLUSIVE MINIFIGURE FOR YOU

The exclusive minifigure that comes with this book is a commemorative minifigure for the 25th anniversary of LEGO *Star Wars*, inspired by the very first release in 1999. Five years ago we released a line of classic designs for the 20th anniversary, so now we're doing something similar for this book. Darth Maul was there in 1999 for the very first release, and we're re-creating his look from that year but with a special 25th-anniversary logo on his back.

Set Index

Senior Editors Tori Kosara and Selina Wood
Senior Designer David McDonald
Cover Designer James McKeag
Senior Production Editor Jennifer Murray
Senior Production Controller Lloyd Robertson
Managing Editor Paula Regan
Managing Art Editor Jo Connor
Publishing Director Mark Searle

Edited for DK by Shari Last

ACKNOWLEDGMENTS

DK would like to thank Randi Kirsten Sørensen,
Heidi K. Jensen, Martin Leighton Lindhardt, Jens Kronvold
Frederiksen, Lucy Bilgin, Niels Bundesen, Christian Minick
Vonsild, Jason Zapantis, Gus McLaren, Madison Andrew
O'Neil, Jme Wheeler, Jan Neergaard Olesen, Henrik
Andersen, César Carvalhosa Soares, Martin Fink,
Jackson Hughes, Michael Lee Stockwell, and Michelle
Martinsen at the LEGO Group; Jennifer Pooley,
Jennifer Heddle, and Mike Siglain at Lucasfilm;
and Chelsea Alon at Disney.

The publisher would also like to thank Huw Millington
and Giles Kemp for their help with previous editions;
Gary Ombler for his photography; Elizabeth Dowsett,
Jason Fry, Simon Beecroft, and Simon Hugo for writing;
Megan Douglass for proofreading; Julia March for
indexing and proofreading and Olivia Campbell
for editorial assistance. For his contribution to
the first edition of this book, DK would like
to thank Jeremy Beckett.

PICTURE CREDITS

Images supplied by the LEGO Group.
Additional photography by Gary Ombler,
Jeremy Beckett, Sarah Ashun, and Brian Poulsen.

Braided hair piece
tops four Leia
minifigures

White is the
traditional
color worn
by Alderaan
royalty

Rank of
rebel
leader

Princess Leia from
Millennium Falcon
(set 75192)